BERTRAND RUSS[...]

[...] WEEGEE • PAUL FUSCO • MARSHALL [...]

ERNST HAAS • MRS. WILLIAM O. DOUGLAS • HARRY S[...]

[...]MacLEISH • M. F. ASHLEY MONTAGU • FRED MAROON • [...]

MARC RIBOUD • GENE SHALIT • JOHN[...] OGDEN NASH [...] BERTRA[...]

[...]ARALES • ERNEST HEMINGWAY • [...] C. P. SNOW • GRO[...]

[...]EBERMAN • DAVID DOUGLAS DUNCAN • JULIAN HUX[...]

[...]EEGEE • IRVING PENN • JOHN F. KENNEDY • [...]

[...]KIRKLAND • WALTER LIPPMANN • PHILLIP HARRINGTON[...]

[...] PEARL S. BUCK • JOHN VACHON • JACQUELINE KENNE[...]

[...]HALL McLUHAN • WILLIAM F. BUCKLEY, JR. • WILLIAM S[...]

[...]RÉSON • ARNOLD NEWMAN • EUGENE O'NEILL • STANL[...]

[...]DOUGLAS • ERNEST HEMINGWAY • OGDEN NASH • MAR[...]

[...]S KIRKLAND • WILLIAM MANCHESTER • S. J. PERELMAN[...]

[...]ARD M. KENNEDY • DAVID DOUGLAS DUNCAN • C. P. SN[...]

[...]E ROBINSON • M. F. ASHLEY MONTAGU • FRED MAROON[...]

[...] WILLIAM SAROYAN • GALE SAYERS • ARCHIBALD MacL[...]

[...]OD • JULES FEIFFER • WILLIAM F. BUCKLEY, JR. • GENE S[...]

[...]ARTHUR ROTHSTEIN • WALTER LIPPMANN • PHILLIP HA[...]

[...]EN NASH • WILLIAM MANCHESTER • S. J. PERELMAN • T[...]

[...] PHILLIP HARRINGTON • EDWARD STEICHEN • DOUG[...]

[...]NN • JACQUELINE KENNEDY • JOHN F. KENNE[...]

[...]I STEVENSON • JACQUELINE KENNEDY • MARGA[...]

[...]RL S. BUCK • JOHN VACHON • MILTON GREENE • [...]

[...] STANLEY KUBRICK • PAUL FUSCO • MARSHALL McLUHA[...]

[...]'NEILL • WILLIAM F. BUCKLEY, JR. • ALLEN DRURY • WIL[...]

[...]JULES FEIFFER • WILLIAM SAROYAN • GROUCHO MARX[...]

[...]OW • MICHAEL VACCARO • JULIAN HUXLEY • WILLIAM M[...]

[...]MAILER • RICHARD AVEDON • GALE SAYERS[...]

[...]NORMAN MAILER • MARVIN NEWMAN • CORNELL[...]

[...]TRETICK • [...]LLIAM ATTWOOD • [...]

To the many men and women who made LOOK
a successful and influential magazine
over a 35-year period.

THE LOOK BOOK

LOOK: The exciting story of people...

JOEL BALDWIN

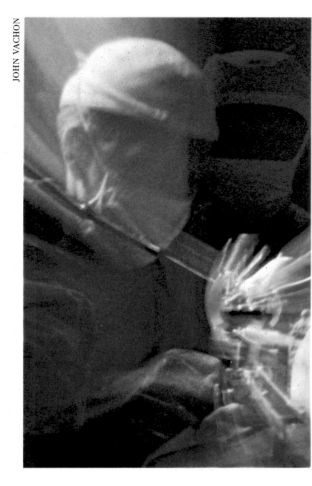

JOHN VACHON

what
they
do...

NASA

MARVIN NEWMAN

what they feel...

...what they want

...what they think

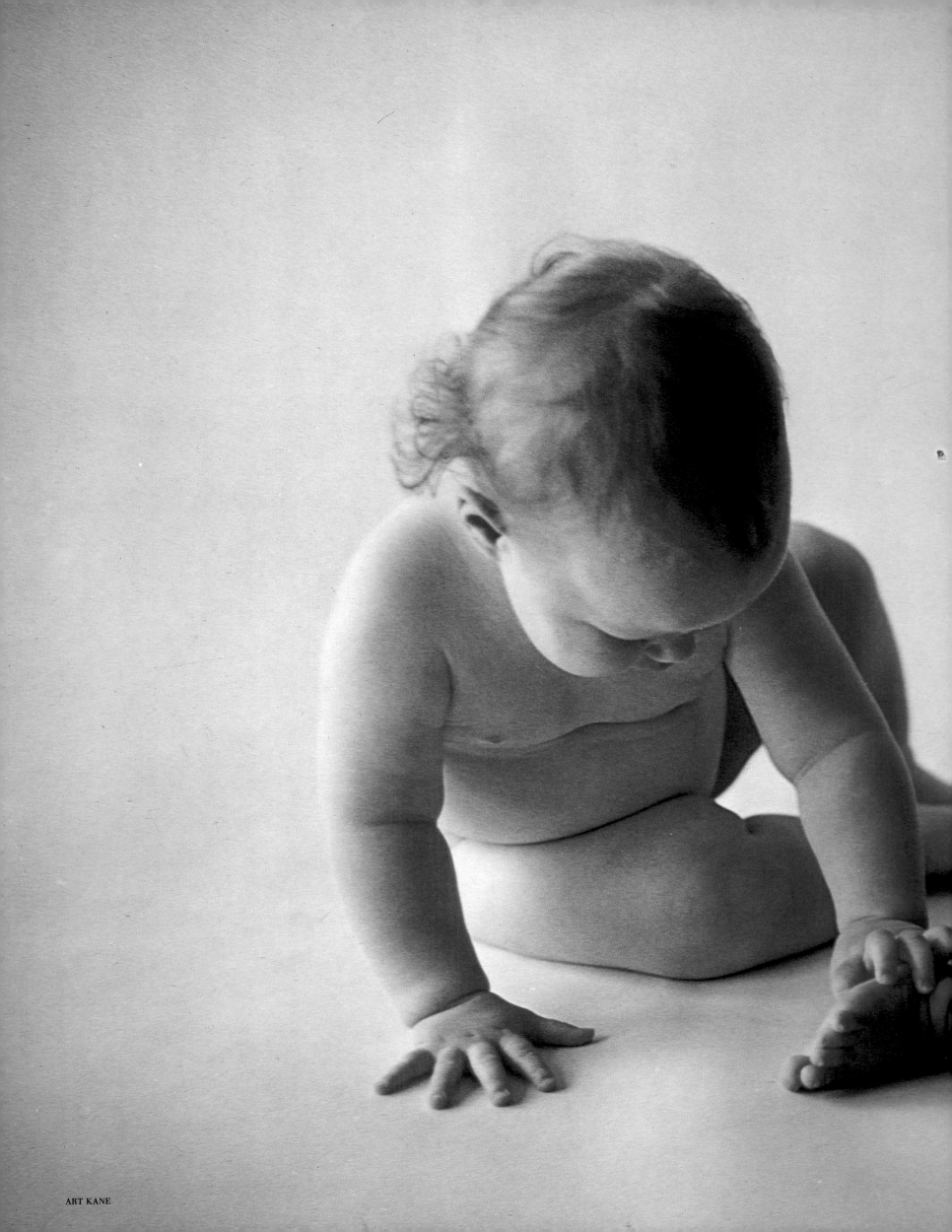

ART KANE

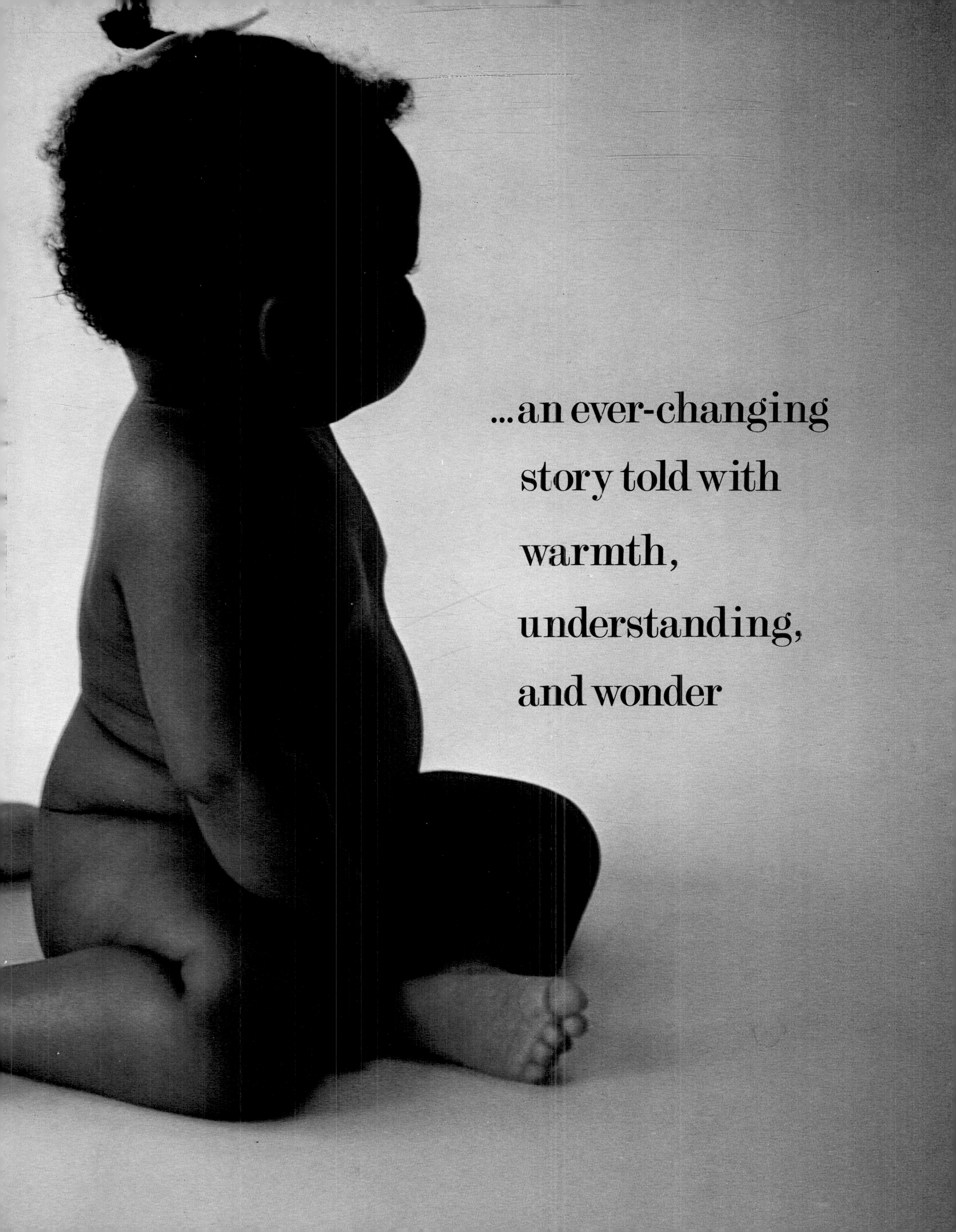

...an ever-changing
story told with
warmth,
understanding,
and wonder

Edited by LEO ROSTEN

Foreword by GARDNER COWLES

THE LOOK BOOK

Harry N. Abrams, Inc., Publishers, New York

Nai Y. Chang, *Vice-President, Design and Production*
John L. Hochmann, *Executive Editor*
Margaret L. Kaplan, *Managing Editor*
Barbara Lyons, *Director, Photo Department,*
 Rights and Reproductions
Claudia J. Kern, *Researcher*

Library of Congress Cataloging in Publication Data
Main entry under title:

The LOOK book.

   1. LOOK . I. Rosten, Leo Calvin, 1908-
AC5.L84   081   75-15853
ISBN 0-8109-0316-4

Library of Congress Catalogue Card Number: 75-15853

First issue: February, 1937.

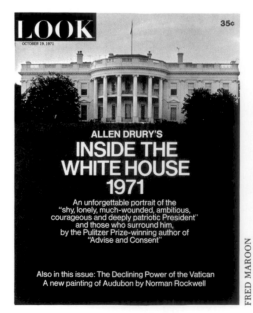

Last issue: October 19, 1971.

FOREWORD

I founded *Look* with great excitement in January, 1937. I announced its death, with the utmost sadness and reluctance, in September, 1971.

Americans bought over four *billion* copies of the magazine. We published 903 issues. Our March 7, 1967, issue sold 9,270,830 copies. More than seventy million people (eighteen years and older) read one or all of the four issues in which we printed William Manchester's remarkable *Death of a President*. (We paid $665,000 for publication rights.) In 1969, we printed 200 million copies.

Why, then, did *Look* fail? Our final issue, after all, sold over 6,500,000 copies. We had outlived the *Saturday Evening Post* and *Collier's* and other competitors. We had passed *Life* in circulation—which we cut back, because of sharply rising costs.

Look had to cease publication because of the beginning of an economic recession, the flight of advertising from magazines to television, a strike at General Motors which compelled that company to cancel some $9,000,000 worth of ads (a sum which could never be recovered), the soaring costs of paper, printing, distribution, and the staggering increases in postal rates. (We were delivering 5,500,000 copies of each issue through the mails.)

Now, a curious and fatal paradox governs huge circulation figures: the larger the sales, the greater the monetary *losses* if advertising revenues decline. You must remember that the price at which a mass magazine is sold is far smaller than the costs of producing it. The difference—and any profits—must come from advertising.

The hard, unalterable fact is that *any* journal designed to reach millions of readers must generate huge revenues from advertisers to break even, much less earn a profit for its shareholders. When our advertisers shifted their spending to television, and away from magazines, *Look*'s fate was sealed. And one year after *Look* "folded," *Life* ceased publication—for the same reasons.

As I think back over the thirty-five years in which I published and edited *Look*, it grieves me to recall that the magazine was long characterized as "sensational"—even after half of our contents, issue after issue, covered world affairs, national politics, advances in medicine and education, religion and science, and the arts. These features won *Look* a great many honors, of which I shall always be proud.*

Our investigative probings often incurred the wrath of political leaders and pressure groups across the nation. Hardly a week passed without my receiving outraged protests, demands for retraction, scurrilous criticism, threats of libel suits. Neither I nor my editors were taken by surprise, for we expected that hard-hitting articles on controversial themes would subject us to violent hostility.

In 1952 we published a story on Richard Nixon entitled "Is This Man Fit To Be President?" We printed an exposé of the use of drugs in high schools long before many knew it was going on—and we were accused of "yellow journalism" designed to gain "cheap" circulation. Long, long before the Civil Rights movement, or the emergence of Black Power, the national furor over Vietnam, or Women's Lib, *Look* was publishing lengthy articles by distinguished authors about these explosive subjects. And before the dreadful scandal of Watergate hit the headlines, *Look* (in its last issue) featured

---

* The first National Magazine Award of Columbia University School of Journalism went to *Look* for "outstanding editorial achievement . . . for editing, imagination, and integrity." We were often cited by the American Medical Association and the Albert Lasker Foundation for our articles on public health. The American Bar Association cited us for consistent accounts of legal problems and needed reforms. The Overseas Press Club singled out *Look* five times for international reporting and analysis. We won the Sigma Delta Chi Award for Public Service seven times. We were given The Freedoms Foundation medal, The George Polk Memorial Award, The School Bell award of the National Education Association, citations from the National Conference of Christians and Jews—and we garnered more awards for art design than I can enumerate.

a story by Allen Drury called "Inside the White House"—a startling portrait of the President "and those who surround him."

During one period of political hysteria and witch-hunting, I was warned, in a telephone call from Washington, that if we did not "lay off" a certain Senator and his committee, *Look* would be "put through the wringer." The caller implied that I would be subpoenaed to explain the "Communists" on our staff (so far as I know, we never employed one), that the FBI would be asked to investigate the dire motives behind our "muckraking," etc. At this point, Leo Rosten quoted this passage from (he said) Dante: "The hottest places in Hell are reserved for those who, in a time of moral crisis, maintain their neutrality."

We never could find out where Dante had written those noble words, but thereafter they hung, enlarged and framed, in most of the magazine's offices.

How did *Look* begin? I was News Editor for the Des Moines *Register and Tribune.* I became increasingly impressed by reader response to the photographs we ran. More important was the public interest in stories which *allied* pictures and text. I asked George Gallup to make a study of these phenomena. Dr. Gallup had developed a scientific polling technique while he was a graduate student at the University of Iowa. His first commissioned poll was conducted for the Cowles newspapers in Des Moines. Gallup's findings supported my own impressions. At that point, *Look* was born.

I had had no magazine experience. I was told by many publishers that a "picture magazine" just could not succeed. (*Life* had not yet appeared.) Had I then known the problems, the risks, the costs and crises which were to plague us, I probably would not have been rash enough to launch *Look*.

It took many years to build a staff of writers, photographers, art directors, of men and women who had journalistic talent, imagination, intelligence—and audacity. I moved *Look*'s offices to New York in 1940.

Not until 1950 did *Look* begin to reach that level of quality for which I had hoped. Year by year, we improved. For that I must credit Marvin Whatmore, President; Dan Mich, Editor; Allen Hurlburt, Art Director; William Arthur, Managing Editor; Leo Rosten, Special Editorial Adviser—and a remarkable staff, I think, of creative editors and outstanding photographers. They made *Look* as exciting and influential as any publisher could have desired.

I miss *Look*. I always shall. I think millions of Americans miss the magazine, too. And I thank Harry N. Abrams, Inc., for bringing out this magnificent book about a biweekly which informed, entertained, and—I feel—helped educate millions of Americans for over a third of this extraordinary and historic century.

GARDNER COWLES
Editor-in-Chief

CONTENTS

INTRODUCTION

...A View From the Inside

LEO ROSTEN

I met "Mike" Cowles (only strangers ever call him Gardner) in 1941, in Hollywood, when I was committing a screenplay. After the customary pleasantries, he asked me what I thought of *Look*. I told him it was gaudy and superficial—far too sensational and shrill for my taste, at least.

He did not wince; he blinked. Then he said, in his even, flat, judicial voice, "I want to make *Look*—well, *respectable*. I'm willing to pour a good deal of money into getting the best writers, the best pictures, and articles as significant as any you can find in a mass-circulation magazine." He paused. "I want to see *Look* on the coffee tables of the homes to which I am invited to dinner."

Pearl Harbor plunged the country into war. President Roosevelt urged Cowles to become Domestic Director of the Office of War Information. After a swift round-the-world trip with Wendell Willkie (they spent three hours with Stalin), Mike took over his duties in Washington. By one of the ironic flukes of fate, he inherited me, a Deputy Director.

He was a pleasure to work for, in days when pleasure was throttled by the awful tragedies of a world whose civilization was threatened by a lunatic, Hitler; a jackal, Mussolini; and the benighted military maniacs of Japan.

When the war ended, Mike invited me to come to New York and become his "adviser." I told him that I was not much of an adviser, that what I most wanted was to write books, that I was allergic to deadlines, and that he would probably fire me within a month because I would make him extremely miserable—simply by commenting on the blemishes of the magazine he owned, loved, edited, and to which he would give the best years of his life.

His answer was dry and slightly amused: "When can you start?"

So I spent twenty-two years at *Look*—half-time. Those years turned out to be more stimulating and productive than I could possibly have dreamed. An author of academic bent is rarely given such freedom to act as gadfly, critic, cynic, obstetrician, and executioner; or such freedom to write articles utterly alien to *Look*'s pages; or such luxury as extensive travel, at the company's expense, to interview a Bertrand Russell or a Luigi Barzini, chronicle a Caribbean cruise, extol the glory that was Greece and the grandeur that was Groucho.

I was never asked to write a paragraph I did not believe. I was never given an assignment I did not originate—or greet with delight. And I *learned* an enormous amount: about mass-circulation magazines, popular "communication," and that remarkable invention of the twentieth century called photojournalism.

Even my best friends seem to think that editors sit at desks and at their leisure examine a flood of fascinating material submitted by authors, authors' agents, photographers, and new geniuses clamoring for recognition. Alas, this is not so. Although we received around 10,000 story ideas a year, the truth is that about 85 per cent of what finally appeared in *Look*'s pages had to be conceived within its own offices and written, photographed, and linked by our own editors and staff into a coherent narrative of pictures, text, and captions. Some brilliant articles and ideas did come "over the transom"—from authors, book publishers, and our voluminous Readers' Mail. But not enough; and not timely enough; and not enough to complete an issue before press time.

In making up a typical issue, the editors saw and screened some 8,000 photographs. In thirty-five years, *Look* published over 180,000 pictures. No one has had the courage to count how many *more* words accompanied and surrounded the cornucopia of pictures.

The commanding "picture magazines" of our time surely were *Life* and *Look*. *Life* was a weekly; *Look* appeared every other week. (Many people think *Look* appeared once a week.) Since *Life* was a weekly, it was committed to covering the news—of the preceding week. *Look* made no effort to cover "spot" news. An issue might open with an article by Ernest Hemingway or an interview with Fidel Castro, a slashing story about racial discrimination or exposé of the disgraces of mental hospitals, an analysis of Harry Truman or John F. Kennedy or a discussion of the tactics of the Politburo.

The fact that *Look* was thought to be a weekly newsmagazine can be attributed to two factors: 1) the skill with which its editors anticipated events; 2) plain luck. We were often credited with uncanny foresight when it was the fortuitous eruption of happenings that gave us "blockbusters." Most issues of *Look* contained at least one story which was picked up by the AP or UPI or Reuters and wired around the globe.

The character of a mass magazine is molded by the interplay between its editors and their audience. *Look* would no more have published an article about, say, a Peruvian *putsch* than the *Reader's Digest* would think of publishing a diatribe against religion. The contents of the *Ladies' Home Journal* or *Esquire* or *Holiday* magazine differed profoundly because each was designed to attract a different kind of reader.

I said that it was *Look*'s staff, not benevolent and ingenious outsiders, who prepared the 903 separate issues of the magazine. It was the Editorial Board who truly created and shaped each issue. Who were they?

Mike Cowles, of course, was the dominant power and personality. He was (and is) a lifelong Republican, and a liberal to his fingertips. But nearly all of his editors were Democrats. I know of no magazine where the "boss" was less partisan, more reasonable, and more determined to publish the widest possible spectrum of opinions.

My first impression of *Look* was of the unusual informality and variety of its personnel. Long before "tolerance" became fashionable, *Look* employed, in positions high and low: women, blacks, Jews, Catholics, a Mormon, agnostics. . . .

My second impression was that unlike other magazines of which I knew something, *Look* harbored no cliques jockeying for power or trimming their sails to suit their employer's politics or flatter his vanity. I believe *Look*'s spacious editorial policy flowed from the ease, the diversity, and the rock-bottom democracy of those who created each issue. These qualities Cowles respected, and he encouraged them by his own example.

Cowles was a very rich young man. His father owned the Des Moines *Register and Tribune*. Mike was sent off to be educated at Exeter and Harvard (he edited the *Crimson*). From his college days on, he was a friend of Nelson Rockefeller and Jock Whitney, of Aldriches and Vanderbilts—and later, of Thomas E. Dewey, Earl Warren, and Bernard Baruch. Some New Yorkers mistakenly thought

Mike a playboy because he loved parties and dancing, was a habitué of the Stork Club and El Morocco, and belonged to such havens of the *crème de la crème* as the Links, the River, the Racquet and Tennis clubs. But his staff knew him to be totally devoid of snobbery. He detested injustice. He gave no quarter to race prejudice. He contributed to civil liberties groups, which raised the hackles of his peers in the Social Register.

Cowles's dominant passion, in fact, was politics. At dinners in his home, one met cabinet members or bankers, senators and movie stars, a visiting European eminence, painters and merchant princes, impresarios of the stage, symphony, or ballet. But the talk usually came to focus on politics.

Cowles combined judgment and impulsiveness. He often came to the office excited about an article he had commissioned from one or another political pooh-bah. His glee was rarely echoed by his editors, who did not greet an article by, say, Herbert Lehman or Harold Stassen with hosannahs of joy. "The Boss" was sometimes talked out of running a dull piece (more often it was rewritten beyond recognition); he then sheepishly confessed error, and promised to restrain his vulnerability to ambitious spellbinders, or turgid careerists.

Cowles loved the constant parade of problems and challenges and negotiations involved in putting out any issue of *Look*. He traveled widely. He valued the entrée which the editorship of a magazine that reached fifty million or more readers (you must distinguish readers—in families, in libraries—from subscribers) gave him to the inner halls of power, whether at City Hall or on Capitol Hill, in London, Nairobi, or Rio de Janeiro. His financial stake in newspapers outside of Iowa (in Florida and Long Island) and in radio and television stations certainly did not diminish the eagerness of presidents and monarchs and powers-behind-a-throne (or a firing squad) to receive him. The day after Adlai Stevenson lost the 1952 presidential election to Dwight D. Eisenhower (Mike knew and liked both men), Cowles offered Stevenson a handsome stipend to take a trip around the world with *Look*'s Foreign Editor, William Attwood; they produced a series of incisive articles and interviews.

Statistics mesmerized Mike. The industry alleged that his command of the "nuts-and-bolts" aspects of publishing (paper costs, printing, binding snafus, distribution headaches, newsstand sales, advertising revenues) was unmatched by the editors of competitive magazines, who were not *publishers* as well. He kept a close, beady eye on the minutiae of expenses, production, and sales. He was at home with the budgets and the obdurate facts of finance.

Cowles did not often attend the Editorial Board's planning sessions, though he lunched weekly with his top editors. But he scrutinized with care every page of every issue before it was "put to bed." He approved or rejected every important political piece that the editors considered.

Each upcoming issue of *Look* was displayed on the walls of the large editorial boardroom, the cover and pages (pictures, texts, advertisements) arranged in sequence. Mike would "suggest" that one or another article be positioned elsewhere or toned down, hopped up, shortened, expanded—or relegated to oblivion. He was especially critical of cover photographs and cover blurbs. He always remembered the mistakes he felt he had made in *Look*'s infancy.

The man who ran *Look*'s editorial operation day by day was Daniel D. Mich. He had worked for Cowles for many years, left briefly for *McCall's*, and returned as Editor, with increased authority, until his saddening death in 1965.

The combination of Cowles and Mich surprised many. Dan came from the sports pages of the Milwaukee *Journal*. He was steeped in sports—and addicted to baseball. He once rejected a controversial article by a celebrated author with this outraged note: "You struck out—and the bases were loaded!"

Cowles was controlled, deliberate, courteous. Dan was rough-hewn, abrupt, often abrasive. He had a fierce temper. (It turned his cheeks as pink as his hair.) He was not diplomatic, but he was respected. He was a good administrator and a tough editor. He despised guile, fence-straddling, or laziness. He had a keen "sense" of news. He was totally fearless, a crusader for the poor and the powerless, an avowed foe of entrenched power—and Republican programs. Intolerance of any sort infuriated him. He never worried about the furor that a hard-hitting article was sure to provoke. But he rarely made a decision about explosive pieces or politically delicate subjects without Cowles's personal approval.

Dan had an uncanny eye for photographs. He insisted upon editorial *drive* and seized upon "stoppers" or action shots. He loved homespun stories and animal features. (He and his wife, Isabella Taves, treated their Dalmatian as their child.) His most exasperating bias was toward short, blunt prose. His newspaper training and temperament saddled him with the peculiar idea that anything could be improved by cutting. Sometimes articles verged on anemia before he really liked them. Yet one could, in the end, persuade him that substance was superior to word count. In time, he came to accept articles of 30,000 words without batting an eye—especially when convinced that a piece "*read* short."

Many members of the staff feared Dan's wrath, but those in his orbit knew that beneath his testiness lay a hard core of soft feelings. He was loyal to those who were loyal to him, and surprisingly sympathetic to the personal problems of his lieutenants. He disliked socializing and rarely gave or went to parties. He was simply so absorbed in *Look* that he edited it day and night, on weekends, and I suspect, in his dreams.

Perhaps you will get the mischievous idea of the differences between Cowles and Mich if I tell you that the former liked to dine at "21" and the latter at Toots Shor's.

William B. Arthur joined *Look*'s staff in 1946, became Managing Editor—and Editor after Dan Mich died. I never met anyone who did not like Bill Arthur. He came from Kentucky and never lost the lilt of border speech. A quiet man, he was easy to approach and to know. He was sentimental and (he will not mind the word) "corny." At thirty-five he was a Presbyterian elder. He went to church every Sunday and often spoke from the pulpit in Larchmont.

At times I suffered the alarming sensation that Arthur was all virtue—unstained and untarnished. He was not at home in the cocktail circuits. But "the Louisville Kid" won such affection and trust from Princess Grace and Prince Rainier that he brought more (and more intimate) picture-stories out of Monaco than any of our rivals.

Please pause. If you think I am uttering saccharine banalities, I beg you to reconsider. I am describing, as truthfully as I can, the governing characteristics and differences of the men who made *Look*.

The revolutionary improvement in the visual quality of *Look*, in its design and layouts, its artwork and use of color and illustrations—in short, its aesthetic excellence—can be traced to the day Allen Hurlburt was appointed Art Director. Hurlburt was incapable of vulgarity. He admired talent—however new, young, or offbeat. He could visualize a feature, or lay out a story, with imagination and taste. He could also turn stubborn and derisive, but time calmed him down. I think he won more awards than any Art Director of a mass-circulation magazine. We worked together on at least 200 articles, most notably four long series: "The Story Behind the Painting," "The Religions of America," "They Made Our World," and "How Much Do We Know About Human Nature?"

I must retrace this chronology. Boundless credit must be given, in any account of *Look*'s transformation, to Fleur (at that time Mrs.) Cowles. She established an independent Women's Section, and thereafter funneled into *Look*'s pages features never before handled with grace: fashions, food, home decoration, art, travel. As much as anyone, she fortified Mike in rejecting the strident and the crude, to reach for polish and (forgive the word) class. She bubbled with ideas and was undeterred by costs.

After Fleur left *Look*, to remarry and live in London, the Women's Department became the province of Patricia Coffin, who was at home with both economy and socialites.

Space prevents my doing justice to many *Look* veterans: Henry Ehrlich; Patricia Carbine, who spent almost two decades at *Look*; Robert Meskill, a meticulous Managing Editor; William Attwood, a crackerjack Foreign Affairs Editor (later the U.S. Ambassador to Kenya and Guinea, he

now publishes *Newsday*); Laura Bergquist; Bob Moskin; Roland Berg, our M.S. expert on medicine; Tim Cohane; Leslie Midgley, a superb newsman; Martin Goldman, the best copy editor we ever had. And although he was Chief of Promotion and Circulation, S. O. ("Shap") Shapiro was a fountain of ideas for stories, covers, cover blurbs. No one wangled more unpaid publicity for the magazine—in gossip columns, on radio and television—than this exhuberant dynamo.

I now praise photographers. Arthur Rothstein, a much-honored craftsman of the lens, headed *Look*'s staff of fifteen photographers. It is hard to describe in words the artistry and technical tours de force of our photographers—and of the many free-lance masters of the camera we commissioned for special stories or from whom we purchased pictures, of their own inspiration, worthy of any museum of the fine arts. Just examine the pages in this book.

I think you must practice photography yourself to appreciate the work of its magicians. A professional photographer, like a painter, simply *sees* differently than you or I do. You might pause to ask how on earth the photographer managed to get such pictures as are in this volume: where was he standing or squatting or hanging from his heels?

No photographer went off on an assignment without an enormous array of cases, bags, pouches, shoulder slings, and knapsacks, all loaded with an arsenal of equipment: five or six cameras (at least), a dozen lenses, umpteen filters and gadgets, flood and/or strobe lights, tripods, clamps, light reflectors, and a muchness of film packets and cassettes in color and black-and-white, in varying sizes for Nikons, Hasselblads, Rolleiflexes. A photographer might shoot forty rolls of film (1200 "frames") for a story that ended up using eight to twelve shots. (The cost of film is negligible compared with the time and salaries of writers and photographers, their air fares, hotel bills, entertainment expenses, and *baksheesh* for the imperative greasing of alien palms.)

Look's writer-photographer teams traversed the world. They half-froze in Tibet, pierced the Iron Curtain, cozened access to the salons of Paris or Cambodia or the White House. They crawled in mud or slogged through buffalo grass to bring back a story. They sought pictures under appalling conditions and fickle light.

Our writers and photographers often worked under gunfire and ominous threats, recording guerrilla actions from Jordan to Chicago or Watts. Story teams were roughed up by zealots in Africa or the Caribbean, fled goons who tried to

smash their cameras or destroy their notes, tore down back roads to escape yahoos from the Ku Klux Klan, or outwitted Communist bullies or Southern sheriffs hell-bent on keeping a story from being told. Young Sam Castan begged for an assignment in Vietnam, and was killed by a Viet Cong bullet.

Does all this sound melodramatic? Blame the facts.

Look's darkroom occupied a substantial cavern on the same floor as the editors. This was imperative; time could not be wasted in the numberless discussions between editors and writers and photo-processors. The dozen men in our darkroom, under Si Solow, performed wizardry with noxious acids on recalcitrant negatives, wresting from celluloid the most extraordinary effects: brightening dark pictures, reducing the intensity of overexposed film, selecting a portion of a "frame" and "blowing it up," eliminating ("dodging out") background junk, "cropping" it, "forcing" or "pushing" a negative to gain one or another breathtaking effect.

A bizarre but momentous aside: the physical production of an issue of, say, 9,270,830 copies (March 7, 1967) involved the printing of 1,112,499,600 individual pages. That is a very large number of pages. Before 1965, magazines were printed on roughish paper (under a magnifying glass it was seen to be pitted by "peaks" and "valleys"). The raw paper

stock was coated, for smoothness, by immense high-speed rollers. These rollers transferred a sticky, hardening liquid to the paper; but when they turned away, some of the coating stuck to the roller, leaving the paper's surface rather like the peel of an orange. Such a surface was incapable of absorbing uniformly the millions of ink droplets (black or colored) deposited in the *printing* process: for the "kiss-and-run" action of the rollers coated the "hills" but passed over the "valleys." Hence, imprecision of registry, smudgings of ink, minute blurring of images.

One day at a Kimberley Clark plant Marvin Whatmore, soon to be President of *Look*'s operations, watched the gigantic rollers whirling across the swift flow of paper stock. He remarked to a supervisor, "What you are doing is like putting the frosting on a cake. Is that right?"

"Yes."

"Well, my wife wouldn't dream of putting frosting on a cake with a rolling pin. The best way to put frosting on a cake—or on paper, I think—is by using a spatula, or a knife."

The remark triggered three years of secret research and experiment—and in 1965 "trail-blade" coating was born: a long knife (not a roller) spread an even, liquid layer deep into the "troughs"—and levelled off on the "peaks." Intense heat welded the coating into the raw stock. This produced paper unrivalled for smoothness and, therefore, printability.

The miracle Whatmore wrought made possible the reproduction of photographs which for sheer brilliance, depth of hue, color "saturation" and subtlety, surpassed anything in the history of rotogravure printing. The new process, registered as *Look-Kromatic*, replaced rotogravure, but required entirely new presses, which could use ten gradations of color (instead of four or five as before). The beauty of pictorial journalism—its visual texture and "punch"—reached spectacular dimensions.*

I think I have reminisced enough, but I would be an ingrate if I concluded without expressing my appreciation to Claudia Kern, as capable and conscientious a researcher as any editor could hope to have; to Nai Chang, who lovingly designed this book; and—of course—to Harry N. Abrams and Martin Levin, who made this entire project possible and enhanced it by their vision.

Let me end by emphasizing one point: this is a *new* book. It is not a catalogue of *Look* features. It does not follow *Look*'s format. It does contain the most dramatic, lyrical, amusing, or memorable pictures, and the most interesting and significant highlights of text that appeared in *Look*'s pages across a span of thirty-five turbulent years.

This is, to my mind, a treasury of what *Look* did best.

*Soon after the *Look-Kromatic* technique was used, in a *Look* color feature on baking fish, Whatmore received the following request from Printing Developments, Inc. (a research and development subsidiary of the *Time* empire): "We would like to receive future examples, to use in our display room." It pleased us to think of the baked fish, apples, bread, spaghetti, avocadoes, muffins—and all the ingenious repertoire of our Food section—which thereafter gleamed on P.D.I.'s walls.

PEOPLE

FACES AND FEELINGS

Nothing in nature is more remarkable than the human face. It is the stage for our emotions. "People have babbling countenances," said Lord Chesterfield, "where they show what they have sense enough not to tell."

The face is a poster—or an impostor. Our features express an astonishing range of feeling: rapture, rage, passion, horror, and the countless nuances of love and fear and hate.

Here is a gallery of faces, more eloquent than words, which would have fascinated Rembrandt—and Shakespeare, who cried, "What a piece of work is man!"

—Ed.

Forever fresh.

◀ The "Jesus Movement" of the 1970's:
America's young turn to new forms of old religions.

◄ Aborigine (Australia).

Indian (New Mexico).

Tribesman (Africa).

ERNST HAAS

JOEL BALDWIN

BETTY AND JACK CHEETHAM

Hippy (San Francisco).

Dancer (Korea).

PHILLIP HARRINGTON

A child races the sun in a golden field.
Where? When? It does not matter.
It could have been a thousand years ago in Anatolia,
or yesterday in North Dakota, or tomorrow in....

The trials and tribulations of love in the second grade—a universal experience:

Johnny's moment of recognition;

The hopeful courtier, the coy fair lady;

Frustration, as a rival takes the field;

Spurned but undaunted, our hero gets the last "word."

California water-babies,
who began swimming when they were two,
frolic for an underwater movie shot.

34

It's always spring in Paris…

…while a new freedom comes to Central Park.

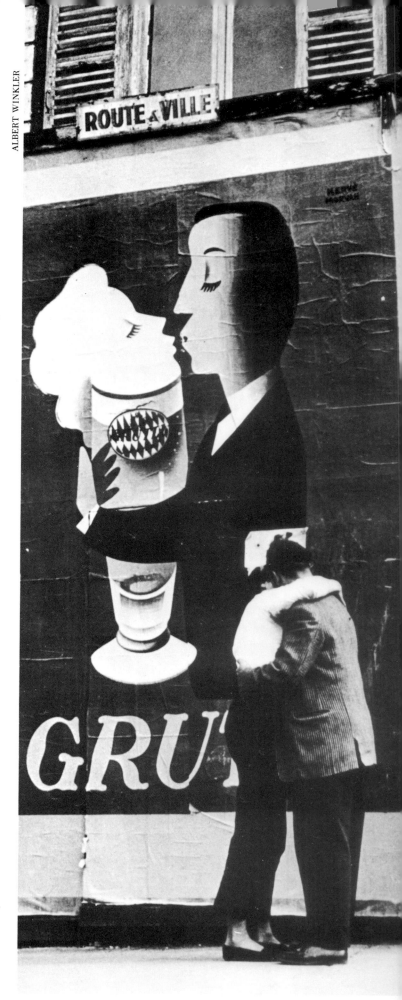

In New York City's Pennsylvania Station, ▶
silent foreboding as waiting prolongs
the anguish of parting.

Pain can be a knife.

O, the shame of it all!

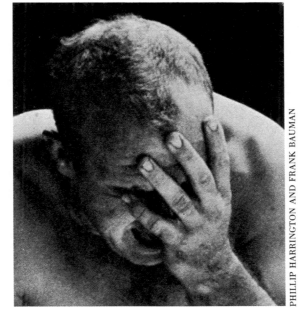

Words failed her.

Humiliation is a headache!

BURK UZZLE

(left). Marine debut: startled rookie, rasping tutor.

(below). The bugle is bigger than the boy—and he's playing it upside-down!

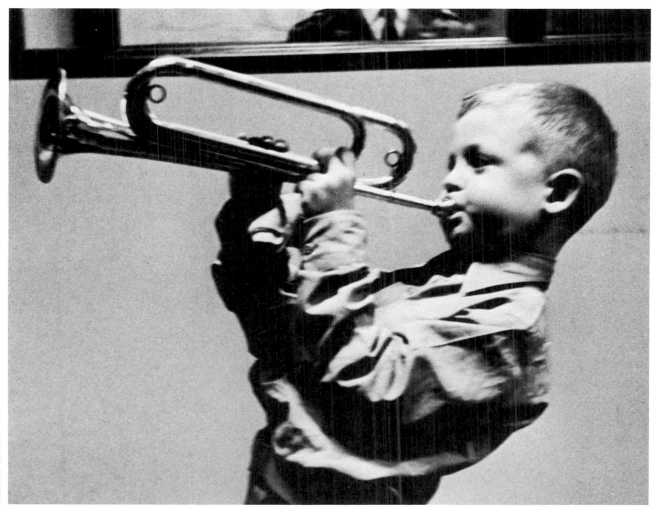

PHILLIP HARRINGTON.

Every boy's ordeal.

Socrates and Plato face a dilemma.

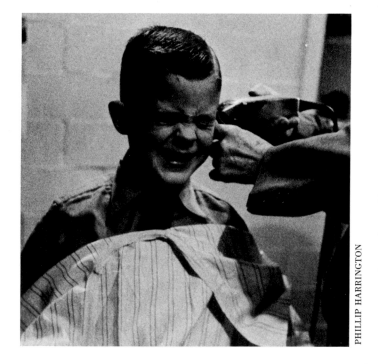

PHILLIP HARRINGTON

BOB VOSE

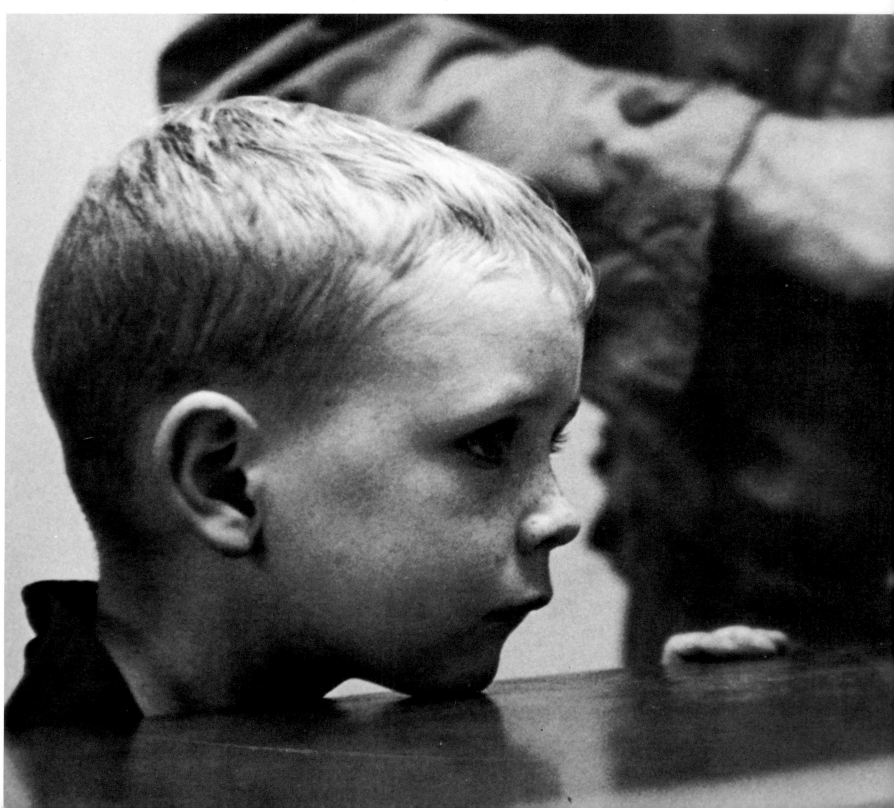

Courtship at the garden gate.

GENE KAMMERMAN

The doctor, the needle, the hero.

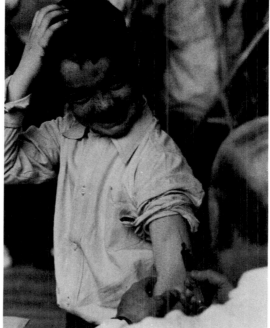

FRANK BAUMAN

BOB LERNER

"I am a horse."

BOB SANDBERG

At the vet's: sick dog,
heartsick master.

41

"I've got it! I know! I know!"

A volunteer from the North ▶
and her southern charge
in mutual discovery.

An Ivory Coast child has been hypnotized for one of the world's weirdest rituals.
Hurled 15 feet, back and forth, her body never touches the knife.

The Rotarian cowboy
whoops it up in
(of all places!)
Provence, France.

Weary but confident
in an ice palace 12,000 feet
in the sky.

Young Laotian Buddhists in training for monkhood.

MARC RIBOUD

Russian lads in Red Square ▶
distrust a foreigner's camera.

47

BOB LERNER

A Maryknoll Sister: serenity of soul; purity of spirit; a dedication to healing.

Pride and power on an American reservation. ▶

Las Vegas: the endless lure of craps...

JOHN VACHON

...and a pip of a belly dance,
an indigenous art form,
at the Silver Slipper.

51

Addicts smoke in pairs,
because cooking opium is a
complex skill not all can master.

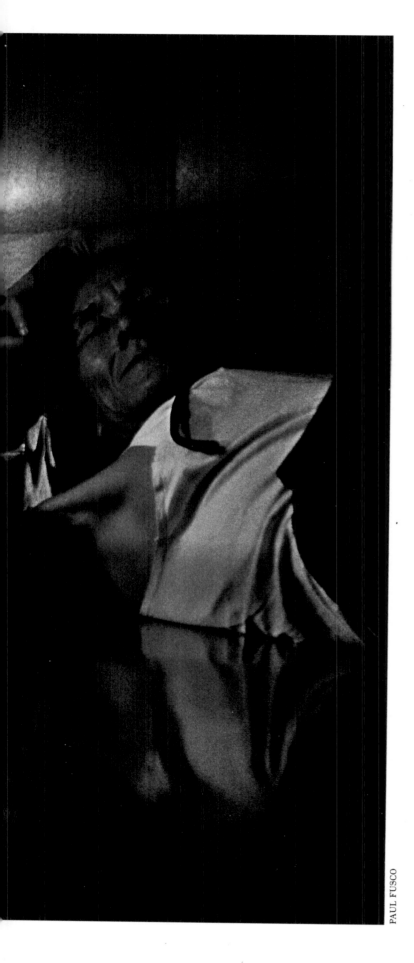

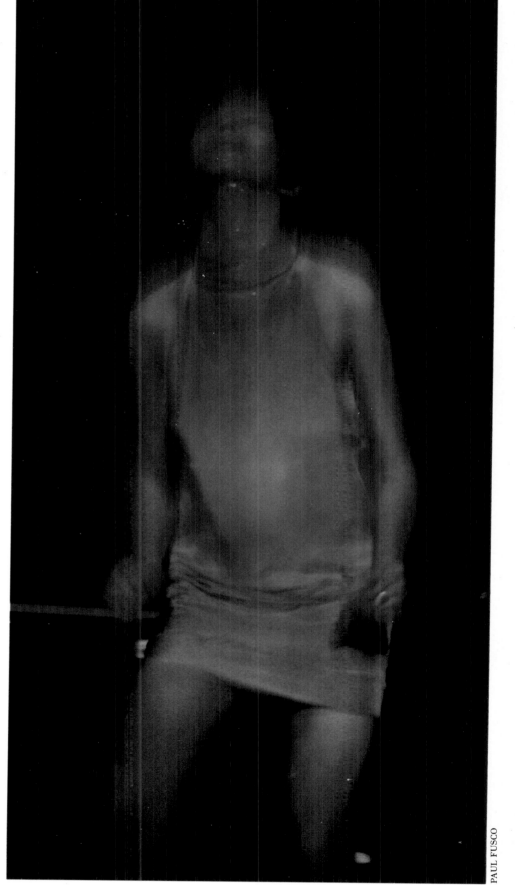

The frug:
a Southeast Asian teenager's
fiery frenzy.

53

◄ Flashy, gaudy hoopla in Miami.

In century-old rites of purification, the faithful bathe and pray in the Ganges.

(overleaf). Isaak Waltons at peace, in bliss, on the river Seine.

Melancholy in Harlem.

The numbed daze of despair. ▶

58

Buying a hat: a trilogy of emotions.

Father and daughter: Sunday in a museum.

"Gawd, it's cold in Montana!"

JOHN VACHON

◄ No greater love....

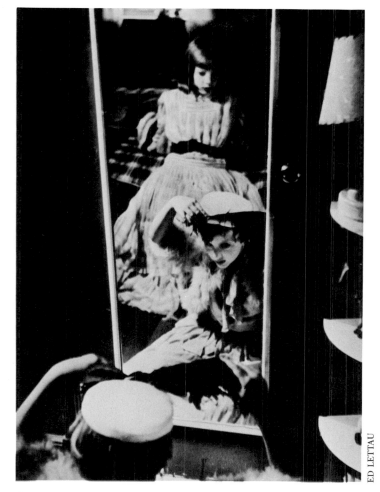

ED LETTAU

Attic treasures, the stuff
of little girls' fantasies.

ED LETTAU

Exquisite, evocative—the photographer turns painter.

◄ O, vanity!

MICHAEL VACCARO

Sheer joy in winged exercise.

Eleven sailors (count them!) ▶
scramble aloft.

◄ Sicilian women: death grips even the living.

BOB VOSE

Shame floods into tears at a military school—
and all he did was lose points for Company "E."

Don't miss the mouth of the pipsqueak below!

PHILLIP HARRINGTON

Southern belles flirt,
and a virago sears her cavalier.

PAUL FUSCO

An ecstatic disciple of Jesus.

A mental asylum,
for those whom life
has crushed.

A Sioux family:
five of America's
long-forgotten.

72

A boy in Bali with a water buffalo.

75

◄ Just before donning her veil,
a bride's pensive moment.

Peeping around China's
bamboo curtain, 1957.
(LOOK was the first American journal
allowed inside Red China.)

Georgia, 1945: fiery crosses carry the Ku Klux Klan's gruesome message.

"CRY HAVOC!"

rom 1914 on, from the rape of Belgium to the horrors of Vietnam, the spinning globe we call Earth was bled and befouled by violence on a scale unparalleled in history.

How many deaths in how many years? How many lynchings, murders, assassinations? How much torture? The toll is too ghastly to be measured, the agonies of the bereaved are too awful to be told in numbers.

In Mississippi or Germany; in Russia Africa, Japan; in mob massacres or bloody revolts; in the clash of immense armies or in the obscene ovens of Buchenwald—the most precious thing we possess, human life, has paid the price exacted by passion masked as politics.

The next pages only suggest the dimensions of hatred writ large.

—Ed.

EUROPEAN

(left). Berlin, 1934:
Nazi torches for Nazi madness.
(above). The Madman from Munich:
30,000,000 human lives paid
for Adolf Hitler's paranoia.

The fruit of war:
grim relics in a field in France,
50 years after World War I.

June 6, 1944, "D" day: the free world's miraculous
invasion of France, gateway to a Europe
overrun by the Nazis. History has no precedent
for so massive, bold, and complex a military
tour de force.

"A half-million people live in Hiroshima. Only one in 15 of them was in the city 25 years ago when an explosion filled the sky as though a piece of sun had broken off, a bolt of white-hot terror that twisted steel into unimaginable shapes, melted iron bridges, and incinerated more flesh than has ever been condemned at one time and in one place throughout the history of the human race."
—*Norman Cousins* (1970)

The holocaust symbolized ▶
in a Japanese girl's eye.

An American corpse waits.

JAMES KARALES

◄ April, 1965: the cannons roar
 in Vietnam's "demilitarized" zone.

CATHERINE LEROY

(overleaf).
"I lose men," the commander said.
"I lose so many men."

War's toll: the half-dead...

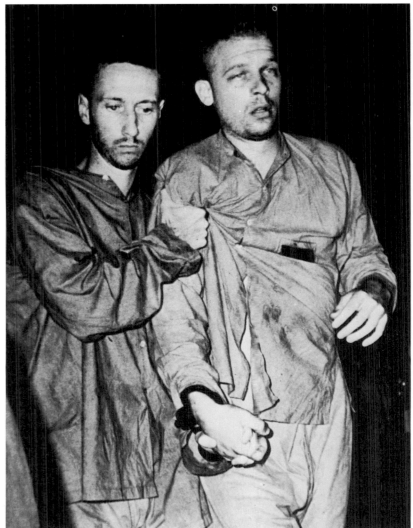

PICTORIAL PARADE

JAMES KARALES

...and the dead.

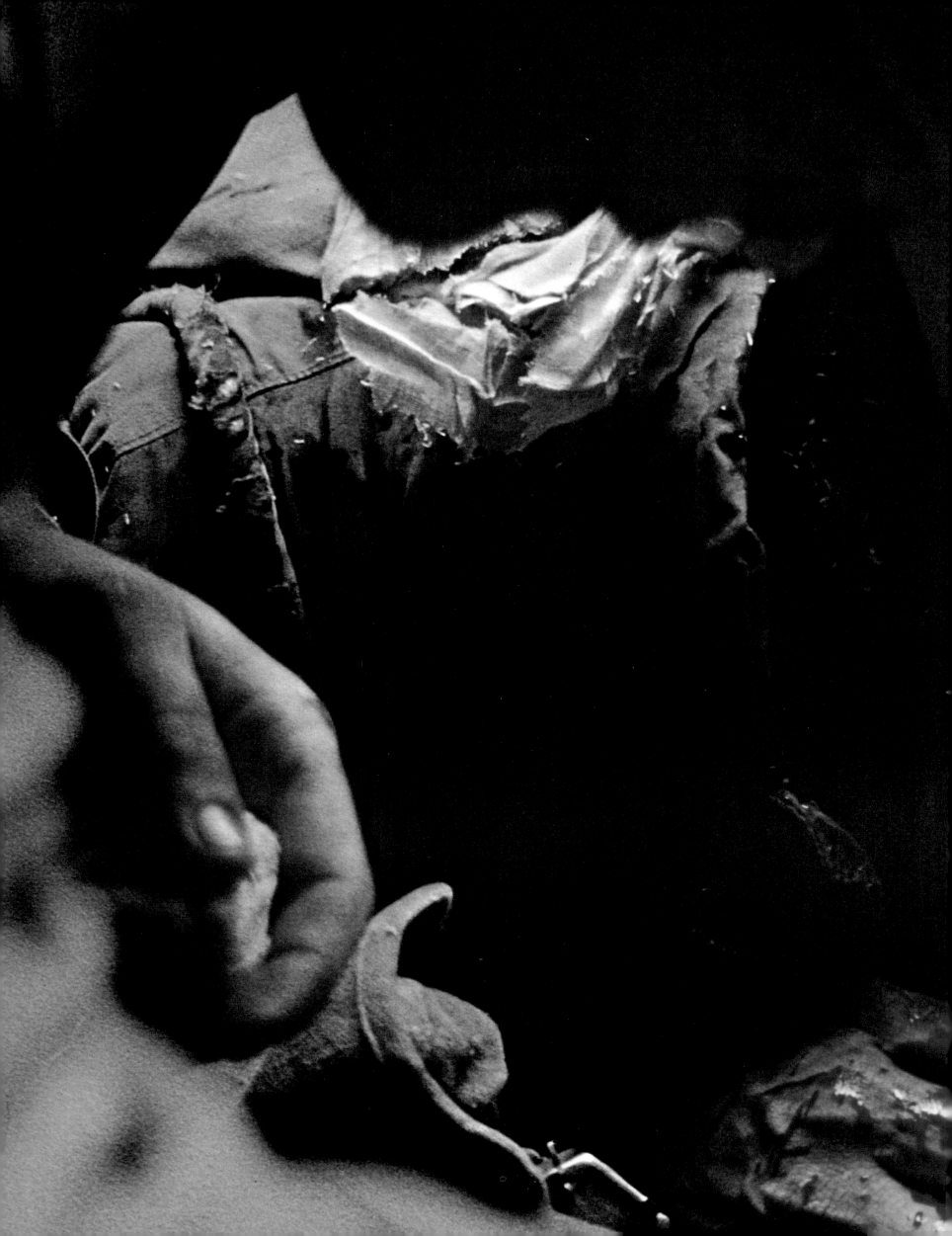

◄ The Reverend Martin Luther King, Jr., "I have a dream...."

The dream on the march....

Racists' hoses pelt helpless blacks.

At the funeral of ▶
a black soldier slain
in Vietnam, the unmeasurable
agony of loss.

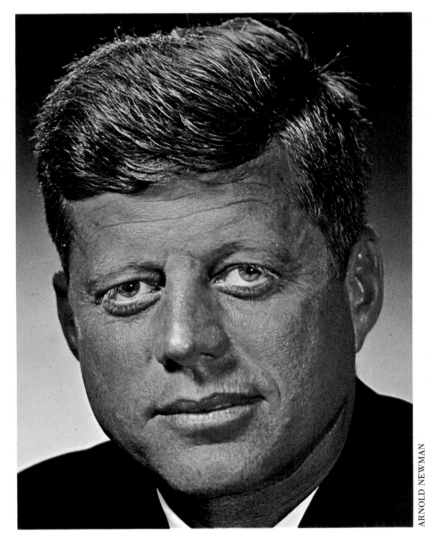

ARNOLD NEWMAN

President John F. Kennedy, 1961.

STEVE SCHAPIRO

Robert F. Kennedy in one haunted
moment of anguished remembrance.

November 25, 1963, ▶
National Day of Mourning:
the President's coffin
before a family stunned
and bereaved.

MARC RIBOUD

At the great peace march in Washington, D.C., 1967,
a "flower child" confronts the massed bayonets
of an uneasy National Guard.

LOOK
TREASURY

What Is Human Nature?

BY MARGARET MEAD

Exactly what does "human nature" mean?

People usually mean by "human nature" those characteristics which are *learned* (rather than inherited) from the way in which we are reared and taught to be human. For we *are* taught to be human. If a human being were not reared and educated by other human beings, he would be "human" only in his physical characteristics; he would not be able to talk (though he could make sounds); he might not even stand erect; he would have neither religion nor table manners; he might not even recognize that another human being was a creature of the same kind.

Is it true that "you can't change human nature?"

When people say "you can't change human nature," they usually mean some undesirable characteristic of other people. But "human nature" expresses itself in so many immensely different ways, from one people of the world to another, that we can only marvel at the capacity of the human race for variation and change.

Consider such basic emotions as fear, shame, grief, anger. They are universal; but the ways in which these emotions are *expressed* depend on social tradition. Anger may be shown by a clenched fist or by chopping down one's own house. Fear may be experienced in the pit of the stomach, the back of the neck, the buttocks or even in the big toe, depending on what parts of your body you were *taught* to identify with the emotion of fear. What any person will feel and do depends on what we call the "culture" in which he is reared—the shared values and traditions which are passed down from generation to generation.

Is it not true that some people are born with greater intelligence or talent than others?

Some *individuals* are born with greater talent than other individuals. Among any *people*—in an African tribe, a French province, an Iowa county—some persons are born with greater talent than others *of the same stock*, even their own brothers and sisters. The same family may contain a genius and an imbecile.

But are there not "racial" characteristics? For instance: Aren't whites more intelligent than Negroes? Aren't Germans better scientists than Italians? Are Jews smarter than Gentiles?

No. So far as we know, there are no differences of this sort. All groups of people have, in degrees which vary from one individual to another, the *capacity* to learn to be scientists or musicians, to be smart or dull, ambitious or apathetic, passionate or unresponsive. The differences in "character" which can be observed today between, say, French Catholics and English Catholics, or between European Jews and Jews who continue to live in the Near East, or between African Negroes and American Negroes—these are all *learned* differences, part of the social inheritance, not part of any basic, unchanging physical inheritance.

Is there not a natural sense of sin in all human beings? Doesn't everyone have a conscience, no matter how he is raised?

Every society teaches people its own concept of what is right and what is wrong, what is good and what is bad. Every human being has *some* kind of conscience. But this does not mean that the sense of sin is either "natural" or "inevitable." There are *styles* in conscience, just as there are styles in marriage patterns or forms of government.

We Americans think of conscience as that part of the self which keeps us good even when no one is looking. Conscience is that part of our personality which is built up out of love and respect for our parents. But in Nazi Germany and Soviet Russia, it was even possible for children to be taught that it was "good" to denounce their own parents to the authorities.

Is there a natural sense of modesty or shame in all human beings?

Whether people respond with a flush of shame or a blush of pleasure is a matter of learning, not "instinct." What people will be ashamed about or pleased about—being caught without a nose bone, or with a hole in a stocking, or with their hair up or their hair down—all these are learned reactions.

How about grief and pain? Don't Orientals endure more pain and show less feeling than the white races do?

People seem unfeeling (or maudlin) to other people when they behave *differently*. The Chinese use white for mourning; some people are required to weep at death; others are taught to smile and play cards on the corpse (the Koryak of Siberia). Some peoples expect anyone who is suffering to wail loudly so that others may give comfort (as among Eastern European Jews).

Does "human nature" contain so much aggression that the human race will never be able to eliminate war?

Warfare is an invention, a way in which one group of people defends itself against others or attacks others—for glory, women, land, slaves or loot. Warfare does not depend upon people's "natural" quarrelsomeness; modern men, indeed, have to be taught to get angry enough to pull the triggers of their guns.

Warfare is a human institution, with rules which are learned and modified from one generation to another. All man's most antisocial possibilities—hatred, vengeance, destructiveness—are used in war. But so are all his most constructive possibilities—loyalty, cooperativeness, generosity, self-sacrifice for his group and his country, his ideals.

War is not inevitable because of "human nature." When we invent other, better ways of dealing with the relationships between tribes or nations, war may become obsolete. Let us not forget that, not so long ago, dueling was considered the "natural" way for gentlemen to avenge an insult, protect a woman's honor or maintain their own self-respect. Whatever man has invented, man can change. War can become as obsolete as dueling.

Can civilization become too complicated for men to cope with?

No civilization has ever been so complicated that a normal baby, reared within it by people who understood it, could not learn how to live in it too. The baby has to learn from scratch—with complete human equipment; he learns to take planes instead of canoes; to communicate by cable or walkie-talkie instead of knotted string; to buy something by check instead of sea shells; to phrase his questions so they can be answered by Univac instead of by a shaman looking at the liver of an animal.

The difficulty does not lie in human *abilities*, which are inherent in our human nature, but in the failure of our social institutions—our schools, courts, leadership, legislatures—to invent new ways of solving new (and old) social problems.

All About Love

BY JULIAN HUXLEY

How much do we know about love?

The first thing we know about love is that, for most of us, it is the most absorbing and interesting subject in existence.

Reprinted by permission of A D Peters & Co Ltd

There is an enormous range of meanings in this one little word "love." There are mother love and self love, father love and children's love for their parents; there are brotherly love and love of one's home and one's country; love of money and love of power; making love and loving food; there are music lovers, sport lovers, bird lovers, sun lovers. Preachers insist that we should love God; Jesus adjures us to love our enemies. Love clearly includes all these usages: but the love in which one can *be* is the pre-eminent love for most of us.

Man is unique in having a brain which can bring all the various elements of his experience into contact, instead of keeping them in separate compartments, as is the case with animals. This not only provides the basis for imagination and abstract thought, for ideals and philosophies and works of art, but also for a battery of complex sentiments unknown in animals—reverence, awe, moral feelings and love in its developed form. It also, however, provides the basis for psychological conflict on a scale unknown in animals. Man's morality, indeed, is a necessary outcome of his inner conflicts.

Love at its fullest can include in its single embrace an enormous range of emotions and sentiments, fusing them all, even those of baser metal, in its crucible. It can combine humility with pride, passion with peace, self-assertion with self-surrender; it can reconcile violence of feeling with tenderness; it can swallow up disgust in reverent worship of beauty; it can sublimate sexual desire into joy and the realization of a fuller life.

Is there a distinction between love and sex?

Surely, that is obvious. It was certainly obvious to Dante, who reserved his highest love for a woman whose hand he had never even touched, but he had four children by the excellent woman he later married: Then maternal love, unlike sexual love, always involves tenderness and care. Only when the different kinds of love become blended does sexual love come to involve tenderness as well as desire.

For true lovers, the act of physical union is actuated not merely (or indeed mainly) by a desire for pleasure, but for the transcendent sense of total union which it can bring.

Sexual desire by itself is lust; it is universally regarded as immoral, and, to many people, the sexual act appears as something dirty or disgusting. In many religions, it is associated with sin.

Is there a difference between love and "being in love"?

Yes. Being in love is love at its most intense, and personally focused in a very special way. Our common speech reflects this fact. We talk of "falling in love," as if it was something into which we are precipitated against our will, like falling into a pond.

Love at first sight is a well-established phenomenon, no less surprising as a scientific fact than as a personal experience. Lovers are obsessed by the image of the loved one, to whom they ascribe every virtue and merit; outside observers of the phenomenon speak of the lover's "madness" or "blindness." The lover experiences a heightened vitality and finds new significance in life. Merely to see the beloved is to feast the soul; and to touch her (or him) is bliss. But when the two souls can interpenetrate, an even more magical state is achieved.

How does love develop in the individual human?

The development of love in man shows a general parallel with its evolution in animals, but there are many important differences. Man relies more on learning by experience, less on inborn mechanisms. But a few inborn stimuli do seem to exist. One is the smile; even a crude, grimacing model of a smiling face will get a smile from a baby. Another is woman's breasts, which act as a powerful sign stimulus to the human male.

The child's basic desires for food, warmth and protection are soon transmuted into love of enjoyment, satisfaction and fulfillment. The child focuses love onto those individuals who provide what is desired—first the mother or nurse, then the father, brothers and sisters, and so on. The widening of the circle of love comes to include love of the beautiful, the strange or the significant.

These complex and nonsexual loves sometimes attain the intensity of passions; the full force of a child's emotions may be bound up with some shell or curious stone; and the experience of beauty can transform his whole emotional life. The experience of loving natural beauty, of self-transcendence in union with something outside oneself —these may change a growing human being permanently, and can enter later into his love of God, for someone of the other sex, or for noble ideals.

Does reason play no part in love?

Falling in love is irrational, or at least nonrational. Emotion in general is nonrational; it tends to all-or-nothing manifestations and resists the critical spirit of reason. And the emotions involved in love are so violent that this anticritical tendency readily overrides our reason. That is why love has a magic compulsion and may become a kind of sickness or madness.

But reason and experience can play a part later. A point may suddenly be reached at which reason gains the upper hand, the lover's eyes are opened, and he falls out of love as he once fell in. Such experiences are useful reminders of the fact that emotional certitude alone is not a guarantee of rightness or truth, in religion or morals.

What social problems do love and sex present to us?

Love presents man with the perennial problem—how to reconcile the claims of the individual and of society, how to reconcile personal desires with social aims. This is perhaps most acute in adolescence. Our sexual desires arise (and in males, at least, arise at maximum strength, as Dr. Kinsey has shown) several years before marriage is desirable or possible. Different cultures have met this problem in different ways. In eighteenth-century England and France, it was the acknowledged thing for upper-class young men to take a mistress. In America, dating and petting—the twentieth-century version of bundling—are the recognized compromise.

Other societies find other ways of gratifying adolescent love. The attitude both to premarital love-making and to postmarital love affairs may differ enormously from culture to culture. In some, the boys after initiation live in communities with the girls; only after some years do they marry, and then extramarital love is severely frowned upon.

What is the relation between love and hate?

In one sense, love and hate are the positive and negative aspects of the same thing, the primary emotional reaction to another individual. From the evolutionary angle, however, love and hate are distinct. Love in animals may have several separate manifestations—parental, sexual and social. The same holds for hate: It may manifest itself in fear, in avoidance or in aggression.

Man's primal conflict is between love and hate. The human baby inevitably loves his mother (or mother substitute) as the fountainhead of his satisfaction, security and peace. But he is also angry with her, as the power who arbitrarily denies him satisfaction and thwarts his impulses. And his anger calls into play a battery of rage impulses and magical hate fantasies or death wishes. But the child's aggressive hate feelings soon come into violent conflict with his love, and the only method available to the infant to cope with this conflict is to repress this hate into his unconscious, as Freud showed.

The infantile conflict between love and hate generates the primal sense of guilt, which is the rudimentary ethical mechanism. Around this mechanism, our conscience and our adult ethics, our sense of right and wrong are later constructed. Of course, reason and experience, imagination and ideals also contribute. But the underlying basis of conscience and ethics remains nonrational and largely unconscious, as is shown by the terrifying sense of sin and unworthiness which besets those unfortunates burdened wih a too-heavy load of guilt.

Consciences, in fact, are not genetically predetermined. They do not grow automatically, like backbones; they need love and its infantile conflict with hate for their origination. This is demonstrated by studies of children who were brought up in impersonal institutions, or otherwise deprived of a maternal love and care, during the critical period between one and three years old. Many of these children never developed a conscience or the capacity for love. They grew up as amoral and loveless beings, creatures without ethics or emotional attachments. The mother is thus the central figure in the drama of love's evolution. Mother love is indispensable for the development of children's consciences and emotions. Mother love has been responsible for introducing tenderness into sexual love.

How important do you, as a biologist, think love is?

As a biologist, but also as a human being, I want to affirm the unique importance of love in life—an affirmation badly needed in a tormented age like ours, where violence and disillusion have joined forces with undigested technological advance to produce an atmosphere of cynicism and crude materialism.

Love is indispensable. Mother love is indispensable for children's healthy and happy growth, both physical and spiritual. Personal love is indispensable both for the continuance of the species, and for the full development of the individual. Love is part of personal education; through love, the self learns to grow. Love of beauty and of all lovely and wonderful things is equally indispensable for our growth and the realization of our possibilities. It brings reverence and a sense of transcendence into personal love, and indeed into all of life. Love is a positive emotion, an enlargement of life; it leads on toward greater fulfillment and counteracts human hate and destructive impulses.

Let the final word be that of a poet who was also a man of science—Robert Bridges: " . . . God's worshiper looking on any beauty falleth straightway in love; . . . love is a fire in whose devouring flames all earthly ills are consumed."

Why We Accept Cheating

BY WALTER LIPPMANN

big change has come into American life. It is not that our behavior is demonstrably worse than it used to be. It may in many respects be considerably better. I have no doubt, for example, that the wars of this generation were conducted more honestly and more efficiently than was the Civil War. The big change in our time is that we are much more lax in what we think about our conduct. We are much more ready to accept and excuse the cheating that is so widespread and so common.

There are some who would argue that this softening of our consciences is a change for the better. It does away, they point out, with much hypocrisy and self-righteousness, with much secrecy and self-deception.

I think they are right. I think that the new candor is letting light and fresh air into many dark and smelly places. It is good to be candid and compassionate, and these are the attractive virtues of our time. But it is bad to be confused. It is bad to shrug off the ideal standards by saying what is no doubt true, but only half the truth, that we are all sinners and fall short of the ideal. This is moral confusion. This is not candor and compassion, which are virtues, but moral ignorance, which is a vice.

Why is it bad to shrug off the ideal standards of honesty in politics, business and love? Because it defeats us and frustrates our lives. If we do not harden ourselves by stretching ourselves to reach upward to these not wholly attainable ideals, we settle into flabbiness and footlessness and boredom. When a generation becomes cynical, it is condemning itself to what a poet once described as the everlasting pursuit of the ever-fleeting object of desire. It is a mistake to suppose that there is satisfaction and the joy of life in a self-indulgent generation, in one interested primarily in the pursuit of private wealth and private pleasure and private success.

On the contrary, a self-indulgent generation, as is this generation, in large part is an unhappy one. We are very rich, but we are not having a very good time. For our life, though it is full of things, is empty of the kind of purpose and effort that gives to life its flavor and its meaning.

The ideals of a good life are not a code of rules defined by old gentlemen with gray beards. These ideal standards of what is good and what is honorable define the hygiene of the spirit by which the good life becomes possible.

When we ask ourselves what should be done about it all, I myself do not despair. It is clear, I think, that moral indifference exists among people who have no purposes beyond their private tastes and wishes and whims and ambitions. It is not surprising that they are so numerous at the present time. For they have been living in a decade which began with the disappointment and disillusionment of the Korean War, and has been followed by years in which private purposes have had the right of way over public purposes.

This will pass. The nation is growing and changing, and the problems which cannot be ignored are mounting. They will generate public purposes. And when they do generate public purposes, they will overcome the moral indifference.

They will organize the spirit of those who are indifferent to-day because they have nothing within them that organizes their spirits.

I have no doubt that the complacency and the in-difference of the fifties will be overcome in the sixties. As the private purposes are overcome by the impact and pressure of our public needs, the way will be opened to a wider examination of our moral condition. It will be open to the larger and more lasting question of the modern age. This has to do with the breakdown of purposes because there has been a failure of the capacity to believe—the capacity to be-lieve that anything really matters very much and that any-thing is really better than anything else.

Men Really
Don't Like Women

BY JULES FEIFFER

I consider most sociology to be emotional autobi-ography. If this generalization is correct—and no study I have read on women indicates otherwise—then I can, without reluctance, proceed to sum up the American woman with full assurance that, like every other expert, all that I am really giving away are some veiled secrets about myself.

The American woman is a victim. She is unique, as far as victims go, in that she has been trained to be ill at ease ad-mitting it. Her trouble is that she is doing comparatively well as a victim—making a buck, running a family; and then, too, there are so many more *imposing* victims around.

For example: Negroes. But Negroes at least have the security of knowing that our society, no matter what it says, basically has contempt for them. They can build an identity on this knowledge, secure roots, invoke defiance. The Negro, by the sheer enormity of the problems we have saddled on him, is a *star* victim.

Woman's position is far less dramatic and, consequent-ly, less conscience-demanding. Lost in the shadow of our greater prejudices, she drags along, her problem not taken seriously by either herself or anyone else, her identity a mess because she has neither a rock of acceptance nor rejection on which to anchor it. Woman is a second-class victim. And what is her problem? We all know it is man.

There is good reason to believe that God created woman not out of Adam's rib but out of Adam's psyche. What Adam needed, he got: a scapegoat to point to for making him

deliciously self-conscious. ("Good heavens, I'm naked! And, good heavens, Eve! So are *you!*")

Man, being the most intelligent of beings, is also the most devious. When physical strength cannot overcome his enemies, he invents weapons; when moral attitudes inhibit his drives, he invents women. They are the instruments by which different men reap different (carefully contained) satisfactions.

Which brings us to a point seldom mentioned in these studies on women. Men really don't like them. Man has always seen woman as his enemy. How in the world can he be expected to love her? He cannot. But, if for no other reason than procreation, he *needs* her.

We are all familiar with the fact that little boys do not like little girls. We pretend to think they outgrow it. They do not. They merely learn to hide it.

What they are hiding, really, is fear for their own po-tency. Man is interested, more than anything else, in his own potency (not always sexual, in fact, in our time, less and less so). Potency today may have more relevance to a man's business life than to his sex life. As moral prohibitions loosen and woman discovers sexual enjoyment, man loses it. As her puritanism lessens, his goes underground. He punishes her with remoteness. When that doesn't work, he tries impotence.

Woman may try to catch up, but she just doesn't have the footwork. When she is practical, man says she lacks romance; when she achieves full romance, man says she's a tramp; when she rejects romance because it hasn't helped her, man says she's frigid; when she argues in her defense, man says she's manipulative; when she makes demands, she is castrating; when she withdraws into alienation, she is the "American Woman"; when she turns bitter and feels sorry for herself, she is the "Jewish Mother." No wonder she has identity problems.

When she's little, boys will have nothing to do with her—the first blow to her sense of self. Girls need the com-pany of boys to feel like girls; boys feel most like boys when they're with more boys—until high school. Girls have their uses in high school: The good-looking ones are to be seen with; the dogs can do your homework.

Boys don't like to be bested—don't best them; boys don't like easy virtue—be difficult; boys don't like unpopu-lar girls—be a tease; boys talk only about themselves—try to listen; boys are terrified by women—stay girlish; boys are most relaxed with boys—become one.

The complexities that we like to claim for the character of women are, largely, male inspired. They are women's reac-tion to a world where men lay down the rules, manage the ethics, inflate the morals and define the stereotypes.

Only a finely honed shiftiness has enabled woman to survive as well as she has. But the fulfillment of the American dream has wreaked havoc on man's picture of himself and has thoroughly frustrated woman's ability to react to that picture. Affluence has taken away man's economic depression and given him, in replacement, psychological depression.

The unblinking attention given by the mass media to the American woman is just another chapter in that old course: Know Your Enemy. Her dissection will follow form; she will come out awful. She will be unhappy, dissatisfied, not knowing her own mind (as we know ours). She will be fragmented, torn between home (where lies happiness) and career (where lies lesbos). She will shortsightedly work against her best interest and wastefully undermine that vast reservoir of goodwill it has taken so many (ungrateful) years to build up.

She will be advised as to what her place is and how to keep it by teams of Aunt Toms who make comfortable careers out of marriagelessly pushing marriage and motherlessly pushing motherhood.

It is sexual McCarthyism. But that it exists at all is a sign of hope. It indicates that something is moving somewhere, and that woman, the most submerged of minority groups, might build for herself a new identity, if only out of the collapse of everyone else's.

What Is Jealousy?

BY DR. RALPH R. GREENSON

hat is jealousy?

Jealousy—"the green-eyed monster"—is not one basic emotion, but a compound of many—grief, love, anger, greed, hatred and envy. Many of these emotional reactions are kept out of our full consciousness because they violate our conventional attitudes. For instance, we do not readily allow ourselves to realize that we sometimes hate those we love—husband or wife, mother or father or even child.

What makes people jealous?

People feel jealous when they lose, or fear they are going to lose, someone they love—to another person. Jealousy always involves a triangle. The fear of losing a loved person's love may be based on real factors or it may be based on imagination or exaggeration. This distinction is very important: It accounts for the difference between normal as against pathological jealousy. Thus, a man tormented by jealousy because of the behavior of his wife with another man is in quite another position from a man who has persuaded himself that his wife is having an affair—when there is no

real ground for this fantasy. The first man may need comfort and advice; the second man can only be helped by psychiatric treatment.

Some people create situations, unconsciously, which will make them jealous. Thus, a jealous wife or husband may insist on taking the spouse to a party where flirtatious contacts are likely.

What is the difference between jealousy and envy?

In jealousy, we feel rejected, rebuffed, shamed; in envy, we do not. Jealousy usually contains a sexual component; envy does not. In jealousy, we feel threatened in envy, we do not. In envy, we simply want something which belongs to someone else.

In envy, the person who has what you want is unimportant—except for his or her role as a frustrating agent. But in jealousy, your reaction to the two other people involved is much more complicated: You want more than possession—you want reactions, emotions, love. When you are jealous, your rival is very important—not only hated, but feared and even admired.

Are men or women more jealous?

Clinical experience suggests that women are more likely to be jealous than men. Clinical evidence indicates that, in the early years, little girls feel that boys have certain anatomical advantages over them. Little girls at play frequently imitate little boys—but rarely do boys imitate little girls.

When and how does jealousy begin?

Very early, each baby has to go through the experience of losing many things it loves. When the baby is weaned from the breast, for instance, it feels that amalgam of frustration, longing, rage and sorrow which forms perhaps the earliest model of the emotions that later produce jealousy. Babies are not born with an instinct to share or the capacity to wait. He wants total, unshared, "selfish" satisfactions. As soon as a child is old enough to recognize that the mother must deprive him in order to care for other members of the family, we see signs of jealousy.

Is it inevitable for brothers and sisters to be jealous of each other?

Yes. Each child is in a position where competition for the love of the mother and father is inevitable. Each brother or sister is therefore a rival for parental love or care, devotion or time; and a rival creates resentment, competitiveness and anger.

How can parents prevent jealousy in their children?

Parents should not try to prevent jealousy. Psychological health depends upon how jealousy is handled, not upon its absence. Even in the happiest families, it is inevitable that one or another child will be given more affection and attention at one time or another. However painful, jealousy is an important emotion and it should be respected as such. If children will learn how to bear the pain of jealousy, they will eventually learn how to avoid or conquer its harmful aspects.

Are parents sometimes jealous of their children?

Yes. The jealous parent is much more common than we realize. It is very hard for parents to admit even to themselves that they really can feel jealous of their own children. The well-known objections of a father to his daughter's boy friends can often be traced to the fact that he is jealous, deep down; jealous that any male should displace him from first position in his daughter's eyes and heart.

In a good marriage, does a husband or a wife ever get jealous?

Of course. Even in the best of marriages, mild, temporary jealousy is bound to arise. A marriage unites two people who were subjected to the inevitable frustrations and conflicts and fears of childhood. Whenever they are humiliated or defeated, the old sources of their fears—particularly the fear of being unloved, the dread of being unlovable—come to the fore. At such times, the husband or wife may seek to "exorcise" feelings of inadequacy by blaming the partner. A spouse is very likely to be blamed when the husband or wife suffers a blow to self-esteem—because at such a time the feeling of being unloved is acute. And with the feeling of being unloved comes that "green-eyed suspicion" which underlies jealousy.

A certain amount of flirtatiousness is encouraged in our society, and this can, on occasion, stir up intense jealousy. Some husbands or wives use jealousy in order to test the love reactions of their partners; others may use it for teasing and even hurting the partner: still others find that jealousy situations, when resolved, make a particularly sweet reunion.

Even in a good marriage, a husband will feel jealous when the first baby enters the family. For the husband is presented with a little "rival" who will undoubtedly take much time and attention away from him. The first baby inaugurates a trying period in any marriage—especially for those fathers who suffered severe jealousy reactions in their own childhood.

In every case, it is the individual's past history, his or her sense of proportion, his or her feelings of security, which determines the intensity and the duration of natural jealousy reactions. In a good marriage—which is to say a marriage in which there is love, understanding and communication between husband and wife—jealousy reactions are managed without lasting harm.

The Christmas Gift

BY ERNEST HEMINGWAY

Various people have asked me what one thinks at the hour of one's death, a rather exaggerated phrase, and what it feels like to read one's obituaries. Your past life does not rush through your brain like a cinema film and your thoughts are purely technical. Perhaps there are people whose past lives rush through their brains, but so far in my life I have never experienced this sensation.

After you have crashed and/or burned in a plane, you are usually in a state of what is loosely described as shock. On a crash-landing where the aircraft has been set down comparatively softly there is not much shock but I believe there is always some. However, if you are conditioned to this by the practice of more or less contact sports, you are familiar with the sensations and can sort them out.

There were four small pops representing the explosion of the bottles of Carlsberg beer which had constituted our reserve. This was followed by a slightly louder pop which represented the bottle of the Grand MacNish. After this, I clearly heard a louder but still not intense explosion which I knew signified the unopened bottle of Gordon's gin. This is sealed by a metal cap and therefore gives an explosion of greater power than that of the Grand MacNish which is only sealed by a cork and, in any event, had been half consumed. I listened for further explosions but there were none.

We then left the scene of the crash in the motor vehicle of a young policeman who had kindly consented to take us to Masindi. In this vehicle was the charming wife of this police officer and Miss Mary and myself, adjusting ourselves to the 53-mile ride which was accomplished on no liquor or any other beverage. This was the longest ride of my life and I am sure it did not seem short to Miss Mary. At one time I remarked to her, "Miss Mary, can you make it okay without our stopping at any friendly place or *dukka* for a small quick one?" It is customary to administer to *Ndege* characters one or two ounces of, preferably, bourbon, after the crash and burning of an aircraft if it has crashed or burned on what is considered a friendly airfield.

"Papa," Miss Mary replied, "I can make it if you can, but it is the hard way."

We held hands with our good hands and rode it out.

There had been what we describe in the parlance of the

R.A.F. as the meat wagon present at the scene of our second crash. It was in charge of an African practitioner who was extremely cordial, deeply moved, but so excited that he forgot he was to administer certain first-aid treatment.

Miss Mary was in great pain from the broken ribs and did not sleep well. However, the howling of this beast reassured her and made her feel that she was back in the dear old days of the Kimana Swamp before she had accepted the Christmas present of this trip in the *Ndege*.

There is nothing you can do about broken ribs anyway, except to hope you receive them in the ninth round of a ten-round fight rather than in the first. Strapping them up only means that the plaster must be removed and even for a girl whose body is less hirsute than that of a man, the removal of plaster may be extremely painful.

After we had been treated, we traveled by motor car from Masindi to Entebbe. This is a rather dull and dusty drive—result of the continued failure of the rains in the north—and there is not much to see until you hit Kampala, the City of the Seven Hills, which is an exceedingly charming town. The journey is, however, one of some 135 miles and it affords ample time for thought and reflection.

This thought is conditioned by the fact that the so-called thinker has suffered a major concussion and therefore is not responsible for his thoughts. This type of concussion induces the type of thinking which sometimes tends toward violence. I believe this violence is a phenomenon of concussion due to the violent demise of the aircraft. In any event, it is to be deplored and I hereby disavow any responsibility for the thoughts which passed through my head, but here is what some of them were.

First, I wished that Sen. Joseph McCarthy (Republican) of Wisconsin had been with us at the crash of both aircraft. I have always had a certain curiosity, as one has about all public figures, as to how Senator McCarthy would behave in what we call the clutch.

Then I remembered Mr. Leonard Lyons, my very old friend, and his experience with the .577 when we tried out 20 rounds of ammunition in the proving booth in the basement of Abercrombie & Fitch in New York. It was old ammo and it was necessary to determine if it was still reliable. Mr. Lyons, who is extremely gallant, well built but a little short on weight, fired the .577 and the recoil lifted him from his feet and laid him against an iron doorway at the back of the proving ground. He dropped the .577 but it was uninjured, and for some miles I pondered happily on this incident and on other incidents that happened to me with Mr. Leonard Lyons.

I then commenced to ponder, in my still disordered condition, on Mr. Toots Shor. Pondering on Mr. Shor, you may pass many miles quite happily. I remembered Mr. Shor's unfailing courtesy. Mr. Shor is supposed to be extremely rude to everyone but I doubt if we have ever exchanged an impolite phrase. I was able to reconstruct Mr. Shor's

countenance in my mind, which is a considerable feat under the circumstances. Mr. Shor's countenance resembles much of the broken country unsuitable for farming that we were passing through.

At this point, I reluctantly abandoned the thought of Mr. Shor, whose place seemed far distant, and started to remember another friend of mine, Mr. Joe Russell, popularly known as Sloppy Joe, who ran a saloon in Key West. Mr. Joe Russell was my partner and friend for many years in many ventures. I then spent several miles remembering the manner of his death.

I thought, since now my brain was somewhere round 52nd and 53rd Streets, of Mr. Earl Wilson and his gentle loyalty over a period of many years. I thought of Mr. Walter Winchell and how we used to sit up late together with Damon Runyon, when Mr. Runyon was still a living man and fine companion and not yet a Fund, and I hoped that Walter and Lenny Lyons would cease feuding.

In this time, my brain had become benevolent and wished good will to all men. I thought of many other friends and of their great assets and their occasional defects. My brain refused to have anything to do with my past life, contrary to the usual reports.

It was at this point that I commenced that strange vice which I believe could become extremely destructive to one's general equilibrium and cause one, perhaps, to lose one's status as a completely well-adjusted person. I had always run as an adjusted person though various tinhorn biographers had attempted to prove otherwise.

This strange vice was the reading of one's own obituaries. Most of the obituaries I could never have written nearly as well myself. There were certain inaccuracies and many good things were said which were in no way deserved. There were, however, some rather glaring inaccuracies in the account of my unfortunate death. One in the German press stated that I had attempted to land the aircraft myself on the summit of Mount Kilimanjaro, which we call "Kibo." It seems that I was landing this aircraft accompanied by Miss Mary in an effort to approach the carcass of a dead leopard about which I had written a story in 1934. This story was called *The Snows of Kilimanjaro* and was made into a motion picture which I unfortunately was not able to sit through so I cannot tell you how it came out. Perhaps the end was that I crashed an aircraft accompanied by Miss Mary at the extreme summit of this peak, which is 19,565 or 19,567 feet high entirely according to which surveyor you believe. Maybe it rises and falls.

If the German obituaries were romantic and full of *Götterdämmerung* although extremely laudatory, the Italian obituaries passed them in many aspects. There were appreciations of us by people who described themselves as our only true and intimate friends and who knew the innermost contents of my heart.

Since I myself have no idea of the innermost contents

of my heart and would not trust it for a minute if I did, some of these obituaries came as a surprise. Actually in regard to the innermost contents of my heart, probably a most foul place, I would rather have a good cardiograph report. However, I was touched deeply by the friendship that was displayed.

We love Italy very much and more than that we love many individual Italians. Maybe too many individual Italians. None of those we truly loved wrote obituaries. They were instead, I believe, at Mass and many old friends would not believe that we were dead unless they saw the bodies.

The British papers I know about only through a cutting which was sent to me by a friend, and opinions seemed to be quite mixed.

What gave one most pleasure was to read in some papers, not the *Times* nor the *Observer* nor the *Guardian*, descriptions of one's habits and character and the exact circumstances under which one's death was achieved. Some of these were the work of great imaginative writers. We resolved to attempt to live up to them at some future date.

In all obituaries, or almost all, it was emphasized that I had sought death all my life. Can one imagine that if a man sought death all of his life he could not have found her before the age of 54? It is one thing to be in the proximity of death, to know more or less what she is, and it is quite another thing to seek her. She is the most easy thing to find that I know of. You can find her through a minor carelessness on a road with heavy traffic, you could find her in a full bottle of Seconol, you could find her with any type of razor blade; you could find her in your own bathtub or you could find her by not being battle-wise. There are so many ways of finding her that it is stupid to enumerate them.

If you have spent your life avoiding death as cagily as possible but, on the other hand taking no backchat from her and studying her as you would a beautiful harlot who could put you soundly to sleep forever with no problems and no necessity to work, you could be said to have studied her but you have not sought her. Because you know among one or two other things that if you sought her you would possess her and from her reputation you know that she would present you with an incurable disease. So much for the constant pursuit of death.

It is a facile theory to hold though and I can see when someone has to write an obituary in a hurry it would be a quick solution to a complicated subject. The most complicated subject that I know, since I am a man, is a man's life. I am sure that a woman's life is most complicated if she has any ethics. Lately, these have seemed, from my reading of the newspapers, a fairly lost commodity, but I know that they still exist in the people who do not spend their time in the newspapers nor in the acquiring of alimony, and I have always considered that it was easy to be a man compared to being a woman who lives by as rigid standards as men live by. No one of us lives by as rigid standards nor has as good ethics

as we planned but an attempt is made.

At this point, I went to sleep and had a dream. Fortunately, I dream a great deal and the night is almost as much fun as the day. They are all nocturnal dreams, for so far I have never daydreamed, being too busy observing or having fun, and latterly reading my obituaries, a new and attractive vice.

In my nocturnal dreams, when they are not the bad kind that you get after a war where other people are killed sometimes by your fault, I am nearly always a very gay and witty person faintly addicted to the more obvious types of heroism and, with all, a most attractive type. In my nocturnal dreams, I am always between 25 or 30 years old, I am irresistible to women, dogs and, on one recent occasion, to a very beautiful lioness.

In the dream, this lioness, who became my fiancée, was one of the most delightful creatures that I have ever dreamt about. She had some of the characteristics of Miss Mary and she could become irascible. On one occasion, I recall she did an extremely perilous act. Perilous to me, that is. When I recalled the dream to Miss Mary and Denis Zaphiro at breakfast, they appeared to be appreciative of the dream, but they seemed slightly shocked. Denis invited me to share a bottle of beer with him, a thing that I almost never do at breakfast, and I sat drinking this beer and remembering with great pleasure the night I had spent with the beautiful lioness.

One of the aspects of this dream that I remember was that the lioness was killing game for me exactly as she would for a male of her own species; but instead of our having to devour the meat raw, she cooked it in a most appetizing manner. She used only butter for basting the *impala* chops. She braised the tenderloin and served it, on the grass, in a manner worthy of the Ritz in Paris. She asked me if I wanted any vegetables, and knowing that she herself was completely nonherbivorous, I refused in order to be polite. In any case, there were no vegetables.

The Nairobi police, yawning and stretching their arms, descended from a truck carrying them to their various morning posts and moved at far from a brisk pace up the street. Natives went by going to market and later returning, the women heavily laden, the men walking beside them in admiration of their wives' strength and beauty. Many Hindus passed on financial errands. A car went by, its top covered with baskets of beautiful flowers. No spivs were yet to be seen. None of the beautiful big cars parked outside the hotel were in action. No two-pistol men were in view. Hundreds of bicycles of all types passed ridden by Africans and Asiatics. Then, yielding to my new vice, I began reading the obituaries I had not been able to finish.

When I had gotten well into the obituaries to the point of the fullest fulfillment of my new vice, Miss Mary woke up and said, "Haven't they brought the tea? And what are you reading?"

When sex—under the influence of Freud, factories, the automobile and world wars—came out into the open to become SEX, a peculiar thing happened: People were *supposed* to be free and frequent with their sexual activity. Women were *supposed* to turn from Victorian propriety to passionate responsiveness. And yet the basic ideals of maleness and femaleness continued unchanged.

The frequency of intercourse may decrease in the future *because of* a real revolution in attitudes toward, feelings about and uses of sex, especially concerning the roles of male and female. What are those young men with long, flowing hair really saying? In what may seem a ludicrous overstatement, they are sending a clear message to all who will listen: "We are no longer afraid to display what *you* may call 'feminine.' We are willing to reveal that we have feelings, weaknesses, tenderness—that we are human. And, by the way, we just may be ridiculing all of those up-tight movie males with cropped hair and unflinching eyes. We're betting they can't touch our girls." Indeed, the long-haired boys' appeal is not esthetic, but sexual; not private, but corporate.

Bear in mind that the Beatles' dazzling early success, long before their remarkable musicianship came clear, was conferred upon them by millions of young *females* who were transported by those pageboy hairdos and those sensitive faces. And the Beatles were not the first in a modern lineage of girl-movers. A younger, slenderer, tenderer Frank Sinatra, and then a hip-swiveling Elvis Presley, had reduced earlier sub-generations to squeals and moans. It takes a particularly obstinate blindness not to realize that an ability to free emotions, and not a fragmented "all-maleness," provides today's most compelling erotic appeal.

If the narrow-gauge male is not laughed out of existence, he may, literally, *die* out. Specialized, competitive man is particularly susceptible to the maladies of the involuntary muscle, nervous and vascular systems. A U.S. male's life expectancy now is seven years less than a female's. Figures on earlier times are impossible to verify, but one thing is sure: the gap has never been greater. Men who operate inside the boxes of fragmented civilization—whether bus driver, production-line worker or professional specialist—die off at an alarming rate from the heart and gut diseases.

In the most isolated primitive tribes, those whose members still operate as free-roving hunters, digestive disorders are practically unknown and the usual civilized heart troubles are rare. Significantly, these people make little distinction between the ideal qualities of male and female. As the noted British anthropologist Geoffrey Gorer writes concerning the peace-loving Pygmies of Africa, the Arapesh of New Guinea and the Lepchas of Sikkim: "Men and women have different primary sexual characteristics—a source of endless merriment as well as more concrete satisfactions—and some different skills and aptitudes. No child,

however, grows up with the injunctions, 'All real men do . . .' or 'No proper woman does . . . ,' so that there is no confusion of sexual identity: no cases of sexual inversion have been reported among them. The model for the growing child is one of concrete performance and frank enjoyment, not of metaphysical, symbolic achievements or of ordeals to be surmounted. They do not have heroes or martyrs to emulate or cowards or traitors to despise; . . . a happy, hard-working and productive life is within the reach of all."

It would seem that "being a man" in the usual, aggressive Western sense is, if nothing else, unhealthy. To live an ordinary peacetime life in the U.S.—as a recent Army study of the "nervous secretions" of combat soldiers in Vietnam shows—is as bad or worse for your gut, heart and nervous system as facing enemy bullets. But the present fragmented civilization seems on its way out, and what "being a man" means could swiftly change.

Grotesque and distorted extremes tend to pop out just at the end of any era, a good example being the recent rash of blown-up photographic nudes. The foldout playmate in *Playboy* Magazine—she of outsize breast and buttocks, pictured in sharp detail—signals the death throes of a departing age. Already, she is beginning to appear quaint, not sexy.

This is not to say that nudity is on its way out. On the contrary, it will most likely increase in the neo-tribal future. But it will merge into the context of ordinary living, becoming not so much lurid and sexy as natural and sensuous.

Already, new "sex symbols" poke fun at the super female. Notable among them is the boyish young model known as Twiggy.

It is toward a common humanity that both sexes now tend. As artificial, socially-imposed distinctions disappear, the unalterable essentials of maleness and femaleness may assume their rightful importance and delight. The lusty Gallic salute, *Vive la différence!*, rings truer about biology than about mores, mannerisms and dress.

While both sexes will probably change, most men will have farther to go than most women in adjusting to the new life. Many forward-looking corporations, especially in the aerospace industry, already are engaged in sensitivity-training sessions for their male executives. The behavior encouraged in these sessions would make a John Wayne character wince: Manly males learn how to reveal their emotions, to become sensitive to others, to weep openly if that is what they feel like doing—all this in the pursuit of higher profits. Sensitivity *works*. The new technology—complex, interrelated, responsive—demands it. But there is one specific product of modern technology, the contraceptive pill, that can blow the old boundaries sky high. It makes it possible for sexual woman to act like sexual man. The Pill makes woman a Bomb. She creates a new kind of fragmentation, separating sexual intercourse from procreation. She also explodes old barriers between the sexes, bringing them closer together. Watch for traditions to fall.

Romantic Love seems a likely victim. As a specialty, romance was an invention of the late Middle Ages, a triumph of highly individualistic enterprise. It requires separation, unfulfillment. The chase is everything—the man aflame, the maiden coy. Sexual consummation bursts the balloon of yearning. As in the romantic movies, the significant embrace can hardly be imagined without "The End" printed over it. Indeed, what we have called sex in recent decades may be viewed as the lag end of Romantic Love.

As Romantic Love fades, so may sexual privacy. Already, young people shock their elders by casually conversing on matters previously considered top secret. And the hippies, those brash pioneers of new life patterns, have reverted—boys and girls together, along with a few little children—to the communal living of the Middle Ages or the primitive tribe. It is not uncommon to find a goodly mixture of them sleeping in one room. Readers who envisage wild orgies just don't get the picture. Most of the hippies are *not* hung up on sex. To them, sex is merely one of many sensory experiences. It is available when desired—therefore perhaps not so desperately pursued.

(WARNING: Proceed at your own risk. Mr. Perelman's quiz is not equipped with correct answers, genius ratings or even common sense.—Ed.)

Are You a Good Parent?

BY S. J. PERELMAN

At a recent conference of the American Child Study Association, I had charge of one of the panels—the one just inside the hotel bar, on the left as you enter. After examining it for three days through various media, including old-fashioneds and sours, I began asking myself just what kind of parent I was. From this I progressed to asking the same of the barman and waiters, and from this I progressed to the lobby, supported by the manager. Out of this survey came (1) the brain wave below, and (2) a hangover it shouldn't happen to your worst enemy.

1. You catch your son forging your name to checks. You should:

(a) Beat him to a jelly.

(b) Make him practice until he becomes more accurate.

(c) Apprentice him to Jim the Penman.

2. Your heirs have filled the gasoline tank with sand. You should:

(a) Smother them with kisses.

(b) Sell them to the gypsies.

(c) Enroll them in a more progressive school.

3. The children wake you each morning at six. You should:

(a) Gag them before retiring every night.

(b) Make them sleep in the cellar.

(c) Slip a powerful sedative into the cottage cheese.

4. Your little boy has fallen in love with Rita Hayworth. You should:

(a) Worm her address out of him.

(b) Write her notes blackening his character.

(c) Spread stories that he is already married.

5. Your child has a dainty appetite. It is best to:

(a) Give him a cocktail before dinner.

(b) Ram the food down his throat with a stick.

(c) Starve him into submission.

6. Your daughter likes to pull wings off flies. You should:

(a) Glue them back on.

(b) Prepare her for a medical career.

(c) Show her the proper technique.

7. Your child has a slightly coated tongue. It is best to:

(a) Keep it immobilized for a year or two.

(b) Wash it hourly with a bar of yellow laundry soap.

(c) Use it for sealing your letters.

8. Your son has trouble with his spelling. You should:

(a) Worry about it until you develop ulcers.

(b) Throw your unabridged dictionary into the furnace.

(c) Take his teacher out dancing.

9. **Your daughter is interested only in Frank Sinatra. You should:**

(a) Ask Sinatra about his intentions.
(b) Apply hot and cold poultices and give her a reliable purge.
(c) Mind your own business.

10. **You suddenly discover you abhor children. You should:**

(a) Throw yourself on the floor in a tantrum until exhausted.
(b) Go around with a long face.
(c) Have thought of that before.

The Last Will and Testament of an Extremely Distinguished Dog

BY EUGENE O'NEILL

I, Silverdene Emblem O'Neill (familiarly known to my family, friends and acquaintances as Blemie), because the burden of my years and infirmities is heavy upon me, and I realize the end of my life is near, do hereby bury my last will and testament in the mind of my Master. He will not know it is there until after I am dead. Then, remembering me in his loneliness, he will suddenly know of this testament, and I ask him then to inscribe it as a memorial to me.

I have little in the way of material things to leave. Dogs are wiser than men. They do not set great store upon things. They do not waste their days hoarding property. They do not ruin their sleep worrying about how to keep the objects they have, and to obtain the objects they have not. There is nothing of value I have to bequeath except my love and my faith. These I leave to all those who have loved me, to my Master and Mistress, who I know will mourn me most, to

Freeman who has been so good to me, to Cyn and Roy and Willie and Naomi and—But if I should list all those who have loved me it would force my Master to write a book. Perhaps it is vain of me to boast when I am so near death, which returns all beasts and vanities to dust, but I have always been an extremely lovable dog.

I ask my Master and Mistress to remember me always, but not to grieve for me too long. In my life I have tried to be a comfort to them in time of sorrow, and a reason for added joy in their happiness. It is painful for me to think that even in death I should cause them pain. Let them remember that while no dog has ever had a happier life (and this I owe to their love and care for me), now that I have grown blind and deaf and lame, and even my sense of smell fails me so that a rabbit could be right under my nose and I might not know, my pride has sunk to a sick, bewildered humiliation. I feel life is taunting me with having over-lingered my welcome. It is time I said goodbye, before I become too sick a burden on myself and on those who love me. It will be sorrow to leave them, but not a sorrow to die. Dogs do not fear death as men do. We accept it as part of life, not as something alien and terrible which destroys life. What may come after death, who knows? I would like to believe with those of my fellow Dalmations who are devout Mohammedans, that there is a Paradise where one is always young and full-bladdered; where all the day one dillies and dallies with an amorous multitude of houris, beautifully spotted; where jack rabbits that run fast but not too fast (like the houris) are as the sands of the desert; where each blissful hour is mealtime; where in long evenings there are a million fireplaces with logs forever burning, and one curls oneself up and blinks into the flames and nods and dreams, remembering the old brave days on earth, and the love of one's Master and Mistress.

I am afraid this is too much for even such a dog as I am to expect. But peace, at least, is certain. Peace and long rest for weary old heart and head and limbs, and eternal sleep in the earth I have loved so well. Perhaps, after all, this is best.

One last request I earnestly make. I have heard my Mistress say, "When Blemie dies we must never have another dog. I love him so much I could never love another one." Now I would ask her, for love of me, to have another. It would be a poor tribute to my memory never to have a dog again. What I would like to feel is that having once had me in the family, now she cannot live without a dog! I have never had a narrow jealous spirit. I have always held that most dogs are good (and one cat, the black one I have permitted to share the living room rug during the evenings, whose affection I have tolerated in a kindly spirit, and in rare sentimental moods, even reciprocated a trifle). Some dogs, of course, are better than others. Dalmatians, naturally, as everyone knows, are best. So I suggest a Dalmatian as my successor. He can hardly be as well bred or as well mannered or as distinguished and handsome as I was in my prime. My Master and Mistress must not ask the impossible. But he will do his best, I am sure, and even his inevitable defects will help by comparison to keep my memory green. To him I bequeath my collar and leash and my overcoat and raincoat, made to order in 1929 at Hermès in Paris. He can never wear them with the distinction I did, walking around the Place Vendôme, or later along Park Avenue, all eyes fixed on me in admiration; but again I am sure he will do his utmost not to appear a mere gauche provincial dog. Here on the ranch, he may prove himself quite worthy of comparison, in some respects. He will, I presume, come closer to jack rabbits than I have been able to in recent years. And, for all his faults, I hereby wish him the happiness I know will be his in my old home.

One last word of farewell, Dear Master and Mistress. Whenever you visit my grave, say to yourselves with regret but also with happiness in your hearts at the remembrance of my long happy life with you: "Here lies one who loved us and whom we loved." No matter how deep my sleep I shall hear you, and not all the power of death can keep my spirit from wagging a grateful tail.

Ogden Nash
on Tipping

BY OGDEN NASH

I can't stop unless you stop, or, lines addressed to a man making $5000 a year who over-tips a man making $10,000 a year to make himself feel he's making $20,000 a year.

I do not wish to tiptoe through the tulips to Tipperary
And I might vote for Tyler too, but about Tippecanoe
    I am a little wary.
The fact is, that at any mention of any form of tips,
My mind goes into an eclipse.
The world of tips has moved too fast for me.
The price of ransoming my hat has become too vast
    for me.
I have to get used to one thing at a time,
And just as I learn that there is no more such tip as
    a nickel, I find that there is no more such tip as a dime.
If you give a dime to a bellhop,
The skyscrapers buck like broncos, and you can
    almost feel the hotel hop.

If you want to talk to bellhops or porters,
You start with baby-talk, which is quarters.
If you want to talk to head waiters, or, as they now
    style themselves, Maitre d's,
You talk in C's or G's,
And the girl with the tray of cigarettes expects the
    Taj Mahal,
And not a small Mahal, either, but a large Mahal.
This is a sad situation for low and middle income persons,
And when you go abroad, it worsens.
At least on the trains over here
You don't have to tip the conductor and the engineer,
And over here, certainly until recently, it would
    have been considered impudent effrontery
To tip the president of the country,
Whereas, in certain nations that shall be nameless,
The entire citizenry is shameless.
Granted that itching palms
Know no qualms,
Nevertheless people, whether men or mice,
Resent scratching the same palm twice,
Which happens wherever you eat or sleep, on the
    Continent, because a fat percentage is added
    to the bill to cover all tips,
But if you think that no further tipping is expected,
    you'd better learn to carry your own pemmican
    and balance your baggage on your hips.
Oh dear, I think that extravagant tips are an
    unnecessary menace,
Whether in Valdosta, Georgia, or Valparaiso, or
    Vancouver, or Venice.
I think that they are a betrayal of the tipper's unsure
    ego, or not quite-quiteness,
I think that they are a vulgar substitute for common
    politeness.
I think that people could do very well both at home and
    abroad on moderate gratuities or fees
If they would just take the trouble to learn and employ
    the foreign and domestic terms for Thank you
    and Please.

MOVERS
AND
SHAKERS

*W*ho shall rule? How? How much? This has always been the distinctive problem of human society; the animal kingdom knows no politics.

The will to power governs those who govern us: kings, popes, presidents, generals; humanitarian leaders or demagogues and madmen.

"Power corrupts." It also ennobles. It can be used with vision and compassion, or with hideous brutality. It can elevate our values or debase our aspirations. It can enforce justice or decree the slaughter of millions, preserve the peace or unleash war.

The men and women who appear on the following pages wielded power for good or for evil. All exemplify Shakespeare's famous statement: "Some are born great, some achieve greatness, and some have greatness thrust upon them." —Ed.

WIDE WORLD

President Franklin D. Roosevelt: creator of the New Deal; charmer, master of politics and promises. Idol of labor and the poor, he was feared and loathed by big business, the rich, and the Right. A peerless leader, he hammered out victory in the world's most fearful war.

Prime Minister Winston Churchill: ▶ statesman, author, matchless orator and wit. Intrepid and invincible during the darkest hours of World War II, he saved Great Britain and Europe with his "blood, toil, tears, and sweat," and sheer, indomitable will.

Chairman Mao Tse-tung: prophet
and strategist of a new order in the
People's Republic of China; a threat
to Soviet Russia.

President Charles de Gaulle:
incomparable, intransigent; the
saviour of France and leader of its
Fourth Republic.

The Yalta Conference, 1945: "Uncle Joe"
Stalin proved adamant and contemptuous,
Roosevelt too confident and trusting,
and Churchill, wary and prophetic, was
apprehensive and dismayed.

General Omar Bradley: "The GI's General" was the best field commander in Europe.

General Douglas MacArthur: Even those who mocked his flamboyance admit that he was the most brilliant and original strategist of World War II. He restructured post-war Japan.

AP

Adolf Hitler: satanic, deranged,
a modern Ghengis Khan. This
man, whom Winston Churchill
termed a "monstrous abortion,"
almost destroyed civilization.

ACME

Benito Mussolini: strutting
Italian charlatan, founder of
Fascism. He conquered helpless
Ethiopia and then turned
Hitler's jackal.

Harry S Truman: The man
from Missouri confounded all
the pollsters...

...and wielded the awesome
powers of the White House
with iron courage and unexpected skill.

Dwight D. Eisenhower: Supreme
Allied Commander in Europe
during World War II; twice
elected President by a landslide. He warned America of
"the military-industrial
complex." Future historians
may rate him much higher than
contemporary critics do.

"Ike" Was there ever
such a grin?

Nikita Khrushchev: shrewd,
crude, bellicose. Russia's
Premier infuriated Eisenhower
and underrated Kennedy when
he tried to build missile sites
in Cuba.

121

CARL PERUTZ

Helen Keller: blind and deaf; a triumph
of human courage and will.

Eleanor Roosevelt: "The First Lady of ▶
the Globe," in an exchange of good will,
rubs noses with a South Pacific native.

HY PESKIN

Three generations of Kennedys: the grandfather, Boston's Mayor "Honey Fitz" Fitzgerald; the father, Joseph P. Kennedy, multimillionaire, Wall Street wizard, Hollywood mogul, Ambassador to the Court of St. James; and the gawky young Congressman who would become our first Roman Catholic President.

CECIL STOUGHTON

The President in a poignant moment with his invalid father, paralyzed by a stroke.

ARCHIE LIEBERMAN

The President in his prime.

The President relaxes in a golf cart aswarm with the clan's small fry.

STANLEY TRETICK

PAUL FUSCO

◄ Fidel Castro: impassioned, long-winded, defiant, champion of Cuba's workers and farmers. Those who opposed "The Maximum Leader" found no mercy. Many were shot, thousands fled; no one knows if others still rot in Cuban prisons. After the Bay of Pigs disaster, John F. Kennedy said, "Every President has his albatross. Mine is Cuba."

"Che!" (né Ernesto) Guevara: A doctor turned Marxist revolutionary, he ultimately became Castro's "brain" and firebrand. Adored by American college radicals, an inept guerrilla, he died in Bolivia in 1967, when the peasants he came to liberate turned him in to government authorities.

President Richard M. Nixon: intelligent, able, crafty. His foreign policy was bold and enlightened, but the brazen profusion of his lies to the press, the people, and his friends and colleagues detonated the greatest scandal in our history. When the courts forced him to release the "Watergate tapes," he resigned rather than face impeachment.

◄President Lyndon B. Johnson and Attorney General Robert F. Kennedy: Political rivals, they confer in the Oval Office.

ARTHUR ROTHSTEIN

President Johnson entertains Margaret Truman Daniel and her husband as "Lady Bird" displays her unaffected charm.

◄Irrepressible Martha (Mrs. John) Mitchell greets Mamie Eisenhower as Pat Nixon looks on. What tales they could swap!

(left). Prime Minister Jawaharlal Nehru:
Elegant, urbane, a profound idealist, he
succeeded the sainted Gandhi, and held
India's millions enthralled.

(above). Prime Minister Indira Nehru Gandhi:
Hostess for her widowed father during his years
as Prime Minister, she became the first
woman to hold India's highest office.

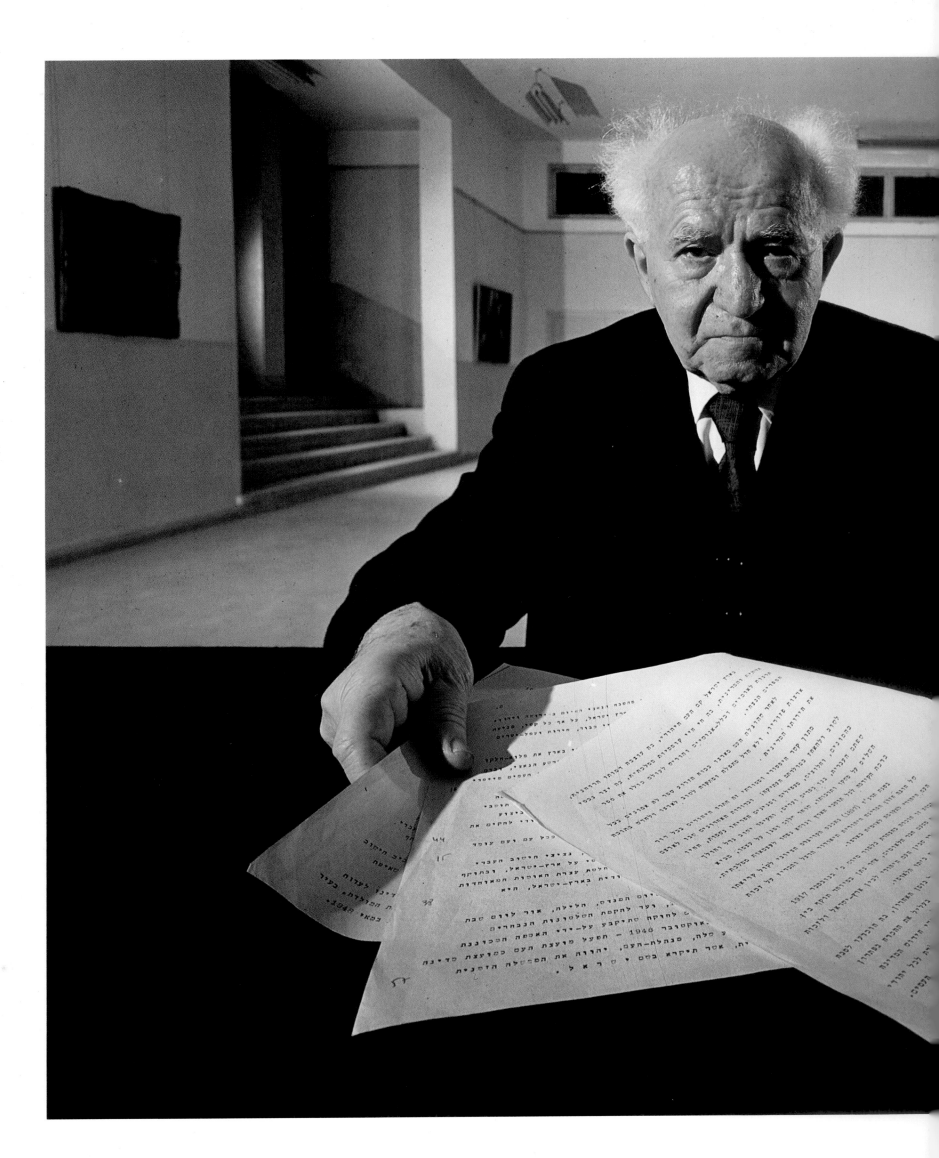

David Ben-Gurion at 81: The little giant
was a prophet, founder, leader of Israel.
Here he holds the Declaration of Independence announcing the establishment
of the Jewish state. On May 14, 1948,
exactly twenty years before this reenact-
ment for LOOK, Ben-Gurion read this
historic document to his cabinet in this
room at the Museum of Art in Tel Aviv.
Few national heroes suffered such tribulations, were deserted by so many allies, or
prevailed over such stupendous odds.

President Gamal Abdel Nasser: With others, he overthrew Egypt's King Farouk and in 1954 he became the head of the Republic. Nasser organized other Arab countries in opposition to a Jewish state and led them to intermittent combat and ceaseless tension with Israel.

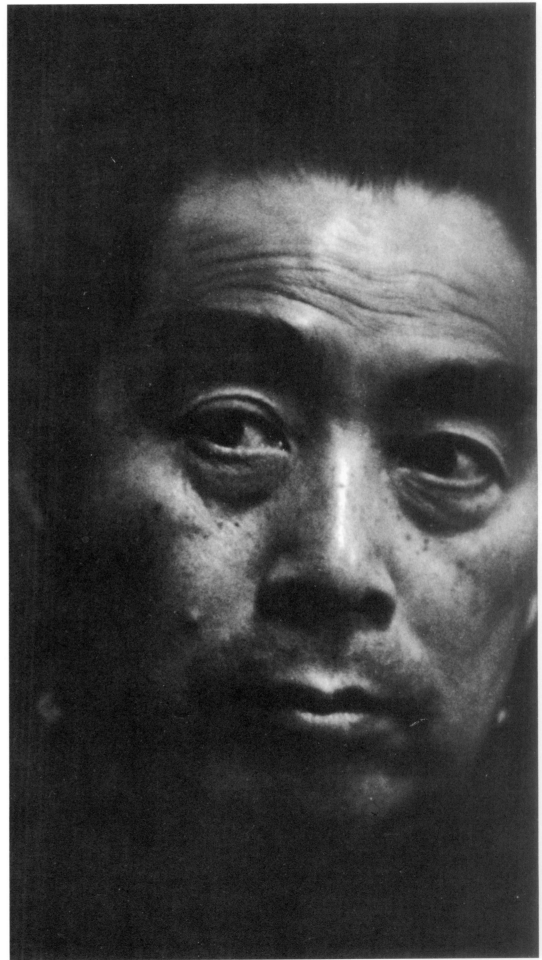

Premier Chou En-lai: Vice-Chairman of the Communist Party of the People's Republic of China, he has been an extraordinarily astute negotiator in the area of foreign affairs.

ARTHUR ROTHSTEIN

STANLEY TRETICK

Prime Minister Golda Meier: Once
a Milwaukee school teacher, she
wept over Israel's dead and wounded
but was iron-willed during peace
negotiations. Now retired, she still
commands the respect and affection
of her fellow countrymen and the
free world

Secretary of State Henry Kissinger:
A former Harvard professor, called
"the most brilliant statesman since
Metternich," he designed our withdrawal from Vietnam and initiated
peace talks in the Middle East.

Ho-Chi-Minh: masterly strategist for
North Vietnam. His name was chanted by
millions of students in the United States
and Europe in support of his drive for
Vietnamese unification.

STANLEY TRETICK

JAMES HANSEN

UPI

J. ROBERT MOSKIN

JAMES KARALES

STANLEY TRETICK

HILMAR PABEL

(top). Nguyen Cao Ky: once Premier of South Vietnam, now a refugee in the United States.

(bottom). Chancellor Willy Brandt: West Germany's democratic lion.

(top). Dean Rusk: J.F.K.'s and L.B.J.'s scholarly Secretary of State.

(center). Averell Harriman: Ambassador-at-Large for Presidents Kennedy and Johnson, with Russian Premier Aleksei Kosygin.

(bottom). Robert F. MacNamara: Kennedy's "wiz kid" Secretary of Defense.

(top). Le Duc Tho: able negotiator for the Politburo of North Vietnam.

(bottom). Chancellor Konrad Adenauer: the reconstructor of West Germany after World War II.

Senator Joseph McCarthy: A publicity-drunk hunter and hounder of "Reds," he split the country with reckless alarums. In the televised Senate investigation of the Army, his double-talk and twisting of "evidence" horrified his supporters. He ended in disgrace, officially censured by his peers.

J. Edgar Hoover: founder of the F.B.I. and its chief for almost fifty years. Immensely able, unyielding, possessed by power, he built a personal empire feared in the loftiest chambers of Washington. No president dared cut his budgets or challenge his authority.

WIDE WORLD

Fiorello La Guardia: fiery Congressman, reform Mayor of New York City. The "Little Flower" loved rushing to fires and blistering his opponents. Yet during a newspaper strike, he read the Sunday comics over the radio to the delight of both young and old.

Nelson A. Rockefeller: From a dozen ▶ posts in Washington, he rose to become New York's Governor and Gerald Ford's Vice-President. Ambitious, attractive, a born politico, he raised New York's taxes and poured so much money into state building projects that he was said to have an "edifice complex." Money is never a problem to "Rocky."

143

Five political stars: Senator Hubert Humphrey, Governor George Wallace, Governor George Romney, Senator Edmund Muskie, and Governor Ronald Reagan, a convert from the glitter of Hollywood, the conservatives strongest Presidential contender.

(opposite page). Adlai E. Stevenson: Governor of Illinois, dedicated liberal. In spite of his magnificent speeches and flashing wit, he twice lost the presidency to Dwight D. Eisenhower. As Ambassador he led the United States delegation to the United Nations.

Malcolm X (né Little): He soared to national fame as a Black Muslim only to be assassinated by rivals within the movement he served.

JAMES HANSEN

James Meredith: The first black admitted to the University of Mississippi, by force of Federal court order, he entered through howling mobs and an army of state troopers.

JAMES KARALES

The Martin Luther Kings sing "We Shall Overcome," the battle hymn of passive resistance in the 1960's.

MARIO TORRISI

Pope John XXIII: "The people's Pope," the humble, immortal Vicar opened the Vatican's doors to internal reform and ecumenical debate.

Bertrand Russell at 96: Philosopher, ▶ logician, mathematician, educator, agnostic, pacifist, social reformer, author of forty books of superlative prose, Russell, a Nobel Prize winner, was one of the commanding intellects of our time. (He died soon after this picture was taken.)

Dr. Benjamin Spock: He transformed baby care with his more flexible approach to child raising, only to become less "permissive" than millions of his readers. His professional reputation brought world-wide attention to his courageous opposition to the Vietnam war.

Bernard Baruch: A dollar-a-year adviser to five presidents, his "office" on spring days was this bench opposite the White House.

150

Albert Schweitzer: unusually gifted organist, world-
renowned authority on Bach, respected theologian.
At the age of 30 he relinquished a university career
of unlimited promise to prepare for his life's work as a
mission doctor in the hospital he built in French Equa-
torial Africa. Revered throughout the world, he won the
Nobel Peace Prize in 1952.

Two remarkable women: Jacqueline Bouvier Kennedy
at Hyannis Port the summer after that tragic November (above);
the indefatigable Rose Fitzgerald Kennedy on
the golf course—at age 80 (right).

RICHARD AVEDON

The Duke and Duchess of Windsor:
As Edward VIII, he abdicated Great
Britain's throne for "the woman I
love," Baltimore divorcée Wallis Simpson.

Charles Philip Arthur George, ▶
Prince of Wales: A dashing bachelor,
he is heir to Great Britain's throne
and one of the largest fortunes in
the world.

(left). Her Serene Highness Princess Grace of
Monaco: Daughter of a Philadelphia millionaire
and one-time bricklayer; Hollywood Oscar-winner,
this rare beauty gave our century a "fairy-tale romance."
(above). In the historic palace of the Grimaldi,
the royal family poses for an exclusive LOOK portrait.

DO YOU REMEMBER?

(for answers see page 160)

1.

INTERNATIONAL NEWS PHOTOS

2.

JAMES HANSEN

3.

8.

9.

UPI

10.

15.

PICTORIAL PARADE

16.

JOHN VACHON

17.

UPI

18.

23.

BOB HANSEN

24.

INTERNATIONAL NEWS PHOTOS

25.

4.

5.

6.

7.

11.

12.

13.

14.

9.

20.

21.

22.

6.

27.

28.

29.

Answers to "Do You Remember?"

1. Juan Perón: twice Argentina's dictator.
2. Norman Thomas: five times the Socialist candidate for President.
3. Cordell Hull: F.D.R.'s Secretary of State.
4. George S. Patton: the "Blood and Guts" general.
5. Christian Herter: Eisenhower's Secretary of State.
6. Allen Dulles: the first Director of the C.I.A.
7. François Duvalier: Haiti's voodoo-practicing dictator.
8. Harry Hopkins: F.D.R.'s closest personal and political adviser.
9. Cardinal Joseph Mindszenty: Hungarian foe of Communism.
10. Clare Booth Luce: playwright, wit, Ambassadress to Italy.
11. Whittaker Chambers: the government's star witness in the Alger Hiss case.
12. Alger Hiss: jailed for perjury in one of history's most sensational trials.
13. Adam Clayton Powell: Harlem's hero in Congress.
14. Josip Tito of Yugoslavia: the first Communist leader to challenge Moscow.
15. Christine Keeler: of Profumo-scandal fame.
16. J. Robert Oppenheimer: "Father of the A-Bomb."
17. Margaret Chase Smith: Senator from Maine.
18. Dr. Ralph Bunche: America's first black ambassador.
19. Eamon de Valera: Ireland's George Washington.
20. Harold Stassen: perennial presidential candidate.
21. Stalin's daughter, Svetlana: defector to the United States.
22. Wendell Willkie: wartime advocate of "One World."
23. Robert A. Taft: Senate leader of Republican conservatism.
24. James Farley: F.D.R.'s campaign strategist.
25. Thomas E. Dewey: crime-fighting Governor of New York, twice-defeated presidential candidate.
26. Alf Landon: Governor of Kansas, defeated by a Roosevelt landslide.
27. Charles Lindbergh: hero of the world, tainted by Nazi sympathies.
28. Frances Perkins: Secretary of Labor, America's first woman cabinet member.
29. Earl Warren: innovative Chief Justice of the United States Supreme Court.

LOOK
TREASURY

Why Asia Hates Us

BY PEARL S. BUCK

Once the peoples of Asia were our friends. Now they are bewildered by us and wounded. They hate us. Harsh words are flung at us from everywhere in Asia.

If I had to simply reason why we are so hated, I would say that it is because the Asians feel that we have deceived them. They feel we have taken sides against them. We have destroyed their ideal of us. There is nothing so necessary as an ideal, at least to an Asian; nothing so precious as the need to trust someone.

We were the trusted, we were the admired. To them we were the good, not really for what we had done, but for what we were.

We had no ports, we did not take the customs revenue, we never fought the Chinese. We had even kept other powers from dividing up China. More than that, in times of famine food came from the Americans as it did not from anywhere else, and American missionaries were kind and good.

But, above all, so far above all for the Asian peoples that it was almost the only significance, America was a republic, a place where people ruled themselves by choosing their own governors, and a place where there was plenty for everybody. It could be done. In Asia, therefore, it could be done. They would learn from America.

That all this is now changed, and that we have come to be hated, is not because we are really hateful. There is nothing in the essential American nature as it is found in the vast average of our people that should be hateful to the peoples of Asia. On the contrary, we are far more likeable to Asians than most of the peoples of Europe are. Our frankness, our humor, our generosity, our practicality, our ability to make friends anywhere, all are qualities that the Asian likes and understands.

It is true that, by the standards of the average Asian, we are vulgar. It is also true that the conduct of Americans in the armed forces did deeply shock the peoples of Asia. The drunkenness alone was repulsive. It was also a shock to the man of Asia to discover the venality of many Americans. Asians are used enough to corruption and bribery, but somehow they did not expect Americans to exhibit these evils. They were too idealistic about us. Nor were the Asians reassured when they saw our haggling over food for India.

But it is not over these things that the peoples of Asia have turned against us. Where we have deceived them, they feel, is in the ideal of freedom.

All the great good of America came, Asians used to say and believe, from the fact that we are a free nation. People must be free, they declared, before they could achieve that wonderful American way of life. As the end of World War II drew near, they looked to us with fervor, hope and certainty.

One day when I picked up the morning newspaper, I saw instantly that we had struck the first blow for our own destruction.

The blow fell at the San Francisco Conference. What happened was reported in The New York *Times* in an article carrying the headline:

"U.S. WILL OPPOSE COLONIAL LIBERTY . . . AMERICANS INDICATE LINE UP WITH BRITAIN AND FRANCE AGAINST AN INDEPENDENCE PLEDGE."

Imagine, if you can, the surge of bewilderment and despair that flooded into Asian hearts when they heard that we were on the side of old empire and therefore against them.

By a few sentences, spoken by an American official delegate in the congress of the peoples in San Francisco, we laid the way for all that has happened since.

Communism is not important to any people in Asia. Freedom is of the first importance, for they are convinced that only with freedom have they the chance to build a better life. Freedom and the chance to build a better life, that is all they ask. If communism does not give them these two conditions, they will reject communism.

We had, and we have, the ability to help them and to help them is to help ourselves. We have thrown all that away and we have instead their hatred, their enmity, so that the incredible, monstrous fact is that the Chinese, who were never our enemies and are not our enemies today, have actually been at war with us, their sons killing ours and being killed by ours.

From the folly of San Francisco, when all Asia sat at our feet, has sprouted, like branches from a noxious tree, one folly after another.

It has been agony to those of us who know Asia, and who have watched helpless; for there was no way to reach the ears, or minds, of those who were committing the follies. The final agony now is to travel among our own people, as I have done, and to find that our people themselves feel betrayed somehow by those who have been so foolish.

The people of Asia are saying that Americans are no different from other white people. They are saying that it was only when we had no material need of empire that we did not attack them as the others did. They think that we have now come to the point of such need and that we will try to make an empire in our time. All empire begins in trade, and so, the Asians fear, will begin our new empire.

It is easy, if one knows Asia's history, to see how the peoples over there would think that of us. It is their final despair.

And what next?

Only that we Americans must work entirely through and with the United Nations in the making of plans and in their execution.

Let us do so without blame to others. I can bear with equanimity the ranting of Russians in public places, but I cannot endure the same behavior, I do not expect it, from our American representatives.

Long ago in China, my old Confucian tutor used to make me write every day this teaching of the wise man: "The superior man blames himself, the inferior man blames others."

Without more waste of time and life in blaming others, let us put to the use of all peoples the wisdom and the experience of our democratic way of life.

Here is our conquering weapon against communism. Here is the way to win Asia back. There is no other weapon, no other way.

No Peace for Israel

BY ADLAI STEVENSON

The long-slumbering Middle East is wide awake today—shaking off its colonial shackles and smoldering with anger. This can't be said too often or too emphatically at home, where we tend to focus our attention on Europe and the Far East.

I traveled for three unforgettable weeks through this turbulent halfway world between Asia and the West: from the oil-rich desert kingdom of Saudi Arabia to an Egypt in revolution; from Lebanon, Syria and Jordan with their camps of sullen, seething Arab refugees to holy Jerusalem, now torn asunder by barbed wire and bitterness. And there, across a desolated strip of no man's land, I stepped into the stony, struggling pioneer State of Israel, where gunfire still crackles almost nightly along uncertain frontiers.

But the story of these three weeks properly begins in Arabia, the heartland and spiritual home of a Moslem community that stretches from Casablanca to the South Pacific.

Dhahran, Saudi Arabia

My first glimpse of the Arab world was this up-to-date American oil city sprawling over treeless sand and stone. Here, under a pitiless sun, the Arabian American Oil Company is developing the fabulous oil resources of King Ibn Saud's immense domain that includes the most sacred shrines of Islam in the "forbidden" cities of Mecca and Medina.

Dhahran is a transplanted fragment of enlightened industrial statesmanship. Along with modern technology, the company has introduced schools, vocational training, hospitals and modern housing for its 25,000 employees, many of them long-haired Bedouins who had never seen an automobile or an airplane until they came—sometimes a thousand miles—to work for Aramco. Now, roads are appearing; camel caravans are disappearing; corn flakes compete with dates; enterprising Arabians are starting contracting firms, traveling abroad, asking questions. A middle class is rising from the sands of feudal Arabia. "Oil has telescoped a thousand years into twenty," and thrust even this last corner of the old Arab world into the twentieth century.

From Dhahran, we flew over the hot sands to Riyadh, the desert-ringed capital where the great Ibn Saud, aging but still a towering, majestic figure, holds court in a mud-brick palace with air-conditioned bedrooms, surrounded by camels and Cadillacs, swimming pools and drought-stricken nomads. His hospitality is legendary: When I absent-mindedly admired an Oriental rug, he promptly presented it to me! Then, flanked by retainers with great ornamental swords, cartridge belts and rifles, we sat down to dinner under the stars with his ministers, the crown prince and some of the King's 36 other sons. (No statistics on daughters are available.)

Afterwards came the water basins and towels, rose water, spiced coffee, perfume and incense to sweeten the hands and beards; but neither tobacco, alcohol nor ladies were visible in that orthodox Moslem court where the new and the old collide.

I wanted to talk about the problems of the Middle East and the impact of Western ways on Saudi Arabia. But at the moment, the chief concern and main topic of conversation was the oasis of Baremi, lying somewhere along the kingdom's undefined southeastern border. In the past—before the discovery of oil—frontiers meant little to the nomads of the Arabian peninsula. But today, Ibn Saud claims Baremi; and so do two adjoining sheikdoms under British protection. The King is mighty angry with the British and insistent on American support. I thought about all our global headaches, from Berlin to Korea, and I honestly told him I didn't know where we stood on Baremi!

Cairo

But the anti-British fling was worse in Egypt—eclipsing, in Cairo, even the bitterness about Israel permeates every Arab country. Two burning issues kindle the passions of the Middle East—the great British military base along the Suez Canal and Israel's lusty little beachhead in a hostile Moslem world. Both are overcharged with emotion and both threaten stability and progress in the whole Middle East. And there is no overestimating the importance of this area. Look at the map, consider the oil, think of the 40 million Arabs and the world's vast Moslem community.

Emerging only now from sleepy centuries and independent for the first time in modern history, the Arab nations face the same staggering social, economic and political problems as the new Asia: ignorance, poverty, disease, feudalism, instability. These are the real problems, but "imperialism" and "injustice" are the universal preoccupations.

In Egypt, I saw the ancient monuments and dreamed by moonlight in the Temple of Karnak, which must surely be "the biggest thing in ruins." I recommend it to anyone suffering from self-importance. I visited the Sphinx on camelback (with protests from the camel), inspected the vast British canal-zone base and jeeped along dusty country roads of the fertile, overcrowded Nile Valley, where 20 million people live off six million acres of land and half the national income goes to 1.5 per cent of the population. I saw poverty and squalor in primitive, fly-infested villages. But all I heard was Suez, Suez, Suez. I heard about it from Gen. Mohammed Naguib, the modest, genial, soft-spoken leader of the so-called Revolutionary Committee that seized power a year ago, kicked out King Farouk and scattered the ruling clique of pashas and corrupt politicians—probably forever. I heard about it from Col. Abdel Nasser and some of the other young, inexperienced but dedicated army officers who make up the committee; from the wise and sophisticated Foreign Minister, Mahmoud Fawzi, and from many other Egyptians in and out of public life.

Although military bases exist on friendly foreign soil throughout the world, in Egypt the press and politicians compete in inflammatory denunciation of imperialism and the British base. And Naguib and his associates believe that no Egyptian government can survive unless this last vestige of the long British occupation is ended. He put it to me this way: "We don't propose to be the doormen in our own house any longer." And he illustrated Egypt's insistence on complete and immediate control of the base with the Arab story of a man who gave his house away but kept one nail for himself. Now and then, the man would drop in to examine and polish his nail. Finally, he hung a dead cat on it—and the occupants moved out.

I also discussed the problem with the British in Cairo and the commanders at the base itself, where airfields, hospitals, supply depots and workshops line the canal for more than one hundred miles. The British insist, not unreasonably, that only trained British technicians can keep the base and its costly British-made equipment in combat-ready condition, at least for the present. They are prepared to withdraw their troops and turn the security of the base over to the Egyptian army—but not the management and operation of their vast installations.

Stripped of the excessive polemics, the situation adds up to this: This great base, perhaps the largest in the world, is a vital link in the free world's defenses.

The Egyptians say that the base on their soil is an intolerable violation of sovereignty and that Britain must evacuate lock, stock and barrel and let Egypt run it with British help and evidently at British and U.S. expense.

The British agree that as a besieged fortress in a hostile Egypt, the base would be useless. But they point out that it would also be useless unless efficiently maintained, and they question Egypt's present state of political stability and technical proficiency for the job. And they raise further questions about the right of re-entry with military forces in an emergency.

The sad thing is that both sides are right (though I think the Egyptians underestimate the skills needed to keep the base in operation). And a logical man would probably say that if the base is indispensable to the international defense structure, the proper solution is internationalization.

Jerusalem, Jordan

In Lebanon, Syria and Jordan, the refrain changes from Suez and sovereignty to Israel and "justice for the Arabs." Communism and Russia are far away, but the 800,000 Arab refugees from Israel are on the doorstep; and America, which "planted and nourishes this cancer in our body," is the villain of the plot.

As in Egypt, the Arab leaders seem to be often the prisoners rather than the leaders of public opinion they themselves helped create, and are more realistic and reasonable in private than in public. They have finally accepted the fact that Israel is here to stay. But their bitterness is profound. They believe that the new State of Israel was created only at American insistence and survives only with American money. Still smarting from their failure to crush Israel in the 1948 war, they are quick to blame the U.S. and the Zionists for their woes, and American prestige and popularity—once so high—have fallen to a low estate.

What exactly do the Arabs want?

• They want the refugees to have the right either to go back to their homes in Israel or to receive compensation for their property.

• They want the boundaries of Israel contracted to the dimensions originally fixed by the United Nations partition plan of 1947.

• They want (with some dissent in Jordan) Jerusalem internationalized in accordance with the U.N. resolution.

• In addition, Jordan wants an outlet to the sea or port

facilities in Israel, and General Naguib resents the fact that Israel severs the land communications of the Arab-Moslem world for the first time in history.

We will hear more about all these demands before peace and neighborliness replace hatred and violence in the Holy Land.

Meanwhile, the thousands of displaced, homeless Palestinian Arabs have been rotting for five years in wretched, sprawling camps in Jordan, Egypt, Lebanon and Syria—supported at a subsistence level by the United Nations (the U.S. pays 70 per cent of the cost). In Jordan alone, some 530,000 refugees constitute nearly half the country's population.

Why isn't something permanent done about them? Some say the Arab states have little real compassion, no place to put them and no money. It is true that Egypt, Lebanon and Jordan are awfully crowded; but Syria and Iraq are underpopulated, and, with some land reclamation, the refugees now multiplying at the rate of 25,000 a year could become a strength instead of a burden.

The best reason for inaction, I suspect, is that to settle the refugees permanently would prejudice the Arab case for repatriation to their former homes in Israel. In the camps I visited, the refugees told me they wanted to "go home," although I am sure they little appreciate the new conditions and environment they would find in Jewish Israel.

It does little good to examine the background of this tragedy. In Israel, they say the Arabs fled voluntarily when the fighting started in 1948, expecting to return in a few days after the Jews had been crushed. The Arabs say they were driven out in panic by the Jews and point accusingly to Deir Yassin—the village where 250 Arabs, including women and children, were massacred by Jewish terrorists in April, 1948. Wherever the responsibility lies, the embattled Jews were not crushed. On the contrary, in the 1948 fighting, they almost doubled the area of Palestine assigned to them by the U.N. partition plan and drove to the center of Jerusalem. The armistice lines were drawn along the battle front, with the result that you find villages chopped in two, Arab farmers with their land in Israel and their homes in Jordan—even houses and outhouses separated—and Jerusalem itself divided by a wide swath of no man's land that marks the boundary between the old city in Jordan and the new city in Israel. I stood with Arab peasants and looked across the barbed wire to their neglected fields and orchards on the other side: I stood on a balcony in old Jerusalem with an Arab lawyer pointing to his house in Israel—which he hadn't been able to visit in five years. And a few hundred yards away, Jews gaze wistfully at the wrecked "Jewish quarter" of the old city, their Wailing Wall and their sacred places—now inaccessible in Jordan.

The results of such unnatural boundaries are continual border incidents; hardly a week goes by without gunfire and casualties. Jews and Arabs blame each other. Jordan authorities admitted to me that refugees often sneak across the line, but insist that the major incidents bear the marks of deliberate instigation. Why? "Because," they replied, "if the Jews appear to be in mortal danger, they get bigger contributions from America."

If not besieged, Israel is certainly blockaded by her Arab neighbors. For years, no oil has flowed from Iraq through the pipeline to Israel's refinery at Haifa. With vast quantities of oil at her back door, Israel imports fuel from Venezuela. No food or raw materials move from the Middle East to nourish the people and limping industries of Israel. Tourists with an Israel visa on their passports can't enter the Arab states. There is no mail or telegraph service between Israel and her neighbors. Armies are too big and too expensive. Everyone suffers.

I talked to most of the leaders of the Arab states, including an old friend, Camille Chamoun, the alert, handsome Christian president of tiny Lebanon, a country stripped of its cedars but not of its culture that belongs to both East and West; and Gen. Adeeb Shishekly, Syria's chief of state, a rugged, friendly, blunt man who quite frankly wants U.S. arms and money more than technical assistance for his development projects. In Jordan, largely dependent on British aid, the story was the same.

From Amman and the land of Moab, we drove down long, rocky gorges, where pink oleanders etched the creek beds, and out into the arid wasteland of the Jordan Valley and the Dead Sea—"the abomination of desolation." And hereafter these Biblical words will have a new and vivid meaning for me. For 90,000 refugees are now strewn along the naked foothills of Judea west of the blessed river. Beside them lies Jericho, the oldest existing town on earth; behind them, the valley of John the Baptist, and on the heights above—Jerusalem.

There, by the gate where Saul strode off toward Damascus, I wondered for a moment who speaks for Christianity in Jerusalem, which has seen so much of piety, heard so much of truth, known so little of peace. And I thought, too, about how much in common have the Arabs, Jews and Christians who have shared the Sacred City for so long; how their common inspiration—faith in one God—sprang from these same rocky hills and deserts; how Jews and Arabs lived together here in harmony for 1300 years; and how the great concepts that unite us converge within the walls of Old Jerusalem. Surely here, one would think, we could settle our differences in the face of peril to our common faith in God. Instead, ill will is growing like the weeds that sprout amongst the rubble of Jerusalem's no man's land.

Jerusalem, Israel

As you come into Israel by the back door after long

months of travel in the East, the first impact is the abrupt change in living standards—no one is barefoot, no one is dressed in rags. Then you notice the modern European aspects of New Jerusalem, the bustling crowds, the new construction. For the Jews are moving their capital to Jerusalem in spite of the talk of internationalization and in spite of the city's division and location, because, as one said to me, "Jerusalem has a meaning for Jews which no Gentile can understand."

"In the next few days, I traveled through Israel from Elath, on the ill-favored shores of the Red Sea, to the mount overlooking the Sea of Galilee where Jesus said, "Blessed are the peacemakers. . . . Do good to them that hate you." And I crossed the Valley of Esdralon where my namesake, Adlai, was a shepherd of King David. It looked more peaceful than politics—or the Middle East.

Much has been written about the modern miracles wrought by Israel, and I will not repeat what others have reported about the camps for new immigrants, the new villages, collective farms, housing, schools and factories. These achievements exceeded my expectations, and I concluded that more human and material progress is concentrated in tiny Israel than in the rest of the Middle East put together. Rather let me report what may be less familiar—that Israel's road is as rocky as its soil.

Imports exceed exports five to one. Last year, Israel earned only about 20 per cent of the foreign currency she spent. The balance came from investments, loans and gifts from abroad, mostly from American Jews and the U.S. Government. Almost three fourths of last year's budget came from abroad. Nearly a third of Israel's foreign debt matures within a year. Productivity is low, costs high, resources meager, industry slowing down for want of foreign exchange for raw materials. And Israel is only about 30 per cent self-sufficient in food. In spite of more than a billion dollars of gifts, loans and investments from abroad in the past five years, Israel is still farther from paying her own way than any other nation. As one official said to me. "Flushed with a victory that had looked so doubtful, we thought we could have everything all at once—unlimited immigration and assimilation, rapid industrialization, agricultural development, social security, high wages and living standards and a big army. We were wrong."

Is Israel doing anything about her present plight? She certainly is. Inflation has been checked; real wages came down 10 or 15 per cent in the last year; supply now exceeds purchasing power and the inflated living standard is declining—as it must before it can go up. With increasing unemployment, there is a great drive to raise agricultural output by diverting more people to the land. And I believe that Israel, possessed of great resources of intelligence and ingenuity and with a record of so many difficulties already mastered, has both the courage and the leadership to take the distasteful steps necessary to earn more and spend less foreign exchange.

Two other factors will ease the situation: Net immigration is down from more than 25,000 a month last year to 900. And Germany has agreed to pay "moral reparations" to Israel in the form of $750 million's worth of goods over the next 12 years.

But as an official said. "We have only a slight margin, if any, for error." At best, Israel will need generous friends for a long time.

More food can be wrested from the soil, but Israel lacks both water and farmers. Water exploration is being pushed with some success, but large irrigation projects would involve her hostile neighbors, Syria and Jordan. Only 15 per cent of the population are in agriculture; the bulk of the 700,000 immigrants (from 48 countries) who arrived since 1948 are urban professional people, shopkeepers, artisans and traders with little taste for farming. The result is that you see too much neglected land, too many machines and sprinklers imported from abroad and too little manual labor in the manner of the Arabs and Asians. This would be understandable if Israel had plenty of money and a shortage of manpower. But the reverse is true; and the resistance to working on the land will continue to be a problem until another generation is trained.

Prime Minister David Ben-Gurion, an energetic, friendly, stubborn fighter who has seen his Zionist dream come true, said to me. "We want to live in friendly co-operation with our Arab neighbors. Our aim is peace." Then I asked him about the Arab demands. He minced no words—nor did Moshe Sharett, the confident, articulate Foreign Minister: "Jerusalem will be internationalized—over our dead bodies. Repatriation? We won't accept a single Arab."

Foreigners sometimes wonder why Israel insists on making her capital Jerusalem—a half-city in a narrow salient. Ben-Gurion explained it in these words: "We are ready to accept divided Jerusalem as it is and we have no objection to international supervision of the holy places. But Israel without Jerusalem is like Zionism without Zion."

As to the boundary changes demanded by the Arabs, the Israeli position is this: "We took no territory from any Arab state in the war; we have no border dispute with Lebanon; we will discuss and settle the small strip Syria claims; we will give Egypt a passage across our southern extremity, with guarantees; we will meet Jordan's port requirements, and we almost reached an agreement with Jordan last year to correct the present frontier absurdities. But to go back to the lines originally fixed by the U.N.—never!"

Sharett put it this way: "The Arabs could have accepted the U.N. boundaries, but they didn't. They forced us to fight for our lives. They can't have it both ways. Our territory was increased by war—and only war can alter it."

The Arab refugees? The Israelis made it plain where

they stood. About 160,000 Arabs who didn't flee during the fighting are still living in Israel, and a few thousand more are being admitted to reunite families. Any more, it is said, would create a security risk and an acute assimilation problem. I suspect any large number of returned refugees certainly would not leave much more room for the 2.5 million Jews still behind the Iron Curtain, who, Ben-Gurion says, would be welcomed.

Sharett preferred to talk about resettlement rather than repatriation of the Arab refugees: "If Israel with its small area and limited resources could within a few years absorb 700,000 destitute newcomers—250,000 of them Jews from Arab lands—it is evident that the bigger and better-endowed Arab countries could find homes for the same number of their kinsmen, if only the will existed."

Israel does, however, recognize an obligation to compensate the Arab refugees for the property they left behind. The Israelis don't know where they will get the money, but, as Ben-Gurion often says, "It can be done because it has to be done."

When do they propose to do something about indemnification? Only as part of an over-all peace settlement. But the Israelis have now agreed to release to the refugees a portion of their $7 million in bank deposits which Israel has frozen for the past five years.

The Arab states fear Jewish aggression. Likewise, the Israelis fear that any arms the U.S. gives the Arabs will be used to attack Israel rather than to defend the Middle East. So again, as in Egypt, it is obvious that a regional defense organization must await the solution of problems that have higher local priority in this part of the world than defense against Soviet imperialism.

As in so many other countries I have visited during this long journey, I was both exhilarated and depressed by what I found in Israel—exhilarated by what has been accomplished by the pride of the ordinary people (like the taxi driver who boasted about what "we Jews" are doing to irrigate the Negev Desert) and by the vision in Israel of a better future for all of the Middle East.

And I was depressed by the gulf that separates Israel from the Arab world and by the bleak facts of her economic life. Regardless of world politics and the importance of unity and strength in the great strategic vacuum of the Middle East, the good will of her neighbors is as vital to Israel's survival in the long run as aid from abroad is today. Israel's many friends in America should remember that good relations between Jews and Arabs are the only alternative to endless contributions of money to a permanently beleaguered fortress surrounded by embittered neighbors.

And "peace" is not just a word in a treaty which, signed today, means friendly relations tomorrow. Real, enduring peace is a state of mind which will only stem from mutual confidence and a community of interests between Jews and Arabs. This may take a long time. But the first and urgent step is to settle the four outstanding disputes—over boundaries, Jerusalem, compensation and reparriation.

My own feeling is that insistence on any *major* alteration of Israel's boundaries is unrealistic.

As to Jerusalem, it is hard to see how a city divided against itself can stand, let alone flourish, and certainly *all* the faiths are concerned.

The refugees constitute the hardest problem, and it is crying tragically for settlement. Indemnification for their property is no more than fair and just. As to repatriation, I doubt that any substantial number of Arab refugees would care to live as Israeli citizens under conditions and in an environment quite different from what they remember; and especially if opportunities were opened to them to resettle with help and hope among their kinfolk in Arab countries.

Finally and most emphatically, the Arab states must be made to feel that America's friendship for Israel does not mean we are "anti-Arab" or esteem them the less. But this will take far more than words.

Perhaps it is too much to expect that solutions will be worked out—as they should have been long ago—by the Arabs and the Jews sitting down together. But they might welcome reasonable solutions imposed by outsiders willing to be damned by both sides.

If this sounds like tough talk, I recall the pleading words of a sad-eyed old Mohammedan *caid:* "Two sick men need a doctor." He said it in Nazareth.

Churchill

BY C. P. SNOW

I remember — I shall not forget it while I live — the beautiful, shining, desperate summer of 1940. I was listening with a friend, for we were never far from a radio that June, to one of the great speeches. It must have been either after Dunkirk, or after the fall of France. The growling, lisping voice came into the room. The accent is odd, to modern English ears: it is nothing like the clipped upper-class English of today: but we didn't notice that as we listened that night, and other summer nights. For that voice was our hope. It was the voice of will and strength incarnate. It was saying what we wanted to hear said ("We shall defend our Island") and what we tried to believe, sometimes against the protests of realism, and common sense, would come true ("We shall fight on unconquerable until the curse of Hitler is lifted from the brows of mankind. We are sure that in the end all will come right").

My friend and I listened, and at the end went out into the London evening. He said: "We must never deny our gratitude. Don't forget. We must *never* deny our gratitude."

For his patriotism was absolute. It took in the whole of his nature. He was an aristocrat, but he would cheerfully have beggared his class and his friends, and everyone else too, if that was the price of the country coming through. Everyone believed that. The poor believed it, as his voice rolled out into the slum streets, those summer evenings of 1940. The national emotion stayed at that pitch for about twelve months, heightened, if anything, by the air raids. During this period, Churchill spoke for a nation undivided and curiously happy, as it has never been in my lifetime, before or since.

Yet there are paradoxes which will puzzle posterity. During those years, Churchill *ruled* the country more comprehensively, more directly and with a greater measure of support than any Prime Minister has ever done. Nevertheless, he only became Prime Minister in the teeth of the wishes of the overwhelming majority of his own party. He was a Conservative, but the Conservatives had distrusted him for a generation. When Chamberlain had to go, they would have chosen Lord Halifax as Prime Minister. King George VI, who represented decent Conservative opinion very well, thought Halifax "the obvious man," and hated having to send for Winston Churchill.

This was in May, 1940, with the Germans driving into the Lowlands. It looks as though Churchill would never have been sent for if it had not been for the absurd but providential chance that Halifax happened to be a member of the House of Lords. When Churchill as Prime Minister was making his first speeches in the House, he got very little applause from his own party. His real support, as well as trust and affection, came from the Labour benches opposite.

Had he died in his sixties, he would have been one of the picturesque failures in British politics—a failure like Charles James Fox, or his own father, Lord Randolph Churchill. In fact, as early as the twenties, his staunch foul-weather friend Lord Beaverbrook—one of the toughest friends he has ever had—was already writing about him as a brilliant failure. His life, right up to the time when most men have finished, had been adventurous and romantic, but he had achieved little. Except among his friends—and I mean his real friends—he had never been popular. In most of his political life, he had been widely disliked.

For years, he could do nothing quite right. He was an excellent First Lord of the Admiralty (in U.S. terms, Secretary of the Navy) before and at the beginning of the First World War. But his best ideas came to nothing. He was responsible for the development of the tank, but the weapon was wasted. His major strategic conception of Gallipoli was a brilliant idea: but, partly because he had made an unwise choice of his chief professional adviser, who betrayed him, he could not carry it through.

So he went through his middle age. The record of brilliant failure got longer. He changed his party [once] again and rejoined the Conservatives. Not that that helped much. He enjoyed himself, much too flamboyantly, in suppressing the general strike of 1926. He had a lively but unsuccessful spell as Chancellor of the Exchequer (1924-29). After that, the one point on which all Conservatives were agreed was that he had to be kept out of office at any cost.

Thus he managed, until he was old, to be disapproved of, for quite different reasons, by the right and the left. To the left, in particular to the British working class, he was simply a reactionary.

On the right, among his own kind and his own Conservative party, the distrust was more serious. In some quarters, it lasted longer. Most of its origins were discreditable, and were rooted in sheer blind envy. He was by any standard the most miscellaneously gifted man in politics. He had the kind of aristocratic magnanimity which, instead of reducing the amount of envy, seemed to provoke it. He behaved like a prince, at a time when princely behavior had gone right out of fashion. He was not good at dealing with the official class, very influential in Britain. His habits were not theirs, they had no use for his friends. The officials were themselves good listeners and expected politicians to listen. That was not his chief gift.

But all that was trivial. He was too distinguished, he was envied, he didn't get on with lesser men. They had just one rational criticism of him. Within limits, there was something in it. It consists of one word—judgment, or rather lack of it. For nearly fifty years of public life, the orthodox remark in Britain was: "Churchill? Brilliant, of course. But no judgment."

I don't think there is any burking the fact that Churchill's judgment has, on a good many occasions in his life, been seriously defective. Compare him with an admirable but far less brilliant man, George C. Marshall. With both of them sitting round a table, Marshall seemed inarticulate, almost dull, by the side of Churchill. He wouldn't have claimed any of the sparks of imaginative genius that Churchill threw out, whatever he was touching. Yet, on the affairs which they were jointly tackling, Marshall's judgment was by long odds the better. The history of World War II has yet to be written. Churchill's memoirs are marvelously heartwarming and persuasive. As one reads them, one is entirely on his side. But it is certain that, over a good many crises of judgment, history won't be.

Yet ironically this same obsessive quality, which often

distorted his judgment and led him into errors, was also the force which saved us.

Judgment is a fine thing: but there are a fair number of statesmen with good judgment: there is only one Churchill. There are ultimate crises which we have lived through and in which, thank God, he took the great decisions, where judgment itself can, though it need not, be a source of weakness.

When Hitler came to power in 1933, Churchill did not use judgment, but one of his profound insights. This was absolute evil, and there was no way round. *That* was what we needed. It was a unique occasion in our history. We needed that insight, and that absolute strength.

That is why we shall never deny our gratitude. There is also a great deal else, not so near life and death, to be grateful for. For all his conflicts, his turbulences, his egocentricities, he has, all through his career, sweetened British life. That is a curious phrase to use of a man always in the middle of the battle: yet I am sure that, despite the hatreds which once collected round him, it is true. He is a singularly magnanimous man. With a few exceptions, he has forgiven his enemies—enemies who had often done their best to ruin him, and who found it hard to forgive *him* just because he was so generous. He has been the loyalest of friends, has taken risks for those he loves, and has paid a heavy cost. He stood by Lloyd George in the most dangerous scandal of his friend's life—and that was counted one of Churchill's crimes in high Conservative circles. He showed chivalry and devotion to Edward VIII over the abdication, and that too took a long time to be condoned. He has never denied his affections, nor betrayed a friend. He has lived his life in the most generous style. He has worn his virtues as cheerfully as his absurd hats. He can put on the grand manner, but he has never lost the rip-roaring Corinthian gusto for living. Eyebrows have been lifted at his brandy and champagne, his cigars, his hosts' yachts, his liking for the company of the international rich. Eyebrows have been lifted, and much he cares. In everything that doesn't matter, he has done precisely what he wanted, and not given a damn. In everything that does matter, he has lived much more strictly than most men, according to a strong and gallant moral code.

He has not only helped to save us from dying. He has shown us a pattern of how life can be lived. These virtues and graces, for they are mixed up together, are in danger of slipping out of our gritty everyday existence. Courage, magnanimity, loyalty, humor, gallantry—these are not often held up for admiration in our literature, or in fact depicted at all. Perhaps we are losing the knack of recognizing them. While Churchill lives, they are there. There they stand, as unshakable as his will. I am not sure that isn't my deepest reason for hoping that he never dies.

Inside F.D.R.

BY JOHN GUNTHER

The first time I ever saw Franklin Delano Roosevelt was at a press conference on December 7, 1934—midway through the all-but-forgotten pressures and turmoils of the first term, and seven years to a day before Pearl Harbor.

Was he a great man? Of course. But what made him so? His career, by almost any criterion, is one of the most extraordinary in modern times. But exactly why? What did Roosevelt himself contribute to his own proliferating destiny? What came from the *Zeitgeist*, what from him?

Roosevelt's most effective quality, I once heard it said, was his receptivity. But he also transmitted. He was like a kind of universal joint or rather a switchboard or transformer. The whole energy of the country, the whole power of one hundred and forty million people, flowed into him and through him; he not only felt this power, but he utilized it, he really transmitted it.

He led by following, which was one of his great sources of power. He lifted people above themselves, and hence no one was ever able to take the masses away from him. Yet more than any modern President, he split the country, which is one of the more obvious Roosevelt paradoxes.

Why was he hated so, calumniated so? Because he took from the rich and gave to the poor. But that is only one explanation. Why, five years after his death, is he still hated so? Because what he did lives after him. But that too is only part of the story.

Roosevelt stood for the "common man" (though this ambiguous phrase is a cliché earnestly to be avoided) but he was certainly not common himself. In fact, he was a storybook Prince Charming, a fairytale hero to the millions. He ruled with a wand—even if it was a brittle ivory cigaret holder. Out in the rain men and women strove—literally—to touch the hem of his cape as he passed, this man who could not walk.

Probably what it boils down to is a matter of contribution. He did not create a country as did Masaryk, or a continent of the imagination, like Beethoven, or a new world of science like Freud. But if you measure a man practically by the work he leaves, F.D.R. ranks very high. Certainly he belongs in the category of Washington and Lincoln as one of the three greatest Presidents in American history, whether you like all he did or not.

There are all sorts of courage, and F.D.R. had them all, including the courage to make tremendous, lonely decisions and to stick to them. Think of Pearl Harbor. Some pretty disgraceful things happened in Washington that night; panic ran in some very high places indeed. There were men who behaved like somebody howling "Fire!" in a crowded theater, but one spot where absolute calmness and resolution reigned was the White House. F.D.R. set in motion that very night the processes by which the United States soon moved expeditionary forces to Australia and Northern Ireland.

A good authority has stated that in the whole time Roosevelt was in the White House he had only two sleepless nights. I asked Mrs. Roosevelt about this once, and her reply was characteristically candid and discriminating: "My husband never had a sleepless night. But it is quite true that there were two nights when he could not sleep, because of interruptions. To be sleepless is one thing. To be kept from sleep is quite another."

General Eisenhower had never met F.D.R., except for one brief, impersonal contact, until he was assigned to go to England in 1942 as commander of the American forces there. He expected some pretty heavy talk, but the President's opening remark was, "I've just had to spend an hour on your baby brother. He's giving me an awful lot of trouble."

"My brother Milton?" Eisenhower replied, startled.

"Yes. Four different government departments want him, and I have to decide which will be lucky enough to get him!"

Roosevelt's capacity to win new people was unparalleled. I recall how Frank Knox, the publisher of the Chicago *Daily News*, told me in 1934 not to bother to see the President. "He'll just glad-hand you, kiss you on both cheeks. Don't go near that son-of-a-blank." Not so many years later, Knox himself was Roosevelt's devoted and hardworking Secretary of the Navy.

The famous smile was not so much an adjunct of Roosevelt's charm as might be thought: people would succumb even when on guard against the "synthetic" smile. A few people remained impervious to his wiles no matter what.

At Teheran, for instance, F.D.R. took time out for 40 minutes to win over a British official he had never met. Roosevelt was like a violinist playing a cadenza, but the Englishman disliked and resented the performance. He felt (a) he was not worth that much time; (b) Roosevelt could not be "sincere," and must simply be using him to sharpen his bow on; (c) it was superb showmanship, but not quite nice.

Was Roosevelt a snob? In some ways, yes. He adored kings and queens and such. Why not? He was a prince himself. He was much taken by names and titles. It is somewhat ridiculous that he should have been impressed by creatures like the Sultan of Morocco, whom he met at Casablanca, but this was part of the fun of his position.

More interesting were Roosevelt's relations with the millionaire class, most members of which hated him so venomously. For a long time, he had close social relations with Vincent Astor, William Rhinelander Stewart and various Vanderbilts; later many rich men served him with complete devotion. Then, too, he was something of a snob so far as his own huge family was concerned. He detested the parvenus and the white trash of cafe society. All this brings up complex issues.

Mr. Roosevelt was a gentleman. This may seem only too obvious, but it is important to state; not all American Presidents have been gentlemen by any means. I mean gentleman in the literal sense. He was decent; he was civilized; he was kind. He loathed anything disagreeable; he hated unpleasantness and abhorred crudities in personal behavior. His casual letters are, one sometimes feels, almost too "nice," even effeminate; it would be a relief if he would break out, get mad, and sass somebody. But what a pleasant touch he had!

He had considerable affection for two of his chief political opponents, Landon and Willkie; he despised Hoover intellectually, and resented what he thought had been some wanton rudeness on Hoover's part, but he was sorry for him on the whole; he disliked and feared [Thomas E.] Dewey, but did not hate him.

It was never made clear who had final authority to do what. The President always saw to it that he was the last judge and arbiter. He was quite frank about his idiosyncrasies in this direction. Once he laughed at a press conference, "I have a single responsible head, and his name is Knudsen-Hillman."

When he had a "bad" situation between Hull and Morgenthau, he called in an officer much junior to these two and said, "You go over and get Cordell and Henry together on this. Knock their heads together." The junior officer was appalled. "Good God, Mr. President, you want *me* to tell *them* that they're both crazy?" F.D.R. pondered and replied, "Well, if you don't, I'm afraid I'll have to create some new board." He was perfectly serious.

F.D.R.'s extreme loquaciousness was another outstanding characteristic.

Why did the President talk so much? Partly because he couldn't walk. This is of course an oversimplification; the fact remains that conversation was his favorite method of relaxing.

Normally a man can pace the room during a tense discussion, shift in his chair, cross to a bookcase, open a window, or beg to be excused for a moment or two; anything to shift the mood of a tight conference, take a little time out, readjust perspective, knit a group together. Roosevelt could do none of these things. So he relieved himself by gossiping, asking questions, interrupting and telling stories. He liked to do things that didn't take too much out of him; stamps were one and talk another. Conversation was his golf, his tennis and his badminton.

Now we swing back to qualities more positive or mixed. One major trait was patience. A cruel master taught him patience—his own illness. F.D.R.'s almost diabolically subtle sense of timing was a related characteristic. I have heard this explained by the remark that "he was in tune with history."

Again, one does not think of Roosevelt as being industrious in the manner of a beaver or an automaton; he had too much variability, nervousness and informality. Yet the amount of work he did was murderous.

The President's omniscience and erudition covered a very wide arc indeed; he knew a little about almost everything, from where to get good beer in Georgetown to which wives of cabinet officers gossiped most. The three subjects about which he knew *most* were American politics, American history and geography in general.

Mr. Roosevelt, too, loved to laugh. His sense of humor was, as everybody knows, hearty and robust. He was no great wit, and he had little gift for drawing-room repartee. His humor was seldom subtle or profound; it was somewhat heavy, smart-alecky, broad and based on exaggeration. But what a relief to the nation in 1932 to have a President with any sense of humor at all!

Once he had to make a public appearance before the Daughters of the American Revolution. He didn't want to go, but he did. The proceedings were stupefyingly formal—until F.D.R. began his speech with the words, "Fellow immigrants!"

Finally, consider the essential quality from which the other human traits derive—F.D.R.'s intense and overwhelming joy in life, and particularly joy in his job; his love of the simple fact of living and being chief was inexhaustible.

Almost naïvely, he said to a friend once, "Wouldn't you be President if you could? Wouldn't anybody?"

My View
of the Presidency

BY HARRY S TRUMAN

As I have studied the many attempts throughout our history to change and restrict the powers of the Presidency, I

feel that most of them stem from a basic misunderstanding of the office and the duties of the President as set out in the Constitution of the United States. The President must have the unfettered right to be in a position to act promptly when an emergency arises. He must, therefore, have the broadest powers, limited only by the Constitution and his term of office.

It is nothing short of a miracle, when you think of it, that the framers of the Constitution had the genius to create an office, the Presidency of the United States, which can function as responsively and as easily in this rocket and atomic age as it did in the age of the stagecoach, the sailing ship and the powdered wig.

Most of the powers that a President exercises today are authorized by the Constitution. Other powers have been built up by custom created by time and by events in emergencies met by our stronger Presidents. I have deep admiration for our strong Presidents who clearly understood their powers and acted to meet difficult situations as they arose. Grover Cleveland said in one case, "We are faced with a condition and not a theory." He met the condition.

I assume everyone knows that   belong to the Democratic party. One of the deciding reasons for my being a Democrat, after intensive study of the history of the United States, was that the Democratic party, in the last decades of the nineteenth century and the first half of the twentieth, has always supported strong Presidents, while the Republican party has been constantly suspicious of strong Presidents, even one of its own (Teddy Roosevelt), and timid about supporting Presidential powers and duties.

I wish that every citizen of this republic would help to keep the office of the Presidency as strong and flexible as it is now, and resist efforts to cut its powers or to harass it.

As a citizen, if you are not satisfied or happy with the way that the office is conducted, you have the right and the duty to go to the ballot box every four years and vote for a man who you think is more suitable for that office. But as a practical matter, the President has only those powers that are delegated to him by your own ballot and the Constitution of the United States.

The efforts in the past to hamper and restrict the office of the Presidency fall largely into two categories—attempts to contract the inherent powers of the President, or to cause him to lose prestige.

At the top of the list of endeavors to handicap the Presidency is the XXII Amendment to the Constitution. This amendment limits the number of terms a President may hold to two. It also limits the Vice-President who succeeds to an unfinished term of a President to one full term if the one to which he succeeds runs longer than two years. Because it restricts the Presidency and thwarts the right of the people to choose any President they desire, this amendment is a monstrosity—one of the worst ever added to the Constitution. It is as bad as that short-lived Prohibition amendment. In the event the nation is confronted by a grave emergency, it could be tragic.

Some plans that look plausible on the face would also tend to constrict the Presidency by indirection. The proposal to establish a national Presidential primary is in this class. A national Presidential primary would force a candidate to raise a huge sum of money in order to tour the country and make his good points known. No poor man or even one fairly well fixed could finance a national campaign. The money would have to be raised and contributed by the wealthy and the special interests. The nominee would become obligated to contributors, and that would not be good for the country. The President should not be faced with any obligations to special interests, or powerful groups, or wealthy individuals.

Now let us consider the efforts to injure the prestige of the Presidency and belittle the man who holds the office.

There is no excuse for people who loose attacks on a President for his use of the facilities and prerogatives of the office. I have no patience with them. They are scandalmongers and character assassins.

The President has the same right to relax from the heavy burdens of the greatest of offices as has any other executive, whether he works for a great corporation or a small city. But to criticize the President because he uses a helicopter to fly to his home or to yap at him when he plays a game of golf is unfair and downright picayunish. A President cannot fight back against personal charges. In this respect, he is defenseless. As the chief executive of the leading nation in the world, it is beneath his dignity to answer personal attacks.

No man can be President without realizing the immense influence of the office. When he becomes the head of this nation, he does his best to maintain the prestige of the office. President Hoover and I probably stand opposed on more political issues than any two men alive, yet we respect and have an affection for each other. I am sure that the tie that binds us is the experiences we had in the Presidency.

Healthy and strong contacts with White House personnel are, in themselves, essential to the proper functioning of the President's office. Power attracts all kinds of men. Most of those who work with a President are sincere and high-minded men. A very few are not. There always are men who want to take advantage of their acquaintance with the members of the staff of the President for their own aggrandizement.

But when these contacts are used for unethical purposes, the offenders should be dispensed with. Every President has had some trouble with this problem. I was no exception.

Of course, I do not think that the office of President is perfect as it stands. An erosion of its influence can take place by custom as well as by law or amendment. For one thing, I do not like this present trend toward a huge White House staff.

The President must make his own decisions. He cannot pass the buck up or down. Therefore, he must keep in close touch with the men who run the Government at his direction. A layer of Presidential aides has been placed between the President and his appointed officials. Mostly, these aides get in each other's way. They tend to insulate the President. The President needs breathing space. The smaller the staff around him, the better. Information is what he needs. When he has the right information, he is in a position to make the right decisions—and he, and only he, must make them.

There has been a lot of talk lately about the burdens of the Presidency. Decisions the President has to make often affect the lives of tens of millions of people around the world, but that does not mean that they take longer to make. Some men can make decisions and some can't. Some men fret and delay under criticism. I used to have a saying that applies here: "If you can't stand the heat, get out of the kitchen."

An administrative Vice-President has been proposed. The advocates say that this No. 2 President could take a lot of work off the President's shoulders. This is merely another form of buck passing.

Another new custom I don't like is televised press conferences. The President's press conference is a great institution. When I was President, I felt that I always learned more about what was on the minds of the people from the reporters' questions than they could possibly learn from me. Television, I think, brings out the exhibitionist qualities of some reporters, and they tend to make speeches to the President.

Television and radio reporters should have the same access to the press conferences as newspaper reporters, but this on-the-spot camera business with spotlights and entertainment touches detracts from the give-and-take of serious questioning. A public show makes it a kind of circus beneath the dignity of the Presidential office and waters down efforts to obtain facts.

Some people think it demeans the office of the Presidency for a former President to run for a lesser elective office. I must heartily disagree. When he leaves the White House, the President is an American citizen with a duty to serve his country, state and community to the best of his ability.

I think it not only proper, but it could become a fine tradition, if former Presidents held office. I would have been honored to run for the Senate from Missouri after my Presidential term, but I had too much respect and admiration for the records and the persons of the two Missouri Democratic senators to entertain such a suggestion.

Remember that John Quincy Adams served in the House for 17 years after he was President, and Andrew Johnson was elected to the Senate six years after he left the White House.

To sum it all up, the Presidency is the greatest office in the history of the world in the greatest republic. We should all work to keep its powers broad, unfettered and flexible and its prestige high.

A Visit with
Walter Lippmann

BY WILLIAM ATTWOOD

No political label fits Walter Lippmann. If you call him a liberal, you have to face the fact that he was a sharp critic of the New Deal and that he supported Alfred M. Landon in 1936, Thomas E. Dewey in 1948 and Dwight D. Eisenhower in 1952. If you call him a conservative, you have to consider his long association with the *New Republic*, his disenchantment with Eisenhower and his profound admiration for Theodore Roosevelt, Woodrow Wilson, Franklin D. Roosevelt and John F. Kennedy.

Lippmann wears no one's colors but his own, and his only credo is that man's best hope lies in the exercise of reason. As a result, he has practically made a career of detached observation.

Apart from books, Lippmann reads the Washington *Post*, the New York *Times*, the New York *Herald Tribune* and the London *Times*, as well as several weeklies such as the Manchester *Guardian*, the *Observer*, the *Nation* and the *New Republic*. From many luncheons and dinners and phone calls, from reading and from reflecting, comes the raw material for his columns. They are deceptively quiet, measured in tone but often shattering in their impact. They are never personal, never strident, never really angry. People who disagree with Lippmann seldom dislike him. His prose does not irritate them; it merely bowls over their arguments like a gently moving but well-oiled bulldozer.

Unlike most columnists, Lippmann has little interest in scoops, exposés or sensational predictions. He uses off-the-record information—of which he hears a great deal—only as background for interpreting the printed record. People trust him with confidences because he never violates them.

And his fellow newspapermen regard him with a mixture of esteem and affection rarely accorded to one of their fraternity. In 1959, when he was 70, twelve of his colleagues from all over the world collaborated on a book called *Walter Lippmann and His Times*. Five hundred people assembled in Washington for a birthday party in his honor.

James Reston, chief Washington correspondent for the New York *Times*, spoke for many of his fellow reporters at that party when he said of Lippmann: "He has brought thought to bear on politics, and he has carried that thought from one end of our society to another. . . He has given my generation of newspapermen a wider vision of our duty."

An interviewer of thousands, Lippmann has seldom been interviewed himself. Recently, in his Washington home, he agreed to talk to a LOOK editor.

You have made a career of commenting on current history. Don't you ever regret not becoming more involved—either in government or in politics?

No regrets—though I do think it's a good thing to get involved once or twice. I did as a young man, when I worked for the mayor of Schenectady and, later, for Wilson, at the Paris Peace Conference. I've been offered positions in government since then, but I've never been tempted. I like the freedom of what I do.

Yet you seemed more committed in 1960 than ever before. Many of your readers felt you were frankly partisan. Why was that?

I did feel more committed than usual because the issue in the election was very great. I felt that a new generation had to come into power. A Nixon Administration would have been an extension of the Eisenhower regime. Nixon would not have attracted new brains to Washington. The intellectuals were overwhelmingly for Kennedy—brains, you know, are suspect in the Republican party.

We needed younger, more experienced and educated men running the government, so a Nixon victory would have been a very bad thing—although I suppose the country could have stood it.

Last spring, you advocated a Stevenson-Kennedy ticket. What made you do that?

About a year ago—after Eisenhower's budget message—I began to feel that we had to have a change in Washington. But I wasn't sure about Kennedy. I was certain that he would be nominated after West Virginia but I wasn't at all sure that he could be elected. And I wasn't exactly on fire for him after the convention. It was his Houston speech in September—when he faced those ministers—that convinced me he was a thoroughbred. Looking back, I wish that [Adlai E.] Stevenson had nominated him at Los Angeles.

Kennedy has been compared to the two Roosevelts. Do you agree?

He doesn't remind me of Franklin Roosevelt at all. Kennedy is much more serious. Physically, he is more like Theodore—who used to bound upstairs at the White House and play games with his children. But Kennedy is more politically educated and more disciplined than either of the Roosevelts. This doesn't mean he will be more successful. Franklin had the vital gift of knowing what the masses felt. We don't know yet whether Kennedy has this gift.

Last July, speaking of a strong President's qualities, you said: "The first thing is his ability to see through the latest headline to what is permanent and enduring. This second sight is the quality of great leaders." Of the Presidents you have known, which ones had this "second sight?" Does Kennedy?

Theodore Roosevelt had it. I don't think he is appreciated by this generation. He realized we were a world power. He also understood that we were no longer a 19th-century rural society and that regulation had become a national responsibility.

Wilson had it. He taught America and the world that a universal society would have to be created—and that the League of Nations was the first step.

And Franklin Roosevelt had this second sight too. For he understood the truly revolutionary condition of the United States when he took office—and he knew he had to act. There is no doubt that he saved capitalism in America.

As for Kennedy—it's too early to tell whether he has this second sight. I hope he does.

You also said in July that "the biggest single job of the next President will be mobilizing the country to meet the Soviet challenge." Are you satisfied that Kennedy will do this?

I know that he has every intention of doing it. I don't know whether he will succeed. He undramatizes things. That's his style. But this may well be the style of his generation. And he is a popular President. The only reason the election was close was because of the Catholic issue—I think Kennedy lost five million votes because of his religion. All that's finished now and, I suspect, forever.

Why did Kennedy come to see you after his election?

To talk about some of his appointments. And I have seen him from time to time since then. But this doesn't mean that I will play any role in his Administration. On the contrary—I intend to be just as critical as I have always been.

Did you have much personal contact with the last three Presidents?

I never met Eisenhower after he became President. I seldom saw [Harry S] Truman—he preferred the newspapermen who covered the White House. Roosevelt I would meet frequently. We were old friends—also, I was one of a small group of newspapermen who attended his "secret" press conferences during the war.

You supported Eisenhower in 1952. Yet, by 1960, you had become one of his sharpest critics. What happened?

I supported him because I felt that he would be able to end the Korean War—and get away with it—and because he would be able to liquidate [the late Sen. Joseph R.] McCarthy. If Eisenhower had lost in 1952, the Republicans would have followed McCarthy. After being out of power 20 years, they would have gone mad.

Well, Eisenhower's first term wasn't so bad. The war was ended and McCarthy was discredited. But Eisenhower never should have run for a second term. It was a fatal mistake for him to accept the nomination after his illness. He lost his sense of balance. He did not see the danger in a relatively stagnant economy. And this slowdown caused great damage to our national strength both at home and abroad.

A year ago, in *LOOK*, you wrote about the moral climate of America: "There has been a failure of the capacity to believe . . . that anything really matters very much and that anything is really better than anything else." Do you think this will change in the sixties?

Yes. This is a most peculiarly Presidential country. The tone and the example set by the President have a tremendous effect on the quality of life in America. The President is like the conductor of a big symphony orchestra—and a new conductor can often get different results with the same score and the same musicians.

Right now, there is a curious exhilaration here in Washington. There is a new generation in charge, with a new style and a new seriousness. And people are beginning to feel that we can *do* things about problems after all—that everything is possible.

Is it like the early days of the New Deal?

In a way, yes. But there is an important difference between the New Frontier and the New Deal. The New Deal was in a true sense a revolutionary movement. It was the American equivalent of what was happening in Europe. The old order—the 19th-century order—seemed to be crumbling everywhere.

The Roosevelt reforms changed radically the balance of

power in the country. This is what made the New Deal revolutionary.

But Kennedy comes in at a time when there is no thought of changing the balance of internal social forces. His program is not radical at all. It does not call for a revolution, but for a renewal. Kennedy's task is not to create a different kind of society in America, but to make the one we now have work better. And the one we now have embodies the New Deal.

Would the mood of exhilaration you speak of exist if Nixon had won?

No. The feeling of a fresh start would have been missing. And he could not have found the talent that makes government exciting. Nixon was not trusted by the intellectual community—by the kind of people who are needed. They are quite a powerful element in this country, but Eisenhower pretended they didn't exist.

You said last year that the prospects for ending the cold war were "pretty good." If you still feel that way, what steps will lead to the end of the cold war?

I am still hopeful, if by "cold war" you mean the dangerous, explosive situation we have lived with for so many years. The reason I am hopeful is that I am convinced that the primary concern of the Soviet leaders is not in spreading revolution—not the conquest of Laos or Cuba—but the development of their domestic economy.

If that premise is correct, I see no irreconcilable conflict over the Congo, Berlin and other trouble spots. Rather, I see a series of steps in which the cold war will be de-fused. And the way to take these steps is by quiet diplomacy—by talking things out with the Russians at many levels without announcing defeats or victories. If the Russians would send a good man to the United Nations—as we have—much could be discussed right there and very privately.

But the cold war will go on for a long, long time, even if we succeed in reducing its dangers. There is a good analogy in the struggle between Islam and Christianity. Despite their rivalry—which has lasted for centuries—the two systems have found a way to live in the same world.

The Russians are showing signs of wanting an accommodation with us. Do you think they mean it?

I do put credence in a realistic estimate of their interests. For example, we know that it's to their interest not to have a nuclear war. Therefore, we do have a common area of agreement. And in the light of their own interest, I don't think they can afford to build up much more tension in places like Cuba. We shall see.

These signs of wanting an accommodation have been going on for some time. They were visible before last May. Then the U-2 incident compelled [Nikita S.] Khrushchev to pursue a tough line that was not at all in his own interests. He was so humiliated that he began to act more like a revolutionary Bolshevik than a Russian statesman.

Now that Eisenhower is gone, Khrushchev's personal grudge is ended. He can, if he wants, resume the role of statesman. I think this would have been true even if Nixon had been elected.

Will Red China be admitted to the U.N. this year?

I don't think so. There aren't enough votes to kick Formosa out, and the Communists say they won't sit in the U.N. with the Nationalist Chinese.

You said recently that "our greatest influence comes from proving that we can make a big democracy like this work." Hasn't it been working?

Not as it should be. Not when we don't really educate our children—and that's a terrible indictment. Not when our cities are increasingly inconvenient places to live, even though we are an urban society. Not when we lose influence in countries that don't want to be Communist at all.

Why do you suppose the Latin Americans loved Franklin Roosevelt—who actually did so little for them —and not Eisenhower? The reason, I think, is that they felt close to Roosevelt because he was dealing with important problems at home. He was doing things they understood.

Didn't you say once that the Soviet challenge may yet prove to have been a blessing in disguise?

Yes, because if we weren't challenged, we might very well go the way of the Romans—we would become contented and corrupted and decayed. Of course, we ought to keep doing the things that keep a society vital and dynamic, but most people would rather sit back unless they feel challenged. Today, we are no longer the only successful society in the world. We are confronted by a society that doesn't want to be like ours and that wants to be successful. This challenge will keep us on our toes.

You have seen a good many political triumphs and tragedies over the years. Which ones stand out in your mind?

I think it was a tragedy that Dewey wasn't elected in 1948. If the Republicans could have come to power under an able and intelligent man like Dewey, they would have become a responsible party. And the damage of McCarthyism would have been avoided.

And I would rate as a great triumph Roosevelt's success in getting Congress and the nation to accept Lend-Lease at a time when we were neutral. This probably saved the war from being lost before we got into it.

What journalistic achievement are you proudest of?

In 1926, when I was editor of the New York *World*, I think our efforts stopped the United States from occupying Mexico. We raised such a clamor that even [Calvin] Coolidge took notice. Instead of troops, he sent Dwight Morrow to Mexico as Ambassador.

What was your greatest journalistic blunder?

In 1940, I wrote some articles suggesting that we go to war with the Soviet Union over Finland. That was bad judgment on my part. It was emotional and, potentially, the biggest mistake I ever made.

How has Washington changed since you first moved here in 1938?

I moved here because it was changing then. Up until the New Deal, New York was the place to be. We knew more about what was going on in the country and the world than they did in Washington. But Washington became the real capital of the nation in the thirties.

Since then, Washington has become even more important. It has become the capital of the world.

Has the quality of Washington reporting improved or deteriorated since you settled here?

It has improved. There is a whole new generation of newspapermen in Washington who are educated people. The old-timers never did much thinking. I used to be a freak down here because I had never been a police reporter. There is still too much emphasis on getting scoops, but at least the reporters *think*.

Why did the press treat Eisenhower so gently?

First, because most newspaper publishers are Republicans. And second, because he was accorded—or allowed to acquire—a divinity that belongs to kings. That won't happen with Kennedy, even though the reporters like him.

What qualities should a good Washington reporter have?

Endless curiosity plus equanimity. I mean curiosity without the desire to see the facts differently from what they happen to be.

Why do you feel that being a Washington reporter is an important job?

Well, I made a speech about that a year or so ago, and this is what I said: "If the country is to be governed with the consent of the governed, then the governed must arrive at opinions about what their governors want them to consent to. How do they do this? They do it by hearing on the radio and reading in the newspapers what the corps of correspondents tells them is going on in Washington and in the country at large and in the world. Here we perform an essential service . . . we do what every sovereign citizen is supposed to do, but has not the time or the interest to do for himself. This is our job. It is no mean calling, and we have a right to be proud of it and to be glad that it is our work."

That is how I have always felt and why I am still a newspaperman.

The Death of a President

BY WILLIAM MANCHESTER

A Catholic clergyman was probably the one stranger who could slip through the concentric circles of sentinels around her. The outer guards would conclude that the Catholic widow had sent for him; the Boston Irishmen who were closest to her would defer to him. And this is precisely what happened, exposing Mrs. Kennedy to what would be remembered as "the episode of the priest." Later, Presidential aides Ken O'Donnell, Larry O'Brien and Dave Powers wondered whether he had been a real priest. No genuine cleric, they felt, could have behaved the way he did.

He was real enough. Father Thomas Cain was the superior of the Dominican Fathers at the Roman Catholic University of Dallas, six miles from Parkland. He was also an eccentric. An energetic, bespectacled cigar smoker with thinning gray hair and a turkey-gobbler neck, Father Cain was, even on serene days, a man of erratic mannerisms. He talked a great deal, sometimes disjointedly, gesticulating loopingly with his long arms, and he tended to swing between cycles of impulsive activity and remorse. When the academic dean of

From pp. 295-6 in "The Death of a President" by William Manchester, as it appeared in LOOK Magazine. Copyright ©1967 by William Manchester. By permission of Harper & Row, Publishers

the university had called him at his priory and told him of the shooting, he had had but one thought—a Catholic President had been wounded, and he belonged at the President's side. The fact that other priests would be closer was irrelevant, for he had something they did not. In a green bag in his office, he kept an ornate crucifix, containing within it a minute splinter from the True Cross encased in plastic. Changing to his robe and collar, Father Cain had pocketed the bag, bounded out to his car and headed for the hospital. He drove the accelerator straight to the floor. It was, he admitted afterward, something of a miracle that he wasn't killed. He left the car in the anarchy of badly parked automobiles and dashed in past the Dallas policemen, the shift commanded by Agent Roy Kellerman, the two uniformed generals and the Mafia. On the way, he heard someone say that the President was dead.

Mrs. Kennedy looked up and saw him hovering over her. His eyes were wild.

"When did he die?"

"In the car, I think," she said haggardly.

Father Cain loosened the bag string. "I have a relic of the True Cross."

He held it out and asked her to "venerate it." She kissed the crucifix, not quite understanding what this was all about. Then he said he wanted to take it in to the President. She thought, *This must mean a lot to this man*, and, *If he wants to give it to Jack, how touching*. O'Donnell nodded; the priest went in. But he didn't leave the relic. He merely walked around, waving it ceremoniously in the air above Vernon Oneal, the nurses, the orderly, the plastic and rubber sheeting and the six rubber head bags.

Coming out, he said, "I have applied a relic of the True Cross to your husband."

She stared. It was still in his hands. She thought, *You mean you didn't even give it to him?*

O'Donnell edged toward him. Father Cain, however, wasn't to be dismissed that easily. He was dancing around in a state of excitement, his larynx bobbing. He pressed her hand and tried to put his arms around her, addressing her by her first name, calling her endearing names and promising to write her a letter. Just as Ken and Larry and Dave thought they had the priest cornered, he jerked away from them. Scurrying back into the trauma room, he pranced around Oneal, pranced out, confronted a group of hospital employees standing against a wall and led them in a recitation of the Lord's Prayer. He returned to Mrs. Kennedy and reached for her hand again. She yanked it away. "Please, Father. Leave me alone."

Now, O'Donnell stalked him in earnest, and now he backed away, clutching the bag. They could hear his voice drifting across a cubicle wall, chanting prayers feverishly. They thought they were rid of him, but he was only a few feet away, and he had no notion of leaving.

I should have known that it was asking too much to dream that I might have grown old with him.

A Remembrance

BY JACQUELINE KENNEDY

It is nearly a year since he has been gone.

On so many days—his birthday, an anniversary, watching his children running to the sea—I have thought, "But this day last year was his last to see that." He was so full of love and life on all those days. He seems so vulnerable now, when you think that each one was a last time.

Soon the final day will come around again—as inexorably as it did last year. But expected this time.

It will find some of us different people than we were a year ago. Learning to accept what was unthinkable when he was alive, changes you.

I don't think there is any consolation. What was lost cannot be replaced.

Someone who loved President Kennedy, but who had never known him, wrote to me this winter: "The hero comes when he is needed. When our belief gets pale and weak, there comes a man out of that need who is shining—and everyone living reflects a little of that light—and stores some up against the time when he is gone."

Now I think that I should have known that he was magic all along. I did know it—but I should have guessed it could not last. I should have known that it was asking too much to dream that I might have grown old with him and see our children grow up together.

So now he is a legend when he would have preferred to be a man. I must believe that he does not share our suffering now. I think for him—at least he will never know whatever sadness might have lain ahead. He knew such a share of it in his life that it always made you so happy whenever you saw him enjoying himself. But now he will never know more—not age, nor stagnation, nor despair, nor crippling illness, nor loss of any more people he loved. His high noon kept all the freshness of the morning—and he died then, never knowing disillusionment.

> " . . . he has gone . . .
> *Among the radiant, ever venturing on,*
> *Somewhere, with morning, as such spirits will.*"*

*John Masefield, "On the Finish of the Sailing Ship Race."

Reprinted by permission of Macmillan, Inc., Publishers, from "Poems" by John Masefield copyright ©1915, 1943

He is free and we must live. Those who love him most know that "the death you have dealt is more than the death which has swallowed you."

Jacqueline Kennedy

Inside the White House

BY ALLEN DRURY

Former high Nixon staffer, anonymous, amicably resigned, still friendly and concerned: "There seems to be a reluctance in the White House to come to grips with certain problems, both of personnel and of policy. Consequently, a lot of people are still hanging on who are diametrically opposed to the Nixon program and they simply can't seem to get up the guts to get rid of them. Bob Haldeman and John Ehrlichman have gotten too far too fast. They have not really been tested in getting where they are. They don't have the experience. They don't really have the backbone about various things. Also, there seems to be a reluctance on Nixon's part really to go after some of these people who are obstructing him. It is a curious thing, which extends also, it seems to me, to foreign policy and what seems to be a reluctance, sometimes, to come to firm grips with the challenges that face him as President from the Russians and elsewhere around the world."

Murray Chotiner (former Nixon aide): "I think the President is amazing in his self-control. I have seen him over the years when he has been uptight about things, but somehow he has learned over the years to control and subdue his emotions. After losing the Presidency in '60 and the governorship of California in '62, he seems to have become completely relaxed. That seemed to settle something inside him.

"It's amazing to me how a man like President Nixon, with all the problems he has and with his past history of political defeats, can sit back with his feet on the desk, so to speak, and be as relaxed as he is. But now he doesn't have to shoot from the hip—he doesn't have to make snap decisions.

"The White House staff operates efficiently. I think sometimes they are a little overprotective, but as far as his being isolated, that's malarkey and a lot of baloney. I don't see any isolation. I think people who want to get answers can get them either from him or from Bob Haldeman. And when he wants to see any of us he can. So I don't think there is any real isolation."

The press (columnist, male, veteran, longtime friend of the President): "I am very puzzled by Nixon. He does things that an experienced politician wouldn't do. It seems to me that there's almost a feeling that he just isn't interested somehow, almost as though he doesn't want to run again. I can't believe this, but look at some of the things he's done. The Carswell nomination—Carswell's a nice little guy, but he has no more business on the Supreme Court than I do. Firing Wally Hickel from the Interior Department—the only man in the Cabinet who has any kind of reputation for being a conservationist—and then appointing Rogers Morton, who has no interest in it, when the Democrats are making hay over the conservation issue. Some of the things he has done in foreign policy also seem very puzzling to me.

"I'm disappointed because I like Nixon, I want him to succeed, and I think it is vital to the country that he do so. And yet I feel in a sense that he is letting down his country and his party because there's just this curious lack of political smartness about doing things it seems obviously necessary to do—things that a smart politician would not overlook if he were really on top of the job. . . . I find many things the President does very puzzling these days. It just doesn't seem to hang together, somehow."

At approximately 4:45, the buzzer sounded and I was taken into the Oval Office. The huge room is now almost devoid of furniture except for the President's massive desk and a few chairs and sofas along the walls. "The first thing I'm going to do," he told me soon after his election in 1968, "is take those damned television sets out of the Oval Office." He has done so.

The windows were opened to the cool winter evening and the curtains billowed out from time to time with the wind. Photographs were taken for the first couple of minutes while we chatted about innocuous things. Then the photographer and the others left. He leaned his head in his hands, rubbed his eyes, stayed that way for a moment. But when he looked up he did not look tired, and that was the only time during our talk that he gave any sign of being tired. Mostly he looked, and talked, and appeared to be, entirely relaxed, comfortable and as though he did not have a care in the world. It was perhaps the single most impressive thing about him at that moment. Tiredness and strain are easy to spot: they were not present here this particular late afternoon.

He sat back and chatted for half an hour, ranging from the press, on which he has some definite and occasionally acrid ideas, to the nature of the questions I wanted to ask.

I said that some of them might be critical in nature, but

that I didn't intend to offer hookers: I would simply be seeking answers to some of the opinions I was running into around town.

"Don't worry about that for a minute," he said. "Give me any hookers you want. Be the devil's advocate, make them just as tough as you like. After all, it's my job to answer these criticisms, and if you simply ask me bland questions without any bite to them—'Mr. President, what did you do to save the world today?'—the interview won't add up to very much. I'd prefer to have you make them tough whenever you feel it is justified."

I asked him if he wished to impose any restriction that his answers be paraphrased rather than quoted directly and he said no, he would be perfectly willing to turn them over to me and let me use them in direct quotes as I pleased—with the exception that on some extra-sensitive subjects it might perhaps be wise to paraphrase. In that case he would do it himself, dictating, "It is known that the President believes—" or, "The President is understood to feel—" or some such protective, if easily detected, formula.

He was very curious as to whether I was getting sufficient cooperation from the staff and suggested that I be sure and talk to such people as the chef and others on the domestic staff as well as the professional and political staffs. He said both Julie and Tricia would be good sources about White House operations, as both were very thoughtful and perceptive young ladies.

"You should try to talk to a lot of people and not just these gray men around here"—and from his tone it was impossible to determine whether he meant the description as it stood or was dryly mimicking the press attacks upon them.

I said I would.

Aside from a couple of minor items, I did not ask him anything particularly vital, since he had suggested written questions and I intended to ask them in that form; but I was impressed with how fluently and easily he did talk about things.

Intimate comments from one in a position to know: The President is "unusually inhibited by strangers," but once he gets used to someone on the staff, "it is very comfortable, and he hardly pays any attention to the routine work we do for him around here.

"Sometimes he is under strain, and when he is, he shows it in ways that those of us around him can tell. On the whole, however, he remains very calm. One thing that struck me about him when I first came here is that he is quite profane. This startled me when I first heard him speaking but I've gotten used to it now.

"Most of the good ideas that originate here come from him. He does take much staff advice, but usually the ideas are his own. When he does something, it will be on the basis of his own thoughts and those of many others on the staff. The opinion real-ly flows in from the staff. He solicits the staff's advice on every point. Sometimes he is overruled by the staff—which means that when the weight of evidence or the weight of argument is against him, he will sometimes yield to the advice. Then if the staff is wrong, he will not say anything in particular, but he will let us know by his manner or his way of saying things to us what he thinks of us for having given wrong advice.

"He does not like to bawl people out and he gets upset when he has done something or said something harsh to us. I remember that on a couple of occasions when he has chewed me out, which I deserved, he has never apologized for temper the next day but he has done some little extra, thoughtful thing, which is his way of saying that he is sorry for the argument and hopes that it will not happen again."

After a pleasant and comfortable half hour, already 15 minutes late for the congressional reception, but not really seeming to mind so very much, he rose and started toward the door: "Now I have to go and shake hands with four hundred congressmen."

Confused a little by the Oval Office's several hidden doors and thinking he was showing me out, I followed him, for he gave no formal farewell but simply moved along still talking. In a moment, we found ourselves outside in the arcade along the Rose Garden and I realized he was on his way to the Mansion. I asked directions to Steve Bull's office, he told me, I said, "Good night, Mr. President," and turned back into the empty office. He waved and walked away, all by himself in the chill winter night: a suddenly lonely and touching moment.

Back in the hallway outside Steve Bull's office, I found some consternation on the part of Steve and the Secret Service. "Where is he? Is he gone? Has he left for the Mansion? Is he by himself?"

This was apparently against all the rules. It was hard to escape the feeling that he had taken one of those small, secret delights known only to Presidents, in going off, thus unescorted and unannounced, to where he wanted to go.

The press (male, veteran, many years' experience covering Presidents, longtime friend of Nixon): "Nixon is like all Presidents—he can be brutal about people sometimes. Maybe it's the Merlin complex or something, but he thinks he can use you for something and then go away for three years and when he comes back you're supposed to be standing there waiting and still be just as much of a friend as you were before. He expects you to maintain your loyalty to him regardless of whether he's shown any loyalty or interest in you in the meantime. They all do it, it's a funny thing. . . . I've talked to him several times and I've generally found him so serene and untroubled that I sometimes wonder a little whether he really knows what's going on, or what could hit him if things go wrong. I think he does, but I really wonder sometimes. . . . They give you this picture of everybody loving everybody else on the White House staff, and it's probably truer in this Administration than in any other I've known in four decades. But when you get up near the top, there's a lot of jockeying for position behind the scenes. I don't think it's erupted into any real feuds like we've had in some Administrations—yet—but there are frictions there, though they try to hide them. You can't avoid it when people are human beings—and these, although they seem a little bland and faceless sometimes, are human beings. There's this great desire to get near the President, to be the one who's always seeing the great man—they can't help it. If they can't do it, they pretend it. I remember the other day, X started to say to me, 'When I saw the President the other day—' I interrupted, 'Now, X, don't give me that crap. When did you actually see the President last?' He grinned a bit sheepishly and said, 'Well, actually, it was about six months ago.' But to hear him tell it, and to read how the press tells it, you'd think he was in there every other day. Among those who really are, there's a lot of competiton for the great man's smile. I think it amuses him. He's an intelligent man. I think he rather enjoys it, like all Presidents. They're really all sons of bitches, in some ways. They enjoy being President and they secretly enjoy what the Presidency does to other people.

The press (bull session with old friends): "He is the most complex man who has ever been in the White House. He doesn't have any intimate friends. Nobody is close to him. He should have at least somebody, but all he seems to have is Bebe Rebozo.

"He definitely tries to get away from the press. The anti-press feeling permeates the whole Administration. He is the first President to duck out of parties early to avoid the press. He deliberately avoids us. He wants to stay away from us." When I pointed out that the press, after all, had been extremely harsh with him over the years, this was conceded. "But the majority of publishers are Republican."

"And the majority of reporters are Democrats and 'liberals.'" Reluctantly this was conceded too. "But—Nixon has no sense of style. No grace. He is always escaping from us. Why is he always escaping?"

I saw him for the second time in San Clemente, on March 30, 1971. The SST had been defeated in the Senate; in Laos, the unhappy invasion had surged in and limped back. It was a typical overcast Southern California day, the sun trying vainly to break through the persistent light clouds. Off in the distance the cold Pacific curled in upon the shore. In the corridors and offices there was an air of quiet, the pace obviously slower, more relaxed, more comfortable than it is in Washington.

The President looked tanned and rested. He apologized for not having taped answers to my questions as he had promised, but explained that he had been rather busy: it was obvious from his comments throughout that he had studied them very closely before deciding on what the staff likes to call his "one-to-one" method. I showed him my newspaper horoscope for the day: *"Consulting with bigwigs opens the door to greater opportunity now but don't try to criticize them in any way."* He laughed and said, "Oh no! Oh no! Don't worry about that!" He played with a single silver cuff link the entire hour and a half that we talked, but otherwise seemed as calm as ever, and as convinced that the course he had chosen was right.

We began, as my written questions had begun, with the Presidency itself. It had held for him, he supposed, "fewer surprises than it does for most. I had been Vice President for eight years, I knew what a President could do and couldn't do. The main thing I had learned was that Presidents come and go, but the bureaucracy goes on forever. I knew that no President who is not in tune with the mood and the ideological bent of the bureaucracy can bend it to his program without a great deal of difficulty and hard work. I also knew how difficult it is to deal with Congress, particularly with both houses in control of the other party, and no such bipartisanship as Eisenhower was fortunate enough to have when Lyndon Johnson was majority leader of the Senate. That bipartisanship is so fragmented now that it practically no longer exists. Mike Mansfield is a very responsible majority leader now, very responsible in his disagreement about Southeast Asia—but he does disagree, and in fact disagreed with Johnson and with Kennedy too on that subject.

"So now it has crumbled away and now we have partisanship—or perhaps not so much partisanship as what you might call a new isolationism, in which the old internationalists and interventionists, who supported World War II, the Korean War, the Alliance for Progress and the rest of the war and postwar programs, are now turning away and trying to turn America inward again.

"They are concentrating now on America's internal problems, the alienation of groups and generations, the economy and all those things which our so-called 'intellectual elite'—self-appointed and self-described—have made their top priorities.

"We now have what could be termed basically a new 'America First' doctrine, not in the sense of 'look to America's defenses and forget the rest of the world,' but in the sense of 'forget the rest of the world and concentrate on our own domestic problems and social commitments.'

"But I don't feel frustrated or disillusioned—I really don't. I went in with my eyes wide open. I knew Congress was against us, I knew we were in a period of great domestic torment, I knew we had Vietnam to face and many social problems. Essentially, of course, those problems would be here whatever happened internationally, and they will continue to be with us long after Vietnam ends. But I want to make sure Vietnam ends in such way that it does not leave us with disenchantment, bitterness, even greater alienation of one group from another. If it ends that way, it will not end, in a sense—it will go on to plague us for many, many years to come.

"I think we are at one of the great watersheds of American history—where America, having acquired world leadership really without consciously seeking it or wanting it, having met that role as best she could since World War II, is now determining whether she will continue to play the part of a leader in world affairs or would prefer to abdicate her responsibility and let it go. If she does, freedom and democracy will go, we all will go. I am convinced that what has happened in Laos will prove in the long run to be as sound as Cambodia. After all, what really matters is what actually happens, not what instant analysts have to say about it. They jump to conclusions, and then a few weeks or months later, they prove to be wrong. Cambodia was an enormous success, and yet you go back and look up what our friends in the press and television were saying about it at the time it ended, and you'll see they weren't about to concede it was any success.

"You have to be quite fatalistic about these things. After all"—with a sudden sharp, direct look—"I know more than they do or you do about it. I know what has happened to the enemy. I know he has taken enormous losses. I know how the South Vietnamese as a whole really behaved, in spite of what three or four units may have done. They proved they could hack it. Everybody ought to wait awhile and see how Laos affects our continuing withdrawal. The enemy will not be able to launch another offensive this summer. He will not be able to interfere with the timetable for the ending of our involvement.

"I know when American involvement will end, though I can't state it, because to do so would be to give up certain tactical advantages, and also to remove whatever chance —little, not big—may remain to have meaningful negotiations in Paris.

"I think we're going to make it, in this situation—I think withdrawal is going to work, Vietnamization is going to work—not in the sense that 'Vietnamization' would mean the withdrawing of all of the American presence, but in the basic sense of South Vietnam being able to handle its own affairs. In the sense of 17 million people having a chance to decide their own destiny and their own future, which is what we will have achieved for them with our help and our sacrifice.

"If we can do this, it will be one of the major achievements of this nation in all its long history—to keep a Communist enemy from conquering our friends, to give a nation the right to live as it wants to live.

"If we fail in that, and if South Vietnam goes Communist in spite of all we've done, then Communism will indeed be the wave of the future in Asia. But I don't think it is, and I don't think that is what will happen. . . .

"Critical to all of this is the way the Vietnam war ends. If it ends in a way that can be interpreted as an American defeat—a retreat, a bugout—inevitably those in the world who are inclined to use force to gain their aggressive or imperialistic ends will be encouraged to do so. And all our friends will be in disarray. The world will say, 'Look at Vietnam. If the United States could not be counted on there, where can she be counted on?' The way to avoid more Vietnams is to be sure that this Vietnam ends in a way that will not dismay our friends and encourage future aggressors. . . .

"The press?" His expression changed, became earnest, stubborn, close to contemptuous. "I probably follow the press more closely and am less affected by it than any other President. I have a very cool detachment about it. I read it basically to find out what other people are reading, so that I'll know what is being given the country and what I have to deal with when I talk to the country and try to influence people for my programs. And of course I read it also because sometimes there will be a very thoughtful article on some subject that is enlightening and of value to me. Presidents are like other people: they don't know everything, it's good to get another point of view on something. Providing, that is, that it's a matter of substance and not just something somebody has dreamed up because he doesn't like Nixon or wants to make points with his own boss or bureaucracy, who don't like Nixon.

"I'm not like Lyndon as regards the press—we're two different people. The press was like a magnet to him. He'd read every single thing that was critical, he'd watch the news on TV all the time, and then he'd get mad. I never get mad. I expect I have one of the most hostile and unfair presses that any President has ever had, but I've developed a philosophical attitude about it. I developed it early. I have won all my political battles with 80 to 90 percent of the press against me. How have I done it? I ignored the press and went to the people.

"I have never called a publisher, never called an editor, never called a reporter, on the carpet. I don't care. And you know?"—a grim but rather pleased expression—"that's what makes 'em mad. That's what infuriates 'em. I just don't care. I just don't raise the roof with 'em. And that gets 'em.

"Anyway, that isn't my style. I don't stomp around. I don't believe in public displays of anger. I don't raise hell. I'm never rough on the staff about things just for the sake of being rough, or making an effect. But they know how I feel. The things we've faced in this Administration have taken a lot of hard decisions and I've had to be firm about things, but I've *been* firm—I haven't shouted about it. There are some people, you know, they think the way to be a big man is to shout and stomp and raise hell—and then nothing ever really happens. I'm not like that, with the staff or with the press.

"I never shoot blanks.

"I respect the individual members of the press—some of them, particularly the older ones—who have some standards of objectivity and fairness. And the individual competence of many of the younger ones. I respect that too, though nowadays they don't care about fairness, it's the 'in' thing to forget objectivity and let your prejudices show. You can see it in my press conferences all the time. You read the Kennedy press conferences and see how soft and gentle they were with him, and then you read mine. I never get any easy questions—and I don't want any. I am quite aware that ideologically the Washington press corps doesn't agree with me. I expect it. I think the people can judge for themselves when they watch one of my press conferences. It's all there.

"I can tell you this,"—and his eyes narrowed, he swung his chair around and stared out across the distant gray Pacific—"as long as I am in this office, the press will never irritate me, never affect me, never push me to any move I don't think is wise. . . ."

What kind of a country would he like America to be when he leaves the Presidency? What would he like history to say Richard Nixon had done for America? His face sobered, he fell silent, stared again out the window at the restless ocean, turned back, spoke slowly and thoughtfully, repeating, refining, rephrasing.

"What kind of country?

"I would like first to get this war ended in a way that Americans can look back upon not ashamed, not frustrated, not angry, but with a pride that in spite of our difficulties we have been totally unselfish—that we have enabled 17 million people to choose their own destiny, and in so doing have preserved and strengthened the chance for peace in the Pacific basin, and probably the world.

"I would like to leave with a new relationship between the U.S. and the U.S.S.R. It will be intensely competitive, of course. We are different peoples with a different history and we want different things—but I believe we are at the critical point where we can finally decide that we must have a live-and-let-live relationship. I think we are making some progress in that direction. I hope we may have achieved it when I leave. I would like to leave some structure on which at least the beginnings of genuine world peace can be built.

"Domestically, this nation is never going to be wholly at one. But I would hope that we can reduce the tensions, reduce the demonstrations, reduce the dissent—not the constructive dissent that is the yeast of a free society, but the destructive dissent that wants only to tear down the system.

"I want everybody in this country to recognize that our system provides for peaceful change—to get people to work within the system and find better methods to make the system work.

"You said something in your questions about how could I, a basically conservative President, propose such 'liberal' things as revenue sharing and the Family Assistance Plan. That isn't 'liberal.' It's common sense. I believe revenue sharing is one way to make the system work better, because it means decentralization of government—and I think decentralization of government is the key. The modern twentieth-century liberal is *for* big government. He likes concentration of power—*he likes power*. I don't go with him in that. I hope to give more people a chance to participate in the action—to believe that what they do counts. I want to restore as much as we can the concept that this country has grown great by adhering to the principle of shared responsibility and peaceful change.

"I would like to make some progress in restoring some sense of understanding and of pride in this country and in its greatness—get away from this idea that America's foreign policy is rotten, its domestic policies are rotten, the whole damned thing is rotten. I know that because of slavery, black Americans have not had an equal chance; I know that there are many injustices in other areas. But we are working, we are trying, we are making progress. I know these things *can be changed*, and in a peaceable and constructive way, through the system we have. When you look at the United States with all its pockmarks, you realize that, nonetheless, a person born in this country has more freedom and more genuine opportunity than a person born in any other country.

"I would like to leave a renewed conviction in America that the system *does* work, that democratic government *is* better than the alternatives, that reforms *can* be made through peaceful change. I would like to leave reestablished the idea that in this system things can be achieved and made better. In foreign policy, the greatest contribution a President could make would be to leave a world in which the United States is at peace with every nation—and has the strength and the will to guarantee that peace.

"In a sense"—hitting the desk firmly with his hand—"it's all right here in this room—right here in this chair. Whoever is President of the United States, and what he does, is going to determine the kind of world we have. His leadership must be strong—and firm—and, we hope, wise.

"But more than that. He must be supported by the belief and the conviction and the faith of the American people, in themselves and in their country. That's why I want to restore some sense of balance, of perspective, of understanding and pride in America's role in the world, and in her institutions.

"This is a noble country in many ways, and somehow

we must restore the feeling that we should take pride in it—that we should believe in its system and its policies and its future.

"The important thing is not our capacity to do things—we have that. The important thing is our will. It is not going to be there unless we restore to Americans more faith in themselves and their country.

"The problem now is the American spirit. This is a crisis of the spirit that we face. The most important thing of all is to restore the American spirit.

"That is what I would like to do before I leave this office."

Ellsberg Talks

BY J. ROBERT MOSKIN

When you turned yourself in, you said you had made the Pentagon papers public as a responsible American citizen. Really, the essential question we want to talk about is: What is the moral responsibility of the citizen who thinks he sees his government doing evil?

I was in a dual position. Like every American, I had a feeling of obligation to the Constitution and to my fellow citizens. At the same time, I was a researcher through most of this period, doing consulting for the Government, and someone whose reflexes in terms of loyalty had been set by 12 to 15 years of service to the Executive Branch—15 years would include the three years with the Marine Corps.

I question the identification of the state or the Government with the Executive Branch or with the President. All the members of the Executive Branch are the creatures of one elected representative of the people, the President. When you look at the entire Executive Branch, you confront this enormous structure of somewhat conflicting institutions in which only one man has been elected by the people. The effects of this are very great.

In the early sixties, before I ever got on the subject of Vietnam, I was granted interagency access at a very high level to study the decision-making process in crises like the Cuban missile crisis, Suez, Skybolt, U-2 and so forth. In fact, the arrangements for that study were set up by Walt Rostow, who was then head of the Policy Planning Council of the State Department.

I was at Rand and was brought to Washington as the sole researcher for what was to be a year's study. That study exposed to me the importance of the President in every one of these crises, the peculiar, very powerful influence of the President's personal judgment and personal preconceptions.

This conflicts with another view of the decision process in Government, which says that the President, although he may look powerful, is given surprisingly little leeway by the bureaucratic agencies under him, in which to influence policy, that he has to fight for influence, to connive, to maneuver, in order to have any impact whatever.

It's a position that's very plausible from within the system. The bureaucrat gets a sense that presidential policy reflects the success of one or another agency in tying his hands. He doesn't have a sense of presidential initiative and power.

The most startling thing to me was to discover how critical the President's role had been, that if his hands were tied at all, it was because he chose to cooperate in having his position forced by one pressure or another.

Because the President is a politician up for reelection, a man who expects to have his reputation recorded in history books, and a leader of a party, a man who is concerned with getting a legislative program through Congress, all these political considerations bear on presidential decisions in a way unlike the decision-making of any other bureaucrat. To take the U-2 example, Eisenhower's decision to announce the truth, rather than tell a lie, was undoubtedly influenced by domestic political considerations. In the opinion of his political advisers, to deny he knew of the flight could be damaging in the 1960 elections and sustain the belief that Eisenhower had been a know-nothing President.

The basic problem is we have a system, then, with a lot of people who don't know what it means to be accountable to the public. The Congress is the enemy, just as the press is the enemy. And the public is seen by members of the Executive in general as the great beast, treacherous, ignorant, irrational, not to be respected, either individually or in the mass.

The polls reveal that most people think we should get out of Vietnam and it was a mistake to have gotten in. I share that view. Obviously, the Administration does not, and many of the former officials who were my colleagues do not. It's not all that hard to explain. The people must face the issues in terms of their own sons and of the impact of the war on their lives, considerations that the man in the Administration—whose life is much improved by the condition of war, which swells the Executive and Executive salaries—doesn't have to face.

Back in 1950, when the Korean War started, I was as antimilitary as anybody else in college. In 1954, I enlisted in the Marine Corps. A friend enlisted in the Air Force, and I remember that we often discussed how come we were the only people in the service at that point and our other friends didn't seem called upon to do this. But I don't know; there was some degree of difference there.

It was the same way when I went to Rand. I spent the summer of '58 at Rand in part because they were interested in my particular academic interest, which was "decision-making under uncertainty," and I found them all hard at work on what came to seem to me the most urgent problem facing mankind. That was the missile gap, and the possibility that we would find ourselves vulnerable to a strike by '60 or '61. I remember that a tutor of mine assumed that I had sold out to Rand for the salary, and I told him very honestly that I would have worked for Rand for nothing. It seemed the most important problem in the world.

Earlier, I had been elected to the Society of Fellows at Harvard, which was the most prestigious academic fellowship, three years for research, essentially at the pay of an assistant professor. That was to begin the month I was to get out of the Marine Corps, in June of '56. Well, I had a rifle company at the time. I was, I think, the only first lieutenant in the Second Marine Division at that moment to have a rifle company. In my own battalion there were captains and majors who were fighting to get my company away from me. But, in fact, it was an outstanding company, and I was allowed to keep it. But I had to give it up just before I was to get out.

Just when I was due to get out, my battalion was scheduled to go to the Mediterranean at the time of the Suez Canal take-over; it would be the duty battalion on the spot in the war zone. So I spent a day thinking about what I would feel like to be back at Harvard and read in the papers about my battalion in combat. I couldn't stand that thought, so I sent a telegram to the commandant of the Marine Corps asking to extend for a year so I could accompany the battalion.

I had the rank of GS-18, which was an official rank in the Government between major and lieutenant general.

Then (Maj. Gen. Edward G.) Lansdale was going; I respected Lansdale from what I had read of his writings, his point of view, his background. So I volunteered to go with him. I was the only volunteer that he ended up taking. I seemed to be the kind of nut he liked to have on his team.

He took me on basically as an apprentice of his trade, which was counter-insurgency. I chose to educate myself on pacification, to learn the realities of what the war was like in the countryside.

The effect of that was that I was probably the only civilian who had served at a high staff level who was then exposed to the realities of the war in Vietnam close up.

What was your reaction to those realities?

That the programs we were pursuing had no chance of succeeding. They were not in any way proceeding as people thought they were back in Washington. Of course, that in itself didn't speak to the question of whether the war was a just one, or whether the aims we were pursuing were right for us to pursue.

Did you do any shooting?

Well, I did a lot of shooting, because in the Delta we were under a lot of fire, some days every half hour or so. I carried a weapon because the alternative was, if you didn't carry a weapon, other people would have to take care of you. I was anxious not to attract attention to myself.

You were quoted as saying that seeing civilians killed face-to-face was the reason you changed your attitude toward the war.

What happened was this: In this particular operation, we were under fire for much of ten days, and we did a lot of firing. In fact, a couple of times when I was with the lead squad going through a paddy, Vietcong rose from the paddy we had just walked through and fired at the people behind us. That kind of experience gives you a very intimate sense of the nature of this conflict and a very strong impression of the opponent we're fighting.

Now we get into the moral question: What did I feel like, firing at these people? Well, I can testify when you're being fired at, you don't worry at all about the moral dilemmas involved in firing back. It was only after I got away from that situation and even from the country that I really began to think harder about the question: After all, why were we there to be fired at? I knew why I was there. But why were *we* there? Why was our battalion there? The guerrillas we were fighting were clearly firing at foreigners to get them out of their own home yards. It was extremely hard to justify what we were doing there.

You simply hadn't asked the question before? You hadn't faced it?

No, it wasn't that I hadn't faced it. It was that I had accepted the official answer to it, namely that there was a civil war going on, that we had a right to intervene and pick one side or the other if our interests were involved, and our interests were involved. That if the wrong side should win this war, it would be worse for the Vietnamese people, worse for the United States and for world peace. It would mean victory for people who wished us ill and who would behave more aggressively in other parts of the world, which we would also have to counter. All the arguments, all the complexities that Dean Rusk can point to, are terribly familiar to me.

While working on the Pentagon study, it was

astonishing, in going through files at the Pentagon, to read the national intelligence estimates from 1950 on. I read all those estimates, probably 40 of them covering a period of almost 20 years, and it was astonishing to discover that, with a few exceptions, they were very realistic, very detailed and skeptical. On the whole, they gave the President quite good predictions of what to expect.

That posed a really enormous puzzle. How did a succession of Presidents bring themselves time after time to increase our involvement, or even to sustain it, when they were being told by the national intelligence estimates that what they were doing would be inadequate to achieve any kind of success and could lead only to getting out in the future or escalating further? Why had Presidents apparently ignored this information?

The simple answer of our interests in avoiding World War III or the total Communistic take-over of Southeast Asia or a great loss of prestige didn't seem to account for these decisions, because the estimates, and even the recommendations made by the bureaucracy, indicated strongly that we would not be able to achieve those interests by what we were doing. So I had to look for other explanations, other interests.

I think that few bureaucrats appreciate, unless they get to fairly high levels—and I was privileged to work at the level of the assistant secretary, as a special assistant to John McNaughton—the peculiar kind of White House influence that goes into policy. The presidential role as a whole is not committed to paper very much, and in particular, the presidential interest in domestic politics does not get on paper because it is a shibboleth that domestic politics ought not to influence foreign policy.

Most people in the Government who had any experience with Vietnam had by late '67 come to feel that the official optimism that was coming out of the top, from Rusk, from Westmoreland, was quite unjustified. This was even before the Tet offensive, and most of the work on the study was done after the Tet offensive.

The startling thing that came out of them was how the same sets of alternatives began to appear to each President, and ultimately the choice was neither to go for broke and adopt military recommendations, nor negotiate a settlement to get out. The decisions year after year were to continue the war, although all predictions pointed to a continued stalemate with this kind of approach and thus to prolong the war indefinitely.

That meant that no one President was responsible in the sense that he acted very differently from his counterparts in other Administrations. It came to seem not like Kennedy's war or Johnson's war. It was a pattern of behavior that went far beyond any one individual that held that position.

I think now to a large extent it was an American President's war. It was a war no American President had,

let's say, the courage to turn down or to stay out of. From a military point of view, you could say he didn't have the courage to go in to win, but on the other hand, he was assured by intelligence estimates—which checked out pretty well, year by year—that the kinds of things proposed by the military would not win.

The explanation seemed to me contained in the very earliest period—'49 and '50—when we did get involved. There one can see the motivation quite clearly. It was the motivation of the Democratic President not to add the fall of Indochina to the fall of China. The very fact the decision-making looked similar year by year from then on, supported the conjecture that no American President, Republican or Democrat, wanted to be the President who lost the war or who lost Saigon.

It was in the early fall of '69 that I began to deliver these documents to the Senate Foreign Relations Committee. Even that was an enormous change for me—to go outside the Executive Branch. It was still within the U.S. Government, but it was a decision for which I expected to go to prison for the rest of my life.

But you felt it was important enough?

Yes, because, you see, the documents themselves had the lesson in them, it seemed to me, that Nixon was the fifth President in succession to be subjected to the same pressures that had led four other Presidents to maintain involvement; that his assurances that he had no intention of staying in Indochina were no more to be believed than other Presidents' assurances; that it was a Vietnamese war, and not ours, and that whatever his feelings were as of '69, the more he got involved, the more sure it was that he would stay involved.

So my first efforts were entirely along the lines of getting Congress and leading Democrats to urge the President, or even require him, to get out, so that the responsibility wouldn't fall entirely on his shoulders.

I sent a letter around to leading Democrats, urging them, in effect, to take the position: it's not your war, Mr. Nixon; it's our war; we made the mistakes; don't you make those same mistakes. Get us out of it. I was communicating with a lot of Democrats, urging them to come out for total withdrawal. They were quite unwilling. So that failed.

At the same time, six of us at Rand who had worked on Vietnam with official access to the documents put out a letter calling for total unilateral withdrawal within a year. But in the President's speech of November 3, he put his stamp so strongly on the policy, making it Nixon's war, that it was clear he would fight any effort to get out faster. From then on, it meant that you couldn't share responsibility with the President; Congress, if it was to get us out of the war, would have to take almost total responsibility.

Now we're getting very much into the question of

responsibility. Congress (including the whole set of doves) recoiled from taking on themselves the whole responsibility for what might happen if we got out of Vietnam entirely.

I think we could have gotten out two years ago if Nixon had been willing to share the risk. I think Nixon's really a true believer in the cold-war premises and does not feel we ought to get out. And this feeling is reinforced by his political reading of what might happen to him if he did.

Since the fall of '69 when I started this, 9,000 more American men had died and hundreds of thousands of Vietnamese had died. Moreover, two more invasions had occurred, and it looked like the next thing facing us was the heavy bombing of North Vietnam, which would undoubtedly fail to succeed and might be followed by an invasion of North Vietnam. So again the urgency seemed very great.

Maybe we could go back to one thing. You asked, was I ready to stand this prison sentence?

Now, I said to myself, if I were willing to risk my life, my body, again and again in support of the war when I believed it was right for us to be in the war, how could I shrink from being willing to go to prison to resist the war, when I feel the war is against the interest of the country and that stopping it is our vital interest?

And I just didn't have any answer to that. I didn't want to go to prison, but, on the other hand, I was confronted with the situation where there seemed a very evident way to contribute to stopping the war, and, for that matter, to contribute to the strengthening of our democratic processes, which had been weakened by lying and Executive usurpation in the last 20 years.

What you were doing was participating in a conflict with the traditional idea of loyalty to the state, weren't you?

Loyalty to the President.

Do you mean to identify the state with the Executive? I feel the President has misled Congress and usurped constitutional powers that belong to the Congress, and manipulated Congress, bypassed Congress. Something that I want to happen as a result of this is to restore or strengthen a certain kind of health to the state by encouraging Congress and the courts to exercise their constitutional responsibilities. I think the courts have been irresponsible in refusing to hear constitutional issues on these matters. As the judges read these papers, I hope they won't shirk those responsibilities any more.

The reality is that whatever the issues are at stake in Indochina for the United States, they are so far removed from issues we faced in World War II in importance, that they could not possibly justify the fact that we have been led to drop in the last two years more tonnage of bombs on Indochina, mostly in Laos with its three million people, than we dropped in all the theaters in World War II. We dropped a little over two million tons in all the theaters in World War II. Nixon has dropped 2.7 million tons, mostly in Laos, in his Administration. Nixon. And that's while we're winding down the war.

Is the charge against you now that you had the documents, not that you distributed them?

That seems to be it; also, that I converted them to my use, which would seem to mean giving them to a U.S. senator, for instance, and later to the press. That shows how unclear the law is. Can they really win a case that I stole the documents when what they are talking about was giving copies of them—not even the documents, the Defense Department still has my set of those—to a United States senator, Senator Fulbright, not for profit? Funny thing. After all, I gave them to the Senate Foreign Relations Committee a year and a half before I gave them to the press. That doesn't strike me as the strongest case in the world for the Government to go in with.

If you want someone reading this to take a single lesson away from the Pentagon papers, what would you say he should get out of them?

I will say this: Everybody knows the slogan "Power corrupts." But have we believed it? For Americans? We've really paid very little attention to the possibility that something like absolute power for the President of the United States could be enormously corrupting.

Do you realize that there's not a hint in any piece of legislation, to my knowledge, that says the President does not have the legal constitutional right tomorrow to send out all the nuclear forces of the United States to explode their weapons in pursuit of our national interests? There is no limitation that he has to consult Congress or the courts or the public or the press before he does that. Nobody else in the history of the world has had that degree of power. It's a very corrupting thought.

To give a man, unchecked and unmonitored, a command of such power is, virtually, to tempt him, over time, to use it in pursuit of interests of the United States as he alone defines them or even of his personal interest when it comes to protecting his place in history or his personal or party interests in getting reelected.

What doesn't have to happen is that he should be allowed to think that without any challenge. And that's what has come to happen.

Most adults have not felt challenged to do anything. Then a few like James Reston recently came face-to-face with the choice that either they were ready to defy the warning of the Justice Department or they would accept press censorship. James Reston said to me, I'd love to go to jail for this principle. I thought to myself, good for you, Reston. I'm glad that history has brought you to the discovery of the principle of nonviolent civil disobedience. So, maybe some adults are ready to get the word.

You said there is still more work to be done. What did you have in mind?

All those officials who say the record of the Pentagon papers isn't complete are, of course, correct. And they should individually take the initiative of completing it by presenting their own files to Congress and to the public. And if they are not willing to do that, I'd like to see the Senate Foreign Relations Committee, or others, subpoena their files and memoranda.

Let me ask you one last question. What happens to your own future? What happens to you now?

The odds are in favor of my spending a long time in prison.

Why We Need a Woman President in 1976

BY GLORIA STEINEM

Five or six years ago, I wouldn't have written anything with this title. In fact, I might have ridiculed the idea of a female Chief of State, all the while feeling that special glow of virtue and safety that comes from conforming to society's notion of a Real Woman.

But the last few years have changed women even more than the rest of the country. All of us have learned two lessons that Conventional Wisdom never taught. First, that women can exercise power constructively and well in "masculine" areas that have nothing to do with the kitchen or the nursery. And second, that this country's existing power structures—including many of the crusading movements themselves—are not about to let us do it.

I learned these lessons ("got radicalized," as the stu-dent Left would say) by watching and interviewing gifted, industrious women as they were turned away, limited in scope, denied equal pay and promotion or simply ridiculed by the institutions that needed their talents most. (Even young and radical men were revolutionary on every subject except women.)

But these women were still trying. They hadn't completely succumbed to the deepest handicap of second-class groups: believing the myths of their own inferiority. (Which is why, I'm afraid, I once scoffed at the notion of a woman President. Even women with hopes for ourselves often believe that females as a group are inferior.) The sadder ones were the conventional wives who were guilty, bewildered or bitter at their inability to find total identity in biological functions and housekeeping, as society had told them they should. Or the unmarried women who weren't taught to feel responsible for their own lives, and so spent their time going from man to man, restricting their development to the demands of the marriage market.

What finally comes from looking at both groups, those learning to love their chains and those still struggling, is an overwhelming sense of waste.

There are Golda Meirs in both parties, but their function is limited to winning elections for men. (Rep. Shirley Chisholm, the first black woman to be elected to Congress, says she has always found politicians more prejudiced against her as a woman than as a black.) And the number of college degrees buried in suburban role-playing is legendary.

Meanwhile, the country, God knows, needs all the human talent that it can get.

A woman President couldn't solve all the problems. The amount of law reform and enforcement necessary to give women an even start isn't likely to get done in four years, much less the changing of consciousness involved. But people will go on supposing the current social order reflects some natural order until the visible one changes. Because the particular is less frightening than the abstract, the real woman candidate will be acceptable to males who would protest wildly at the idea if questioned first. Finally, in this country of heroes and personal charisma, one good heroine—one woman who is truly honored in authority—is worth a thousand court cases, arguments and books. She could help to free the aspirations of half the population.

Men and women progress together, or not at all.

There have been arguments that a woman President would be not only equal, but better; that her mother role makes her closer to the earth, more peaceful, more moral. It seems to me that's a romantic hangover from the days when church and state glorified motherhood beyond all reality as a way of getting the population increased. Women leaders in other countries have often proved it wrong. The truth probably is that women are not more moral, they are only uncorrupted by power.

But the female experience of second-classness *has* produced a special sympathy and understanding for others in the same boat. Historically, women have always been in the forefront of movements for humanitarian reform, including the abolitionist movement 70 years before they themselves endured prison and ridicule to get the vote.

In fact, male-female role-playing itself is probably the greatest long-term threat to peace. Anthropologists have found that the few societies without war are those in which sex roles are clear but not polarized. Women needn't be submissive semi-adults to be women, and men don't have to go to war or dominate their surroundings to be men. Members of society are born male or female, and don't feel much of life must be spent in proving it. Some of the under-30 generation is already secure enough to prefer this cooperative, unpolarized life-style. And by 1976, that's where 40 percent of the votes are going to be.

Of course, there's a long way to go. Women trying to step out of their 19th-century roles will be punished with ridicule, just as Blacks who refuse to act like Blacks are greeted with violence and fear.

Indeed, if the current pattern continues, the first woman President and the first black one may be the same: blackness has saved recent women candidates from ridicule, and their femaleness has reduced the fear. A black *woman* in the White House; now, that might be more politically likely.

If all this seems mind-bending and impossible, think back to the beginning of the '60's. What seemed impossible to us then? Men on the moon? Assassinations? Tanks in our streets? Demonstrations the size of cities?

Surely, a woman in the White House is not an impossible feminist cause. It's only a small, beginning step in the humanist revolution.

Why We Need
a Black President
in 1980

BY WILLIAM F. BUCKLEY, JR.

I ran for mayor of New York City a few years ago, and the headline in the New York *Herald Tribune* . . . was, "Buckley Has a 'Balanced' Ticket: Markey, Mrs. Gun-

ning—All Irish." The professionals rocked with mirth when I announced that I hadn't known that Mrs. Rosemary Gunning was Irish, and hadn't known even that she was Catholic.

I was stung by the criticism of my naïveté and tried to turn it to my advantage later in the campaign by observing that those who sought a religiously balanced ticket or an ethnically balanced ticket were, after all, the ethnically self-conscious and hence the opportunists of discord and of totemic political practices. And I was right . . . I am talking out-of-this-world where, ideally, politics has nothing to do. In this world, it is different—especially different, in my judgment, where the Negro is concerned. The objective at hand is the election of a Negro (no, not any Negro) as President of the United States in 1980 (or thereabouts).

High political office tends, after all, to carry social distinction, and it is for this reason that some Americans . . . voted for John Kennedy in 1960. Not merely Catholics, but others who wished to see broken a religious barrier they believed generically unhealthy and (in some cases) practically inconvenient. It seems to me that the election of Kennedy did have this reassuring general effect. When people are reassured, they tend to become less ambitious in that particular direction.

One senses that the accomplishments of the Jew in America are so pronounced that he no longer needs the Presidency, not because the Presidency is small potatoes, but because the achievement of it is unlikely to add anything to the sense the American Jew now has of being In.

It isn't so with the American Negro. He has not won a dozen Nobel Prizes, or crowded Groton graduates out of Harvard, or coached us in the mysteries of atom-splitting. The debate will continue on the question whether his gifts are genetically other than those of the Caucasian, or only apparently other for reasons of training or environment. I do not myself believe that the final scientific adjudication of that debate will prove to be particularly important, except perhaps in a narrow pedagogical sense. George Washington was less "intelligent" than Einstein, an obvious way of making a point that is nonetheless subtle.

But the American Negro needs the kind of reassurance that Einstein did not need. It is the reassurance that he can move into the reaches of reservations from which he has grown up thinking that Americans whose skins are black are permanently excluded.

There are reasons for urging that final achievement (the black President) that are more important than merely buying the reassurance of American Negroes.

The outstanding charge against America is hypocrisy. It is greatly exaggerated. But where the Negroes are concerned, the practice of inequality directly belies the vision of equality of opportunity, so that the election of Negro public officials (yes, because they are Negro) is a considerable tonic for the white soul.

It helps, but it is not enough, to "encourage" the careers of a Sugar Ray Robinson, a Duke Ellington, a Martin Luther King, Jr. But men such as they will not need, in the 1970's, any particular help, inasmuch as their talents pull them up as inexorably as an escalator. The area in which the Negro will need help is increasingly the area in which raw talent is not mechanically measured.

It is not necessary to experience the goodwill of a predominantly white community in order to confirm that Joe Louis is a better boxer than Max Schmeling. But it is only the white community that can, e.g., express itself—as an act of faith—that it is preferable to elect Carl Stokes mayor of Cleveland, than Seth Taft.

I have had a brief experience with the black militants, and they are as attractive as the Aryans who cheered along the drive of Adolf Hitler for racial purity. These militants receive much attention, as indeed they should: they bamboozle a lot of Americans, most typically those Americans who are happiest believing the worst about America.

But they remain a very small minority of their people, for reasons that reconfirm the health and sanity of the large body of Negroes for whom they presume to speak. The race of the next decade will be over the question: Who will attract the attention of the majority of the American Negroes? A great unpublicized phenomenon is the arrival in America of a class of young Negro leaders who work in the ghettos, in economic cooperatives, in straightforward social work, who are arguing that progress is possible within the System. They are harassed by the demagogy of the racists who say that America cannot make way for the Negroes. But they nevertheless survive—and they proliferate. You can find them in Cleveland (some of them will make it a point to be just a little bit rude, just for the record), in Detroit, learning the politics of adjustment, throwing their weight around in economic and political maneuver; in Los Angeles, calmly (if not openly) countering the witch doctors and practicing a tough-minded idealism (the top people at Watts are brilliant, ingenious, tough, graceful, irresistible).

It is from the ranks of these young men, now 30, 35, 40 years old, that I can imagine someone rising, in the next decade, to national prominence as a presidential candidate. When it happens, I think that it is quite possible that he will be greeted gladly by those who, having satisfied themselves that the point they are about to make will not be at the expense of the survival of the Republic, will join in a quite general enthusiasm over his election as President of the United States; who will celebrate his achievement as a celebration of the ideals of a country that by this act alone, would reassert its idealism—shrugging off, as is America's way, by practical accomplishment the chains of cynicism and despair that the detractors and the cynics wear so gladly, singing their songs of hopelessness.

How shall we sing the Lord's song in a strange land? the prophet asked. Whittaker Chambers wrote 20 years ago of the Negro people that they have been the most man-despised and God-obsessed people in the history of the world, that on coming to this strange land, they had struck their tuning fork, and the sorrow songs, the spirituals, were born. But the sorrow songs are of another age, describing another spiritual plight.

"Jes call me Prez-i-dent Jones," they sing now in the Bahamas, where they have elected their own "Prez-i-dent." It will be even better when "President" Jones is elected by others who, seeking to alleviate the sorrow of the few, lighten the burden of the many.

On Black Power

BY NORMAN MAILER

W*e must understand that we are replacing a dying culture, and we must be prepared to do this, and be absolutely conscious of what we are replacing it with. We are sons and daughters of the most ancient societies on this planet. . . . No movement shaped or contained by Western culture will ever benefit Black people. Black power must be the actual force and beauty and wisdom of Blackness . . . reordering the world. —LeRoi Jones*

Are you ready to enter the vision of the Black Left? It is profoundly anti-technological. Jump into it all at once. Here are a few remarks by Ron Karenga.

"The fact that we are Black is our ultimate reality. We were Black before we were born.

"The white boy is engaged in the worship of technology; we must not sell our souls for money and machines. We must free ourselves culturally before we proceed politically.

"Revolution to us is the creation of an alternative . . . we are not here to be taught by the world, but to teach the world."

Any mystique which has men ready to die for it is never without political force. The Left Wing of Black Power speaks across the void to the most powerful conservative passions—for any real conservatism is founded on regard for the animal, the oak and the field; it has instinctive detestation of science, of the creation-by-machine.

Conservatism is a body of traditions which once served as the philosophical home of society. If the traditions are now withered in the hum of electronics; if the traditions have become almost hopelessly inadequate to meet the computed moves of the technological society; if conservatism has become the grumbling of the epicure at bad food, bad air, bad manners; if conservatism lost the future because it enjoyed the greed of its privileged position to that point where the exploited depths stirred in righteous rage; if the conservatives and their traditions failed because they violated the balance of society, exploited the poor too savagely and searched for justice not nearly enough; if finally the balance between property rights and the rights of men gave at last too much to the land and too little to the living blood, still conservatism and tradition had one last Herculean strength: they were of the marrow, they partook of primitive wisdom.

The tradition had been founded on some half-remembered sense of primitive perception, and so was close to life and the sense of life. Tradition had appropriated the graceful movements with which primitive strangers and friends might meet in the depth of a mood, all animal in their awareness: lo! the stranger bows before the intense presence of the monarch or the chief, and the movement is later engraved upon a code of ceremony. So tradition was once a key to the primitive life still breathing within us, a key too large, idiosyncratic and unmanageable for the quick shuttles of the electronic. Standing before technology, tradition began to die, and air turned to smog.

But the black man, living a life on the fringe of technological society, exploited by it, poisoned by it, half-rejected by it, gulping prison air in the fluorescent nightmare of shabby garish electric ghettos, uprooted centuries ago from his native Africa, his instincts living ergo like nerves in the limbo of an amputated limb, had thereby an experience unique to modern man—he was forced to live at one and the same time in the old primitive jungle of the slums, and the hygienic surrealistic landscape of the technological society.

And as he began to arise from his exploitation, he discovered that the culture which had saved him owed more to the wit and telepathy of the jungle than the value and programs of the West. His dance had taught him more than writs and torts, his music was sweeter than Shakespeare or Bach (since music had never been a luxury to him but a need), prison had given him a culture deeper than libraries in the grove, and violence had produced an economy of personal relations as negotiable as money.

The American Black had survived—of all the peoples of the Western World, he was the only one in the near seven decades of the twentieth century to have undergone the cruel weeding of real survival. So it was possible his manhood had improved while the manhood of others was being leached. He had at any rate a vision. It was that he was black, beautiful and secretly superior—he had therefore the potentiality to conceive and create a new culture (perchance a new civilization), richer, wiser, deeper, more beautiful and profound than any he had seen. (And conceivably more demanding, more torrential, more tyrannical.)

But he would not know until he had power for himself. He would not know if he could provide a wiser science, subtler schooling, deeper medicine, richer victual and deeper view of creation until he had the power. So while some (the ones the Blacks called Negroes) looked to integrate into the super-suburbs of technology land (and find, was their hope, a little peace for the kids), so others dreamed of a future world which their primitive lore and sophisticated attainments might now bring. And because they were proud and loved their vision, they were warriors as well, and had a mystique which saw the cooking of food as good or bad for the soul. And taste gave the hint.

That was the Left of Black Power, a movement as mysterious, dedicated, instinctive and conceivably bewitched as a gathering of Templars for the next Crusade. Soon their public fury might fall upon the fact that civilization was a trap, and therefore their wrath might be double, for they had been employed to build civilization, had received none of its gains, and yet, being allowed to enter now, now, this late, could be doomed with the rest. What a thought!

Let the Indians Run Indian Policy

BY EDWARD M. KENNEDY

Add the American Indian and Alaskan native to the list of minorities who want to take part in the decisions that affect their lives.

From a history of neglect and despair, the Indian is beginning to emerge and to demand his own identity and share of American life. It has been a long time in coming, this new Indian self-consciousness. But it is here, and America must pay attention.

Tribal councils travel weekly to Washington, bringing their grievances and proposals directly to the Congress and the Interior Department, rather than using the local Bureau of Indian Affairs, as had been the custom.

Before I became chairman of the Indian Education Subcommittee, that post was held by my brother, Robert Kennedy. He traveled America extensively in that role, exposing the severity and degradation of Indian poverty and the failure of this nation to help the Indian people.

He saw, as I have seen, the resilience of the Indian way of life, a way of life that has for many generations resisted destruction despite Government blunders that almost seem designed to stamp it out. My brother called America's treatment of the Indian "a national tragedy and a national disgrace."

I second that opinion. And I think it is past time to end this disgrace.

I have seen statistics reflected in the faces of thousands of Indians. Their lives are hard and often filled with despair. Their average income is about $1,500 a year. Their teenagers are three times as likely to take their own lives as are young people outside the Indian community. They have 12.2 times the chance of an alcohol-related arrest as the average white American. Their children are plagued with disease. (One Indian leader told our committee he had lost eight children to disease: " . . . it is a lot of kinds of sickness they die from. Not only one kind. Mostly with whooping cough and measles all together. It hit them one at a time and that way they die.") And their pride decays into a passive wariness of the white man and his misguided attempts to help.

America has been frustrated by the "Indian problem" since the dawn of the nation.

First, we embarked on a policy of isolation, marching entire Indian nations to desolate reservations. Later, we turned toward assimilation, but for the wrong reason—to exploit and expropriate Indian land and Indian resources. We shouldered the "white man's burden" initially by herding separate Indian nations together against their will—then turned around and plunged them headlong into the white man's society, thereby helping to tear them apart. But in any case, so the feeling went, the Indians would be off our conscience, off our land, out of our pocketbooks.

Well, it hasn't worked. Our casual paternalism has done more to hurt than to help. It has disorganized or destroyed this country's Indian communities. It has created a severe and self-perpetuating cycle of poverty for most Indians. And it has brought about an enormous, ineffective bureaucracy that seems to treat the elimination of Indian poverty as a gross waste of Federal funds.

The average educational level for Indian children under Federal supervision is five school years—and the Indian dropout rate is twice the national average. Only 18 percent of the students in Federal Indian schools go on to college, against a much higher national average. And only three percent of these Indians graduate.

Numerous studies, reports and commissions have come forth with their "solutions" for the Indian problem. But the crucial ingredient that has always been missing is the concept that the Indian can speak for himself, can say what is wrong, what he wants and needs, and what our policies should be in his regard.

On numerous occasions, the Federal Government has suffered the embarrassment of putting forth grand schemes to solve Indian problems without really permitting the Indian to determine the policies and programs for himself. This is not only a hypocritical charade that breeds cynicism and frustration on both sides, it is also, more importantly, a perpetuation of our cumulative failures.

The vast Federal bureaucracy charged with "managing" Indians for the United States can never, as presently structured, be expected to change our tragic Indian policies. This is a harsh conclusion. It brings no satisfaction to Americans who believe that ours is a land of equality and justice for all.

So, is there anywhere to turn? We might try turning to the American Indian himself.

That's what he is asking. That's what he is demanding. And ultimately, that's what we must recognize as the best solution.

In early April, the Navajo School Board in Ramah, N.M., completed negotiations with the Bureau of Indian Affairs to bring the community's children home from boarding school to an Indian-controlled high school.

Similar gains are being made in other areas of Indian life. Major economic development plans are being put forward by the Zuñi in New Mexico and the Seneca in New York State. The Crow tribe in Montana is moving toward extensive development of its mineral resources; the Lummi in Washington are experimenting with advanced agriculture; and natives at Bethel, Alaska, continue their cooperative fishing ventures. So, progress is possible—if the Indians manage their own affairs.

191

A DAZZLE
OF STARS

THE MOVIES

Until 1915, Hollywood was a sleepy little suburb of Los Angeles. Suddenly, with the invention of the motion picture, brilliant showmen and hucksters flocked to the town, and the world became aware of "Hollywood, capital of the Motion Picture." However crude in manner or prodigal in spending, these men wrought magic on celluloid, producing first the "silents" and then, in 1929, the "talkies." These creative pioneers made movies the most popular mass medium in history, to be rivalled only by television.

Ignoring the sad, seamy despairs of life and the tragedies of war, economic depression, and racial conflict, the "silver screen" glorified Romance and Adventure. In movie mythology, heroes were always fearless; heroines were forever chaste; villains were always punished; and virtue was invincible. Love conquered all, and happiness crowned "The End."

On screen and off, movie stars became a new international royalty. No aspect of their lives went unchronicled, and for five decades the demigods and -goddesses of "Bagdad-on-the-Pacific" fulfilled our every dream. The stars influenced our manners, affected our dress, dances, courtships, and songs.

Throughout this period, however, certain films dealt with more serious subjects. Gradually, new themes emerged, and by the late 1960's a new breed of actors and actresses appeared on the screen, playing more realistic characters in more complex situations. No longer molded by the studios, they created new trends, projecting a wide range of values rather than a stereotyped code of behavior. In addition, the prohibitive costs of rebuilding Constantinople in southern California made location shooting a greater necessity. As a result, the American film industry has become an increasingly global enterprise. Hollywood can no longer be considered the true "film capital." But while the dream lasted, it was indeed a "lollipop kingdom."   —Ed.

BOB VOSE

(above). Actors can be their own harshest critics. Joan Crawford experiences a range of emotions as she watches the "rushes" after a day's filming of *Flamingo Road* (below). Such projection-room scenes, although rarely photographed, are a typical part of a film star's day.

(overleaf).
In its heyday MGM was said to have under contract "more stars than there are in heaven." No other studio could rival its glittering and lucrative "stable," assembled here specifically for LOOK photographers. Impressive as this gallery is, missing are such MGM luminaries as Gable, Tracy, Garbo, Lamarr, Rooney, and Garland—all off working on location.

STEVE FORREST   PIER ANGELI   DEBBIE REYNOLDS   LOUIS CALHERN   GEORGE MURPHY   CYD CHARISSE

EVA GABOR   ANNE FRANCIS   STEWART GRANGER   VAN JOHNSON

LESLIE CARON   ROLAND PETIT   MERLE OBERON   WALTER PIDGEON   JANE POWELL

TAMARA TOUMANOVA   RUSS TAMBLYN   CARLOS THOMPSON   ROBERT TAYLOR   ELIZABETH TAYLOR

C DAMONE   PAUL DOUGLAS   JOHN ERICSON   TAINA ELG   JOSE FERRER   ANN MILLER

RT KASZNAR   JANET LEIGH   HOWARD KEEL   GRACE KELLY   FERNANDO LAMAS

ORGE RAFT   DONNA REED   ANN BLYTH   MICHAEL WILDING   JEFF RICHARD   ESTHER WILLIAMS

LIONEL BARRYMORE   HELEN TRAUBEL   VERA-ELLEN   GEORGE SANDERS

Greta Garbo: Her classic face is considered the most photogenic in film history. Intriguing, mysterious, inaccessible, she shuns the limelight in a personal life that echoes her now famous line, "I want to be alone."

Mae West: Her lusty, busty demimonde satirized lechery and sparkled with mocking lines, which she wrote, that still tickle our fancy—"C'mon up and see me some time"…"Beulah, peel me a grape." Here she camps it up in the ultimate of camp, *Myra Breckenridge.*

Marlene Dietrich: Although she was 60 years old—and a grandmother— at the time of this portrait, her face retains the mystery and beauty that made her the queen of sheer glamour, a source of endless fascination for cameramen throughout the world.

Barbra Streisand: Singer turned actress, her phenomenal voice and acting skill, projecting both comedy and pathos, have created a new kind of magic.

Raquel Welch: Her incredible body, radiating sensuality, first brought her stardom; recently, her acting has brought her critical acclaim.

Clark Gable in *Gone With the Wind:* The animal magnetism of "The King" made him the idol of both sexes.

(top). Marlon Brando portrays an arrogant Nazi soldier in *The Young Lions.* A superlative actor—earthy, brooding, introspective—he introduced a new kind of hero.

(bottom). Spencer Tracy in *Father of the Bride:* The "actors' actor," he possessed a naturalism, force, and expressive range that were triumphs of talent.

MGM

MGM

PHIL STERN

"The Duke"—John Wayne: The husky
"Westerner" with the trademark stride
has ranked among the top ten movie
draws over a longer period than any other
actor. More a compelling personal presence than an innovative actor, he epito-
mizes confident, elemental masculinity.

MILTON GREENE

MILTON GREENE

MILTON GREENE

EARL THEISEN

MILTON GREENE

MILTON GREENE

Marilyn Monroe: An enduring legend, she was touching, sexy, a wistful waif, and a gifted comedienne. Everyone from baseball star Joe DiMaggio to Pulitzer Prize-winning playwright Arthur Miller wanted to protect her. The beautiful blonde with the beautiful body was more complex than her public image implied. She expressed her personal conflicts in verse—and so admired poet Carl Sandburg that on one occasion she tinted her hair to match his (lower right). Uncertainty still surrounds the circumstances of her tragic death.

"I am a child in the body of a woman," Elizabeth Taylor once cried. Often described as having the most magnificent face in films, she developed such assured dramatic skill that she sacrificed her beauty for an Oscar-winning performance as the blowzy, haggard shrew of *Who's Afraid of Virginia Woolf?*

DOUGLAS KIRKLAND

MICHAEL VACCARO

MILTON GREENE

(top). Judy Garland: Snub-nosed, wide-eyed, she could take over the stage with an electric appeal and a voice that chased rainbows. Off-stage her attempted suicides and drug-laden sufferings were followed by millions of adoring fans who continue her cult even now.

(bottom). Sophia Loren: Italy's gift to the screen is our most voluptuous and mature sex symbol. Her beauty is magnified by a superb dramatic sensibility.

Ava Gardner: The sloe-eyed girl from North Carolina soared to stardom with both acting skill and smoldering sex appeal. (It was so hard to think of her as Mrs. Mickey Rooney!)

Cary Grant: He broke into show business in England as an acrobat, but emerged in the United States as sophistication par excellence. Hollywood's most handsome man developed an acting skill that took comedy, drama, and melodrama in stride. There is not an actress who has not yearned to co-star with him.

Steve McQueen: Another of the new breed of heroes, he is cool, tight-lipped, blunt.

Sidney Poitier: The first black to break many Hollywood taboos, in *Guess Who's Coming to Dinner?* he not only kissed but married a white girl. A director and producer as well as an actor, he is involved in every aspect of filmmaking.

Gregory Peck: His screen image of the decent, courageous man of conscience is consistent with his private life. Modest, dedicated to social causes, he is one of the most admired and best-liked men in the movie colony.

Rex Harrison and Audrey Hepburn in *My Fair Lady:*
An uncharacteristically exuberant Henry Higgins
and his cockney pupil celebrate her first—equally
uncharacteristic—moment of elocutionary excellence.

BOB WILLOUGHBY

WARNER BROTHERS, INC.

Humphrey Bogart and Ingrid Bergman in
Casablanca: A tough, cynical Bogart was
paired with a beguiling, idealistic, and
romantic Bergman in the now classic
"Bogie" flick of love, political commitment, and foreign intrigue.

UNIVERSAL PICTURES

Rock Hudson tries to seduce glamorous songstress
Doris Day in *Pillow Talk.* In film after film her stead-
fast virtue and his determination made their
comedies a delight.

Richard Burton mesmerizes Elizabeth Taylor. His resonant, evocative Welsh voice is equally at home with Shakespeare and Albee. The two superstars shared a life of tempestuous romance, marriage, and lavish self-indulgence that kept them in the headlines, but it all crashed in divorce.

W. C. Fields and Mae West in *My Little Chickadee:* A glorious coward and sardonic "con man," Fields was a supreme charlatan whose special brand of cynicism flourished in scenes with Mae West. When the doxy with the hour-glass figure extended her hand, à la Pompadour, a leering, whiskey-voiced Fields inquired, "May I admire the symmetry of your digits?" To call him unique is feeble; to call her delicious is factual.

UNIVERSAL PICTURES

Charlie Chaplin in *The Great Dictator:* No one thought comedy could be wrested from so hateful a theme as Nazism, but the great actor/comedian brilliantly deflated Hitler in *The Great Dictator.* The movie was his personal vengeance on a man he loathed—"The swine stole my moustache!"

210

Tony Curtis and Jack Lemmon appear in drag for the
uproarious *Some Like It Hot*, Billy Wilder's satiric
jewel about Chicago's gangster era.

Three who took us down many laughing
roads: the incomparable Bob Hope,
radiant Dorothy Lamour, and
bon-vivant Bing Crosby.

Maurice Chevalier: Child of Parisian ▶
streets and music halls, the debonair
chanteur with the lilting accent illumi-
nated the screen with his irresistible
smile. Asked how he felt at age 80, he
grinned: "Wonderful—when you consider
the alternative."

Ray Bolger, Jack Haley, Judy Garland, and Bert Lahr: Seeking a brain, a heart, home, and courage, the Scarecrow, the Tin Woodman, Dorothy, and the Cowardly Lion skip along toward their meeting with the Wonderful Wizard of Oz.

As Huck Finn, Mickey Rooney ▶ projects a timeless image of free and adventurous American boyhood.

Three masters of menace: Sydney Greenstreet, unforgettably malevolent (above); James Cagney, hoofer turned tough, explosive hoodlum—imitated but unequalled (top right); Edward G. Robinson, gangland mastermind, dapper, cool—but vicious when crossed (below right).

Veteran "hams" of horror: lisping Boris ▶ Karloff, mammoth Lon Chaney, Jr., and unctuous Vincent Price.

Jimmy Stewart: A fine comedian and
actor, his drawl and diffidence—and
unwavering integrity—are his trademarks.

Gary Cooper: In *High Noon*, as the town
sheriff, he broke the code of the Western
by showing fear, fleeing from the outlaw,
reluctantly returning to fight (right),
and emerging with contempt for the sanc-
timonious townsfolk. Screenwriter Carl
Foreman created the character; "Coop"
made it immortal.

Recipe for Westerns: "The hero has no past, few friends, seldom pays for a drink; when he gambles, he never loses. He never draws first, never seeks a fight, but always wins it. And the noble bachelor rarely gets the girl."—Peter Homans

(top to bottom). Tom Mix, Harry Carey, Dustin Farnum, and Hoot Gibson.

Ginger Rogers and Fred Astaire in just a few feet of the many miles they danced arm-in-arm.

MGM

Gene Kelly: The dynamo dancer/choreographer who invented one of film's classic dance passages in *Singing in the Rain*, hoofs with gusto on anything from ashcans to freight cars.

With the dramatic power and professionalism that have characterized her career, Bette Davis plays the personification of the temperamental and passionate "Broadway star" in *All About Eve*.

Montgomery Clift and Burt Lancaster comfort Frank Sinatra in a scene from *From Here to Eternity*. Sinatra's crooning career was moribund when he begged to play the role of Maggio, offering to work for a pittance. His performance launched him on a brilliant new career.

The Grapes of Wrath was Darryl Zanuck's milestone departure from the bonbons at which Hollywood excelled. Henry Fonda, the perfect choice for John Steinbeck's Okie, still packs them in at the box office.

In *The African Queen* a majestic Katherine Hepburn co-stars with a boozy Bogart in John Huston's exciting tale of adversity, courage, and redemption.

In the 1960's, new young moviemakers stormed the citadels of make-believe. Aware of the inadequacies of the Hollywood dream and of the ambiguities of human motivations and relationships, they challenged traditional values and accepted definitions of good and evil. Self-assured, independent, they demanded full control over their films. However bold and imaginative, these young directors owed great debts to such pioneers of earlier generations as D. W. Griffith, John Huston, and Alfred Hitchcock (above, top to bottom) and Billy Wilder (right). They also learned from the films of gifted foreign directors, among them Jean Renoir, Ingmar Bergman, Federico Fellini (opposite, left column), and Michelangelo Antonini (opposite, lower center).

The success of Mike Nichols (top center)—whose *The Graduate* broke both Hollywood stereotypes and box-office records—persuaded producers that movie audiences were ready for the ideas of the new generation. The trailblazers of the 1960's and 1970's explored previously forbidden territory with unprecedented frankness. Much that would formerly have been labelled pornography has become accepted and familiar in today's movies. Individual directors, however, in demolishing illusions, have pushed their explorations of sex, drugs, and the convolutions of the human psyche to extremes, and the images of such filmmakers as Andy Warhol (right) still retain the power to shock.

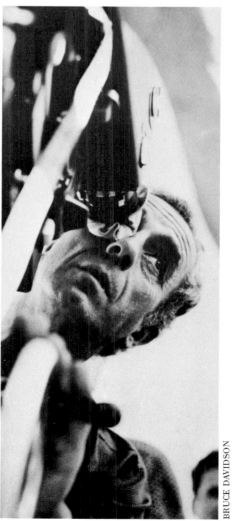

TELEVISION

While Hollywood and Broadway laughed off the "boob tube," television was developing the technology that would make it available in almost every American home and the imaginative programming that would soon win stupendous audiences. Filmmakers did not foresee that while movies charged admission, television fare would be free. Movies carried no advertising; the television industry would reap millions from its hard sell of everything from dog food to the latest, most glamorous model Cadillac.

The movie moguls gasped when they found their theaters deserted every Tuesday night because an outrageous, uproarious Milton Berle was entertaining twenty million viewers in the comfort of their homes. Jackie Gleason's The Honeymooners," Ed Sullivan's vaudeville extravaganzas —even Hopalong Cassidy's old-fashioned Westerns—acquired vast and loyal followings, emptying movie theaters from Hoboken to Hong Kong.

—Ed.

LOOK

Versatile Milton Berle mugs for the cameras in one of his hilarious comic routines.

◄ Dan Blocker, Michael Landon, Pernell Roberts, and Lorne Greene in "Bonanza": Frontier sagas featuring close-knit families, such as Ben Cartwright and his three sons, have always been a formula for television success.

Television entrepreneurs astutely developed new program formats appropriate to the medium. Sid Caesar and Imogene Coca made "Your Show of Shows" the liveliest, funniest comedy around (below). Johnny Carson (below right), succeeding Jack Paar, deluges audiences night after night with famous guests— authors, actors, sports heroes, comedians —who ad-lib personal opinions, intimacies, and gossip to make "talk shows" a bonanza for the networks.

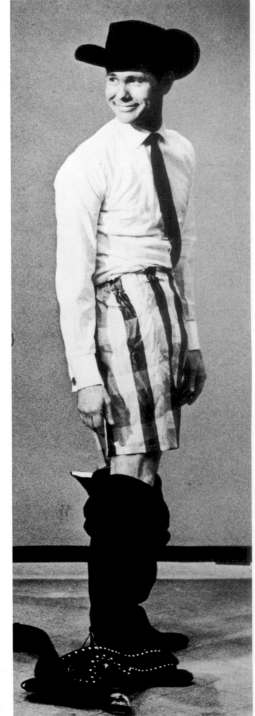

JOHN VACHON

BOB LERNER

Ed Sullivan, TV's king for two decades: He could not tell a joke, imitate an ant, or juggle an orange. But the columnist with the deadpan delivery brought the best and most varied talent money could buy to "the tube" in a format that inter-mixed acrobats, jugglers, and comedy routines with opera stars, orchestras and choirs, and international ballet companies.

Carol Burnett: Her Chaplin is a master-piece of make-up and mimicry. She mugged her way to stardom in weekly comedy skits, ultimately earning her own show, which has been in the "Top Ten" since its first season.

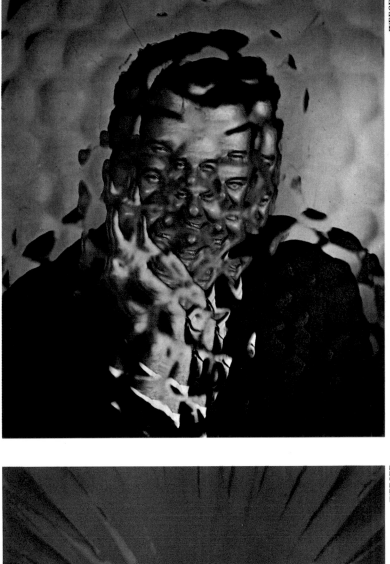

The mischievous portraits on these pages—low-keyed Arthur Godfrey (top), comedienne Lucille Ball (bottom), thrifty Jack Benny (right), and rubber-faced Red Skelton (far right)—are the work of Weegee (he never gave his first name). He printed the negatives through bubbled glass, wire screens, prisms, kaleidoscopes, or whatever he needed to manipulate famous faces and express an outrageous sense of humor.

Television gave every fan a front-row seat
and close-up views such as these scenes of
wrestling, one of the earliest telecast
sports: (above) Baron Arena, an imitator
of "Gorgeous George," lovely as a butterfly; (right) Antonio Rocco executing a
stupendous leap.

Three television staples season after
season—the hospital drama, the detective
story, and the Western: Vince Edwards
as resident Ben Casey, Robert Stack as
United States Treasury agent Elliot Ness,
and James Arness as Matt Dillon,
Marshal of Dodge City.

News on the spot, visual, immediate, became television's forte. A riot, a murder, a march, a political convention—all gained unprecedented impact and urgency when seen in one's own living room.

Edward R. Murrow: Radio's great commentator ("This is London....") became television's "conscience" with his bold, thoughtful, news analysis.

Chet Huntley and David Brinkley: In their new team-reporting format Huntley's solemn delivery and Brinkley's dry wit complemented each other and made them, for many years, television's most popular newscasters.

Walter Cronkite: Calm, credi- ▶ ble, tireless, he is the most influential network anchorman. Recently, thousands of Americans suggested that he become a presidential candidate—an unprecedented expression of country-wide confidence.

"Kukla, Fran, and Ollie": A Punch-and-Judy show with charm and endearing stars, it was immensely popular with the children who grew up as America's first "television generation."

Big Bird: Educational television's "Sesame ▶ Street" transformed children's programming. Imaginatively applying the theories of psychologists and educators, it enchants small fry, teaching them in a captivating way, with the aid of such appealing characters as Big Bird, and helping them to recognize and understand their conflicts and emotions.

THE CLOWNS

From the time of the cavemen, the clown has wooed laughter. Buffoonery has never lost its appeal to young and old, dullards and sages. Court jesters amused kings and queens, artful "fools" set the masses roaring, and the cunning dunce is a fixture in the entertainments of every culture.

America's audiences everywhere adored slap- stick, burlesque, and vaudeville. The silent films snapped up madcap comics to perform in their nickelodeons.

Clowning looks simple because the humor is broad, but it uses subtlety to get laughs. Comedians are often fine actors—but how many actors can win belly laughs from their audiences?

—Ed.

Danny Kaye: Dancer, singer, actor, conductor, mimic, he delights audiences with his comic antics and astonishes them with the multiplicity of his talents. A favorite of children, he has ardently espoused their cause and travels throughout the world to entertain youngsters and raise funds for UNICEF.

Buster Keaton: He used a single expression to get a million laughs. One of the great comedians of the silent-picture era, he fell from favor during the thirties and forties, until television reintroduced his slapstick shenanigans and pantomime skills to enthusiastic viewers.

Jimmy Durante: Whether singing, playing the piano, or talking in his inimitable combination of mispronunciations and malapropisms, the great "Schnozz" brightened night clubs, theaters, films, and television screens with personal warmth—and his hilarious spasms of mock outrage.

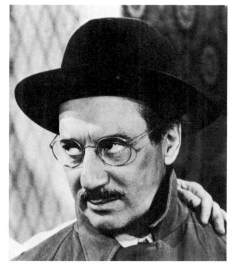

Groucho, O Groucho!: cerebral wit, prince of puns, leering wolf. Multifaced and multifaceted, this Einstein of illogic tosses off mordant wisecracks: "I don't care to belong to the kind of club that accepts people like me as members."…"I never forget a face, but in your case I'll be glad to make an exception."… "I came into my hotel room and found a strange blonde in my bed. I gave her exactly 24 hours to get out."…In 1942, while he was visiting a general, the phone rang; Groucho lifted the receiver and crooned, "World War Two-oo."

242

Red Skelton: His flexible face is an encyclopedia of shifting expressions, but it always retains an aura of childlike innocence. At the beginning of his career he was so poor that he "drowned" twice a day in Atlantic City; when lifeguards "revived" him, Red would entertain the inevitable crowds—and lead them to the restaurant of his employers. He worked in shabby carnivals, circuses, and sleazy clubs for years before his boundless versatility and genius for pantomime made him a nightclub star and television favorite.

Bud Abbott and Lou Costello: Over and over, chubby, gullible Costello was the credulous victim of his suave straight-man sidekick. Their zany dialogue sparkled with classics of confusion ("Who's on first?") that made them a gold mine to their studio.

Dick Van Dyke: An agile comic, he beguiled audiences as the star of one of television's best situation comedies. On film his performance as the irresistible chimney sweep in Walt Disney's *Mary Poppins* was superlative.

MGM

RICHARD HEWITT

DOUGLAS KIRKLAND

Jonathan Winters: The wackiest original on television, he can imitate anything from a wallet to a whale. No one can rival his consummate renditions of bumbling idiocy, or the vocal agility that gives him a repertoire of over 5,000 sound effects.

Jackie Gleason mugs as The Bartender. ▶ Bombastic, boastful, the huge comedian with the colossal talent has created a galaxy of characters whose humorous foibles and failures mirror our own.

Dean Martin and Jerry Lewis: The happy couple
above made a sensational team in nightclubs and
in a dozen dippy, zany, phenomenally successful
movies—and then split up. Working independently,
each has become a star of immense popularity.
Lewis so perfected his wacky clowning and gifted
writing and directing that French buffs regard
him as the century's comic genius. Television
audiences love Martin's image of ease and virility
and his frank self-parody. Not since Perry Como has
a crooner so captivated the public with his deceptive
indolence.

THE ARTS

O*urs is a time of artistic ferment. Rebelling against traditional forms and values, audacious innovators in every field—the visual arts, music, literature—have continued a powerful creative search for new structures and ideas appropriate and adequate to their experience of the contemporary world.*

In painting and sculpture, the revolution that began with Impressionism has generated a series of movements—including Cubism, Dada, Surrealism, Abstract Expressionism, Pop Art, Conceptual Art—each building upon while rejecting its predecessors. A radical commitment to the artist's personal vision and to the expression of his creativity through any medium, used in any manner, has led to the kaleidoscopic variety of contemporary art.

Transformations in music have been equally radical. Composers have experimented with every aspect of sound, exploring complex rhythms, atonal music, the effects of dissonance and chance. The inventions of modern technology—amplifiers, sophisticated recording devices, Moog synthesizers—have made new effects available, expanding our musical horizons. Simultaneously, popular music has developed in richness and scope. Jazz, emerging from American black culture, has gained universal recognition for its vital spontaneity. Rock and folk musicians have explored a wide range of compositional techniques, including those of the Far East, while their lyrics have taken on new subtlety and sophistication.

Literature too has seen the advent of a wealth of new forms. Free verse has become the rule rather than the exception and stream of consciousness prose is just one among many experiments made by authors seeking to capture and convey the elusive complexities of our consciousness. Equally important, writers, abolishing old taboos, have declared all experience and thought to be proper subject matter for art. In both traditional and radical forms, today's writers relentlessly break down our preconceptions, leading us to new recognition of ourselves, our society, and our world.

In all the arts, the rebellious and the visionary defy convention to bring us new dimensions of sight and sound. —Ed.

Pablo Picasso: One of history's authentic geniuses, he initiated a host of movements and worked in almost every available medium (he used bicycle parts to make one of his most famous sculptures), always moving on to explore new styles and new forms of artistic expression. David Douglas Duncan's photograph records the stunning moment when a rainbow, arching overhead haloed the great artist and his French château. "I could not believe my eyes," said Duncan. "I snapped my shutter in a daze."

251

The aged Matisse, his vigorous and lyric creativity unimpaired by illness, uses an 8-foot pole to design vestments for the Chapel of the Rosary at Venice, which he had designed. His joyous, fresh color harmonies remained a constant during an age of artistic upheaval.

◀ In a typically self-publicizing moment, flamboyant Surrealist Salvador Dali kneels triumphantly before the madcap backdrop he devised for an all-Scarlatti program at Venice's La Fenice theater. At his feet is the "soft watch" that has become synonymous with the name "Dali."

◄ Andrew Wyeth: Resisting contemporary trends, he uses an ancient medium—egg tempera—and a meticulous style to depict traditional subject matter. The haunting melancholy of his landscapes, interiors, and portraits links him, however, with the 20th-century themes of isolation and loss.

Grandma Moses displays the greeting card of an admirer, amateur artist General Dwight D. Eisenhower. This self-taught farm wife began painting when she was almost 80. Her beautifully composed "naive" paintings of rural scenes have gained wide critical recognition and have won the hearts of the public.

Alexander Calder adjusts one of his delicate mobiles, abstract metal forms of colored tin subtly balanced to hang and turn in lyrical silence (left). Calder creates the antithesis of these hovering flights and formations in what he calls "stabiles," massive shapes firmly planted on the earth, suggesting a fantasy architecture (right).

Two maestros: In concert, the revered Arturo
Toscanini (opposite). Physically and temperamen-
tally imposing, he inspired orchestras with his
passion for clarity in interpreting the classics. In
rehearsal, brilliant, dramatic Leonard Bernstein
(above), once boy wonder of the baton, wears a
sweatshirt celebrating Gustav Mahler, whose works
he revived and popularized. Independence and
creativity have characterized his career, both as a
renowned conductor and as the composer of symphonies, electrifying scores for Broadway musicals,
and an innovative modern Mass.

Arthur Rubinstein: A piano virtuoso
in the grand tradition, acclaimed for his
moving interpretations of the masters,
he is an untiring storyteller, epicure, and
bon vivant.

◄ Igor Stravinsky interprets one of his
scores for members of the string section.
In the course of a long creative career—
and often the focus of simultaneous
criticism and acclaim—he composed
symphonies, ballets, concerti, and
chorales, experimenting with the new
musical idioms that have become the
vocabulary of 20th-century music.

Pablo Casals: The outstanding cellist
of our time, he chose exile from Spain
when Franco came to power. In protest
against recognition of the dictator's
regime he refused, with rare exceptions,
to perform in public.

◄ Maria Callas: A bel canto soprano, the "fiery diva" brought dramatic talent and personal theatrics to her colorful operatic career.

Leontyne Price: Opera reached new opulence with the arrival of this shining soprano.

Johnny Cash: craggy-faced, moody,
a former drifter and ex-convict. His
resonant voice and fierce determination
have brought him to the top of country
music. He expresses the sorrows of the
dispossessed as well as a new message of
hope.

Diana Ross: In the 1960's, as lead singer
of The Supremes, she launched the
"Motown sound." The group's recordings
outsold those of all competitors but the
Beatles. Going solo, in 1972 she portrayed
Billie Holiday in *Lady Sings the Blues* and
earned accolades as a total entertainer
second only to Streisand.

UPI

© DANIEL KRAMER

Peter, Paul, and Mary: Among the first of the popular contemporary folksingers, they composed hundreds of songs on every subject—from magic dragons to Vietnam. Thousands upon thousands hummed or clapped along at their concerts, and the music business knew it had found a hit group and a new trend.

Bob Dylan: The Svengali of a disenchanted generation, his lyrics offered restless youth the hope of changing times. Emerging from a period of self-imposed retirement, he again offers the promise, but to an older, sadder, and wiser audience.

◄ Joan Baez: Amid the din of rock and roll, she appeared with a guitar, a lyrical voice, and graceful songs that captured an audience of both youth and adults. The Civil Rights movement and Vietnam led her to compose protest songs that transformed her into a rallying point for political activists.

Janis Joplin: Her emotions as raw as her clothes were funky,
the "Queen of Acid Rock," Southern Comfort bottle in hand,
dominated any stage with the raging sound of a voice that
cried in conscious imitation of black soul blues.

A small fan shies from the attentions of a
youthful Frank Sinatra. Even today he
can work magic on audiences who squealed
to his crooning when they and he were
young.

Nat "King" Cole: Many a romance is forever recaptured under the spell of his mellifluous renditions of haunting ballads and old favorites.

PHILLIP HARRINGTON

Elvis Presley: His suggestive pelvic gyrations shocked his elders and shook the young. Hordes of adolescents made the "King of Rock and Roll" a millionaire, and battalions of imitators aspired to equal his erotic aura and appeal.

◄ Louis Armstrong—"Satchmo": The perfection of his trumpet playing and the rattlings of his hoarse voice made the genial man with the mouth like an open satchel one of the immortals of jazz. Armstrong's sweating, grinning infectiousness could no more be duplicated than could the style that made him a star even behind the Iron Curtain.

273

(left to right). Paul McCartney, Ringo Starr, George Harrison, John Lennon.

(left to right). George Harrison, Ringo Starr, Paul McCartney, John Lennon. ▶

Robert Frost: Deceptively simple, colloquial in phrasing, his spare, evocative verse has the enduring strength of the New England tradition in which it is rooted.

BOB LERNER

JOHN VACHON

Carl Sandburg: Lincoln biographer, historian, poet. He shocked the purists, as had Walt Whitman, with the blunt honesty of his free verse and his use of contemporary slang and idioms. But his celebrations of his country—its people, its cities, and its past—have made him Whitman's heir as the singer of American democracy.

Ernest Hemingway: hunter, boxer, ▶ expatriate. In his life "Papa" sought out experiences he could then treat in his fiction. With a cool, lean, and detached narrative technique and laconic prose, his novels deal with elemental conflicts— war, sex, politics, violent death—in stories about tough, cynical, moody men and women who are nevertheless romantic underneath the surface.

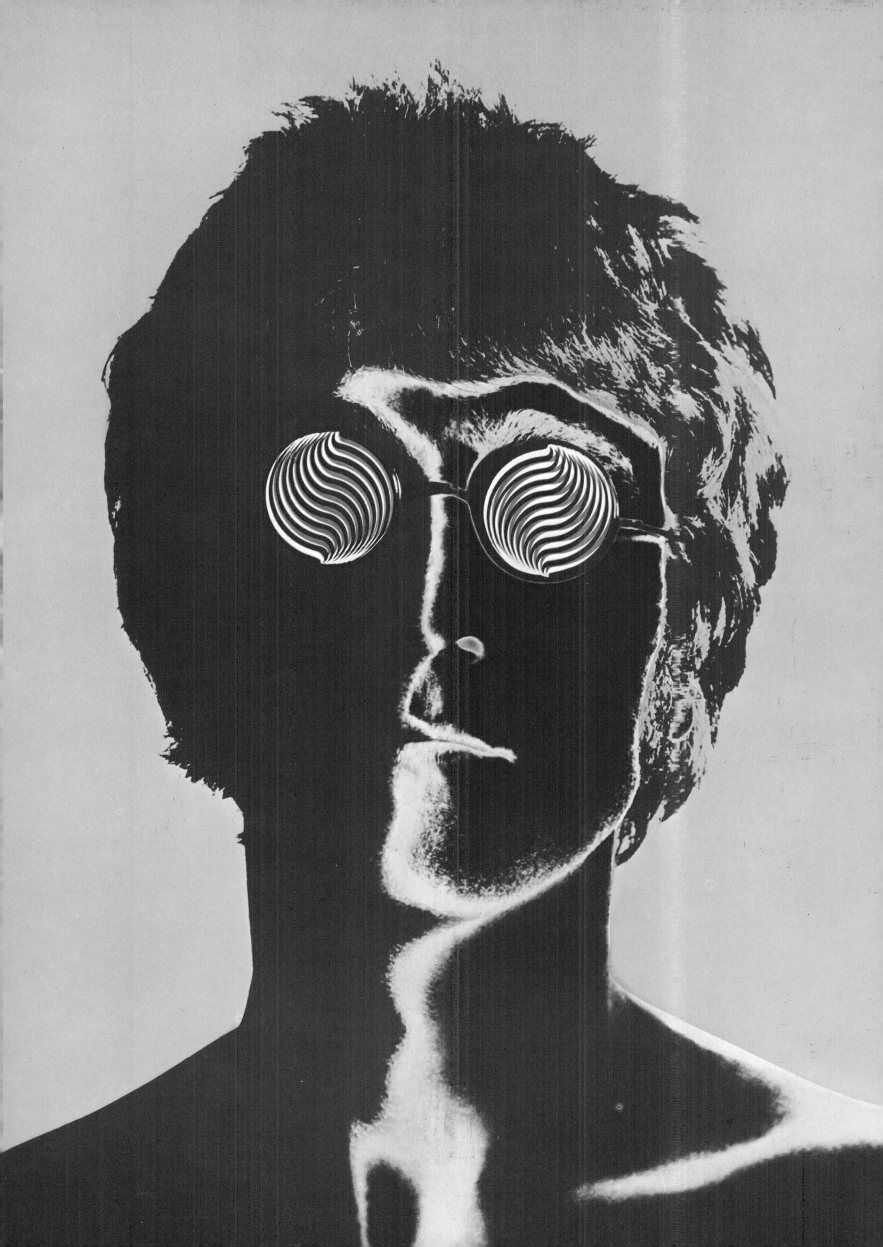

The Beatles: Jelly beans and flowers pelted the stage floor, thousands of teenagers screamed, cried, swooned, or went into delirious transports during the Beatles' deafeningly amplified performances. Original, cocky, magnetic, the four English moppets became the new idols, and around the world shaggy hair replaced the crewcut, "mod" clothes displaced the pinstriped suit. Their early, earsplitting music was the curse of adults and the craze of the young. But their style went through countless transformations, revolutionizing both the sound and the message of pop music. Once considered an affront to the ear, their compositions are now seriously studied as a true contribution to the art of the 20th century. The magnificent composite portrait and the four astounding studies in color by Richard Avedon capture the compelling personalities of the group and the psychedelic mood of their music.

Somerset Maugham: astringent,
detached, Edwardian, a superb storyteller.
Although disparaged by some critics
because of their popular appeal, his
novels, plays, and short stories are distinguished by penetrating satire and
skillful technique. His *Writer's Notebook*
ranks among the best analyses of the
writer's craft.

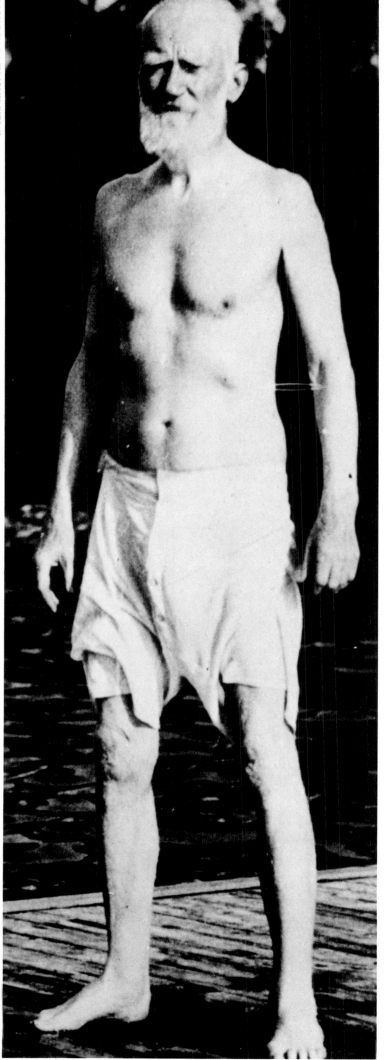

Two critics of society: In his columns spoofing national and international leaders, impish Art Buchwald (above) uses laughter as an effective weapon against governmental absurdity and human foibles. George Bernard Shaw (left) made hypocrisy and social conventions the targets of his biting wit in plays, essays, music criticism, and deliberately outrageous public statements. His plays opened up English theater to political and social themes. His epigrams are priceless: "An Englishman thinks he is moral when he is merely uncomfortable." …"My way of joking is to tell the truth; it's the funniest joke in the world."… "Lack of money is the root of all evil."

William Saroyan: prolific writer, prolific talker. He has been a published writer for 40 years—longer than Dickens, de Maupassant, or Chekov, as he himself has exuberantly remarked.

Arnold Toynbee: erudite, omniscient, controversial. When his 12-volume *A Study of History* was issued in abridged form, it became an immediate best-seller and a source of scholarly dispute. Acknowledged as a universal historian, he has been criticized for the rigidity of the patterns, especially in regard to religion, that he has drawn from his study of civilizations.

James Baldwin: native son turned expatriate; essayist and novelist. One of the first writers to give voice to black discontent, he has viewed the black scene with pitiless candor and galvanized white society to new self-examination.

Sinclair Lewis: the first American to win the Nobel Prize for Literature. His eye-opening novels *Main Street* and *Babbitt* were not only tremendously successful; their titles almost immediately became a part of our language as synonyms for small-town provincialism and a certain type of narrow-minded, go-getting American businessman.

In the expressive mime of Marcel Marceau, actions do speak louder than words. Explaining the appeal of his beloved character Bip, he commented: "With his battered hat and its brave little flower that symbolizes some dreamed-of glamour [he parades] in white-face up and down the boulevards of the world, watching, listening with a timid ear and a wistful face to the laughter, tears, and applause of the people who identify themselves with him."

THE GAMES WE PLAY

Every child first plays spontaneously and then, later, learns the satisfaction of structured games: the exuberance of speed and strength; the excitement of pitting skill and daring against opponents in contests that ultimately may be decided by chance. Greeks wrestled, Egyptians rowed, Roman gladiators fought. To this day the human race loves not only the pleasure of participation but also the spectacle and panoply of sports. Both amateur and professional competitions attract such avid audiences that Karl Marx might have called sports, rather than religion, "the opium of the masses."

Television and closed-circuit screenings can beam any nation's sporting events throughout the country and even the world. Cameras catch the action from every angle, magnifying its excitement and glory. Never before have so many fans (the word comes from "fanatic") thrilled to the performances of skilled athletes and the drama of the unpredictable, which invests any game.

—Ed.

JOHN VACHON

The joyful activity of a carefree child is part of a professional boxer's rigorous training program.

Rocky Graziano: the superb body and fighter's face signal tension before the bell. Powerful but erratic, he remarked: "I'm not a good fighter, I'm a puncher." Yet that punch earned him his nickname, "The Rockabye Kid."

Joe Louis—"The Brown Bomber":
A man of gentle character, he was, at the height of his career, a champion of surpassing power.

STANLEY KUBRICK

LOOK

N.Y. DAILY NEWS PHOTO

An opponent's savage, smashing punch brought Kid Gavilan close to concussion. Such violence and its often irreparable effects have led to repeated public demands that boxing be outlawed.

Muhammed Ali (né Cassius Clay): handsome, ▶ impudent, a cocksure clown who coins doggerel fit for oblivion. A superlative boxer with lethal hands, he has taunted and knocked out more than 30 opponents. At the age of 34, his superb body still "floats like a butterfly" and his fists "sting like a bee."

Y. A. Tittle was the star quarterback of the New York Giants, a peerless forward passer, and an outstanding field general. His enthusiasm and stoic confidence—at various times he assaulted the field with broken wrists, fractured cheekbones, damaged knees, and a collapsed lung— were a constant inspiration to his teammates.

On the bench, "Broadway Joe" Namath intently waits for his chance to reenter the quarter. His strategic genius is backed up by the spitfire power of his throwing arm, but the number of his playing years will depend on the endurance of his celebrated knees.

◂ Millions of American fans turn out every weekend of the season to watch the masterly tactics and passionate melees of pro football.

Brute beauty and flashing valor shine in
the blazing spectacle of pro football.

BOB SANDBERG

The aspiring professional. He may trip over the baggy pants, but only after a determined swing.

Willie Mays gets a bead on the ball ▶ in the California sun. Versatile, a natural-born ballplayer, he is remembered for his agile center-field plays, dazzling base stealing, and championship hitting.

The padding weighs almost more than
the boy whose fond father helps him dress
for the fray.

◄ Hockey: lightning on ice, a rough sport
where collisions of emotions and players
often result in bloody brawls—in which
spectators frequently join.

Bob Cousy's fantastic leap foils a helpless opponent. A brilliant dribbler, shooter,
playmaker, defenseman, he was unstop-
pable in the clutch and led the Boston
Celtics to seven championships.

Towering height and ball-handling
wizardry made UCLA's Lew Alcindor a
natural candidate for the professional
leagues. Now, as the Los Angeles Lakers'
Kareem Abdul-Jabbar, he is the best center
in the game.

Bobby Jones: In the 1920's, when golf caught the American imagination, this elegant amateur became the game's first idol.

Arnold Palmer: He continues the tradition of golfing greats, having won the prestigious Masters tournament a then record-setting four times. His charm and superb sportsmansh endear him to a legion of fans known as "Arnie's Army."

TONY TRIOLA

Jack Kramer: Brash and aggressive, he gave tennis dramatic impact with his "Big Game" and "Big Serve," and professional status with his insistence that tennis prizes be equal to those of other sports.

Arthur Ashe: Long considered a fine player of unfulfilled potential, he was dubbed "always the bridesmaid but never the bride" until 1975, when he roundly defeated the seemingly invincible Jimmy Connors at Wimbledon, the premier event of tennis.

303

ROBERT GOODMAN

In Australia lawn bowling is not only a serious sport, but a social activity. Manners are always genteel, but the competition is stiff.

◄ Judo, karate, and Kung Fu are Eastern forms of the art of self-defense, but they have caught on in America as well. Americans, however, are more impressed by the startling effectiveness of these sports than by their stylized grace.

305

Surfboarding took a surprisingly long
time to move from Hawaii to Malibu. Now
surfers "hang five" on every coastline
around the world.

Crewmen take an unexpected dip as ▶
their craft runs aground.

To devotees of sailing, nothing is as absorbing—and enslaving —as a boat, for sails, like gigantic wings, free men from terra firma.

1.

2.

3.

4.

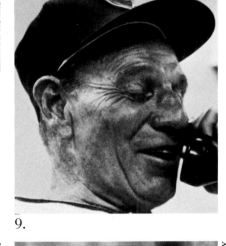

8.

9.

10.

11.

15.

16.

17.

18.

23.

24.

25.

26.

6.

AP

DO YOU REMEMBER?

(for answers see page 312)

CHARLOTTE BROOKS

KEN RARICH

ARTHUR ROTHSTEIN

13.

14.

CULVER PICTURES INCORPORATED

MICHAEL VACCARO

20.

21.

JOHN VACHON

PICTORIAL PARADE

28.

29.

22.

Answers to "Do You Remember?"

1. Mary Pickford
2. Laurel and Hardy
3. Norma Shearer
4. William Faulkner
5. Carole Lombard
6. Ty Cobb
7. Frederic March
8. Irving Berlin
9. Leo Durocher
10. Hedy Lamarr
11. Rudy Vallee
12. Richard Rodgers
13. Gertrude Lawrence
14. Mary Martin
15. Artie Shaw
16. Clara Bow
17. Richard Tucker
18. George Raft
19. John Barrymore
20. Risë Stevens, Lily Pons, Dorothy Kirsten
21. Robert Taylor
22. Twiggy
23. Jeanette MacDonald
24. Jesse Owens
25. Eugene O'Neill
26. Myrna Loy
27. Vladimir Horowitz
28. Al Jolson
29. Irene and Vernon Castle

LOOK
TREASURY

The Arts in America

BY JOHN F. KENNEDY

The life of the arts, far from being an interruption, a distraction in the life of a nation, is very close to the center of a nation's purpose—and is a test of the quality of a nation's civilization. That is why we should be glad today that the interest of the American people in the arts seems at a new high.

Looking at the American scene, I am impressed by its diversity and vitality—by the myriad ways in which Americans find enlightenment, exercise, entertainment and fulfillment. Books have become a billion-dollar business; more money is spent each year in going to concerts than to baseball games; our galleries and museums are crowded; community theaters and community symphony orchestras have spread across the land; there are an estimated 33 million Americans who play musical instruments. And all this expresses, I believe, something more than merely the avidity with which goods of all kinds are being acquired in our exuberant society. A need within contemporary civilization, a hunger for certain values and satisfactions, appears to be urging us all to explore and appreciate areas of life which, in the past, we have sometimes neglected in the United States.

Too often in the past, we have thought of the artist as an idler and dilettante and of the lover of arts as somehow sissy or effete. We have done both an injustice. The life of the artist is, in relation to his work, stern and lonely. He has labored hard, often amid deprivation, to perfect his skill. He has turned aside from quick success in order to strip his vision of everything secondary or cheapening. His working life is marked by intense application and intense discipline. As for the lover of arts, it is he who, by subjecting himself to the sometimes disturbing experience of art, sustains the artist—and seeks only the reward that his life will, in consequence, be the more fully lived.

Today, we recognize increasingly the essentiality of artistic achievement. This is part, I think, of a nationwide movement toward excellence—a movement which had its start in the admiration of expertness and skill in our technical society, but which now demands quality in all realms of human achievement. It is part, too, of a feeling that art is the great unifying and humanizing experience. We know that science, for example, is indispensable—but we also know that science, if divorced from a knowledge of man and of man's ways, can stunt a civilization. And so the educated man—and very often the man who has had the best scientific education—reaches out for the experience which the arts alone provide. He wants to explore the side of life which expresses the emotions and embodies values and ideals of beauty.

Above all, we are coming to understand that the arts incarnate the creativity of a free society. We know that a totalitarian society can promote the arts in its own way—that it can arrange for splendid productions of opera and ballet, as it can arrange for the restoration of ancient and historic buildings. But art means more than the resuscitation of the past: it means the free and unconfined search for new ways of expressing the experience of the present and the vision of the future. When the creative impulse cannot flourish freely, when it cannot freely select its methods and objects, when it is deprived of spontaneity, then society severs the root of art.

A nation's government can expect to play only an indirect and marginal role in the arts. Government's essential job—the organization and administration of great affairs—is too gross and unwieldy for the management of individual genius. But this does not mean that government is not, or should not be, concerned with the arts. A free government is the reflection of a people's will and desire—and ultimately of their taste. It is also, at its best, a leading force, an example and teacher. I would hope that in the years ahead, as our cultural life develops and takes on new forms, the Federal Government would be prepared to play its proper role in encouraging cultural activities throughout the nation.

To work for the progress of the arts in America is exciting and fruitful because what we are dealing with touches virtually all the citizens.

There will always be of necessity, in any society, a mere handful of genuinely creative individuals, the men and women who shape in words or images the enduring work of art.

De Tocqueville, in the 1830's, described how on the remotest frontiers, in a wilderness that seemed "the asylum of all miseries," Americans preserved an interest in cultural and intellectual matters. "You penetrate paths scarcely cleared," said de Tocqueville; "you perceive, finally, a cleared field, a cabin . . . with a tiny window." You might think, he continues, that you have come at last to the home of an American peasant. But you would be wrong. "The man wears the same clothes as you; he speaks the language of the cities. On his rude table are books and newspapers."

The cabin with its tiny window has vanished. Yet we might expect to find its counterparts today in homes which would seem quite as remote from the arts.

To further the appreciation of culture among all the people, to increase respect for the creative individual, to widen participation by all the processes and fulfillments of art—this is one of the fascinating challenges of these days.

Brigitte Bardot, Coco Chanel and Me

BY BETTY ROLLIN

Brigitte Bardot is not in the phone book. If you want to see her, you call her agent in Paris. Exactly five-thirty-one Wednesday afternoon, I appeared at the office of Bardot's agent, Olga Horstig, and, together, we entered a small apartment building, inched into a tiny birdcage elevator and jerked to the top. A young, rather plain secretary opened the door and asked us . . . to ascend a small green-carpeted stairway with green-flowered wallpaper.

At the top, a maid waved us into a tiny, romantic, dark, red-all-over sitting room. I looked around. Between the top of some bookshelves and the ceiling, I noticed a row of about ten drawings of Herself, ranging from the Coney Island variety to a few that were pretty good. The shelves held *some* books, but mostly a plethora of teeny things: Scottish eensy weensies—little tartan boxes and dolls—jade eggs, and a surly porcelain cat whose belly said "God Save the Queen."

The maid suddenly shot in, struck a match and lit four red candles in silver candlesticks on a low coffee table. A moment later, Bardot entered.

She was *adorable*. Not that I could see that much of her. Her hair was stuffed into a black-leather cap that was pulled down over her forehead. A white super-turtleneck sweater almost cleared her chin, and although her black-leather suit (shorts and a vest) was crotch-high, so were (almost) a pair of black-leather boots. So, what showed were two inches of upper thigh and the face. I'm not the best upper-thigh judge, but the face looked pretty good.

The face is not beautiful, just cute. But cute carried to the nth degree. It has fantastic oomph. There are global eyes made up like crazy for eye oomph; there is a nose in perfect miniature for nose oomph; and there is a three-month-old mouth for mouth oomph. And the way her teeth stick out adds what I can only call, at the risk of your throwing up, teeth oomph.

Don't get any funny ideas. I am a girl who likes men—absolutely. But I have two eyes and appreciate another of my gender doing a good job on herself, which is precisely what BB has done.

". . . If I can spen five minutes to nave thee bath in thee sun, I do it." She was winding up some story, the point of which was, I think, that Americans are so serious about their work and don't stop everything to take sunbaths. "I had one American fren," she had started out. "He was from thee movie company, and he come to find me on the beach, to find out if everything was *fantastique*. I say, yes, everything is *fantastique*, but take off your suit and thee tie for a bath in thee sun. He say no. He was so working, you see. It is *fantastique*, thee Americans." She dropped off the eensy settee onto the floor.

I kept getting this odd feeling that Brigitte had spent the entire afternoon with her girl friends, trying on high heels and makeup and listening to records and giggling. "I adore people who are beautiful," she said, when I asked her who her friends were. "All of my frens, they are beautiful. I think a girl looks more beautiful if she is wiz another beautiful girl, you know? I have a lut of faults," she went on, softly. "I am so impatient. I have thee bad temper like my grandfather. I am gay; and five minutes later, I want to die. I can give the best of myself to a man I love, and then I am empty."

I got out of there fast.

"You must go to Chez Castel," she called as I left. "It is a *fantastique* discotheque. It is on Princesse Street. Theenk of Princesse, and you will remember!"

The appointment with Coco Chanel was rescheduled for the day I was flying to Rome. Lunch at two was cutting it close; but apparently, Mlle. Chanel does not get up until one.

(Mlle. Chanel sleeps at her Ritz apartment, but she also has a suite that sits like icing on top of her salon. We were headed there.)

It's blurry now, but I remember passing through a gargantuan door into a foyer where two life-size black Africans (statues) stood with their arms out to welcome us. Then, the sitting room—what wasn't large and velvet was large and gold. There were black Oriental screens, gold, Attila-the-Hun-like mirrors and haughty gold lions under the coffee table. In the dining room, a waiter in tails and white gloves—the cotton kind that stranglers wear in movies—stood like the black statues outside, only he was white. The table glistened with polished wood, champagne, silver and a porcelain monkey.

But nothing in that room glistened like Mlle. Chanel. She sat at the head of the table in one of her own white-wool suits, with gold jewelry everywhere—stuck into the front of her suit, on her hat, clanging wildly on her arms as she gestured—which she did constantly as she spoke, which she did constantly. Three black curls sat like the three monkeys in the middle of her forehead. Her mouth was narrow and lipsticked in blood red. She had pinked her cheeks and penciled her eyes, and she was 86 and she looked great. I didn't understand one word she said, but I was so enchanted, and *she* seemed to be having such a nice time, chattering away like a feathered bird, I just kept nodding and *oui-oui*-ing as if I understood. Later, I found out what she had said: "I have nothing against Cardin. He has never done anything to me, but he's an amateur. I create clothes to last ten years, the others make gimmicks that change tomorrow. Don't ask me to speak about today's fashions. This is a bad period. There is no romanticism anymore, no sense of what is ridiculous. You see a young man in front of you in the street in pants, and then he turns around, and he's a 50-year-old woman. A woman should not disguise herself as a man. I despise eccentricities. . . .

"You know Madame Alphand, the wife of the Ambassador? She works at Cardin. What is an Ambassador's wife doing as a salesgirl? Where would we all be if all ambassadors' wives wanted to be salesgirls?

"I do not like this style of short clothes. Most people's knees are ugly. The dress should hide the knee."

Squeaking slightly, the white statue began to serve lunch. But it was the zero hour for getting to the airport, so, profusely begging apology, I got up. It was quickly translated to Mlle. Chanel that the flight was the last one to Rome, and that I had to work there the next morning. As I got up, she got to her feet as well. I said no, no, you mustn't, and she said no, no, she understood perfectly, and, as she held both of my hands in hers, said that she would speak to the translator the next day and give her the most wonderful interview for me and that I would have a wonderful article, and that she would answer any questions and answer even the questions she was not asked!

The next evening, the translator called me in Rome, as I knew she would, to tell me the result of her interview with Chanel. But, apparently, there had been no interview: "Listen, I called Grumbach, and she said that Chanel told her that if you were so goddamn anxious to interview her, you would have missed your goddamn plane." I sat down on the corner of the bed and rubbed my arm, which I had thrown out of joint swinging at a creepy Roman who pinched me on the Via Bolognese.

Jack Benny's 39 Years

BY WILLIAM SAROYAN

Me, Jack Benny? I should live so long. Thirty-nine years. I was 39 several years ago. He was 39 at least 20 years ago but he keeps saying he's still 39, and the funny part about it is, he is—or younger even. I've seen a lot of 'em 39 and less, but I've never seen one yet who was half as young as Jack.

Of course, I'm not Jack Benny, but I sometimes think I am. It happens when I listen to him. It started happening 23 years ago when I was 23 and Jack Benny was 10 or 20 years older.

What did he have? Style.

Jack Benny had style from the beginning. He stood straight and walked kind of sideways as if he were being gently shoved by a touch of genius—and knew it, and knew you'd know it too, in a moment.

Style. If you've got it, you don't need much else. If you haven't got it—well, I hate to do it, but I've got to borrow from [James] Barrie—if you haven't got style, it doesn't matter what else you've got. Unless it's money. But did you ever see a banker who made you smile; let alone bust out laughing?

Take the case of Benjamin Kubelsky, for instance. Ben was born 61 years ago in a hospital somewhere in Chicago, about 35 miles from the home of his father, Meyer [which was] on an unimportant street in an unimportant suburb named Waukegan, Ill. Meyer Kubelsky ran a saloon for a while, and then a clothing store.

At an early age, blue-eyed Benjamin, Ben or Benny Kubelsky was sent, not with a cow, but with a violin, either to sell it, trade it or play it, and all kinds of strange, terrible and wonderful things began to happen to him too.

With an order of poetic justice impossible to account for, his first name, Benjamin, became Jack, and his last name, Kubelsky, became the diminutive of his first name, Benny, making his name, in full, Jack Benny. Jack Benny, as everybody knows, means an imaginary character performed by a real man who for almost a quarter of a century has stood tall and straight and quietly defied the world not to laugh at him.

Benny is not the only apostle of the democratic qualities of faith and piety and courage, but he's one of the best. The record speaks for itself. Look up the other apostles and you'll find they didn't have the mortal staying power of this boy at all. If you survive, there's always a good reason, and he survived. Him and his valet, Rochester, for instance, and his Maxwell, and his laughing, hearty, overweight announcer. Announcer? In Benny's world, he became the ambassador to Main Street from the fat men of the nation, the man who eats a light lunch of—name it, name a lot of good, wholesome, starchy food. And his bandleader, always a loud and raffish guy with a fine group of musicians who sneak drinks out of the plumbing of their cornets and trombones.

There are a lot of good American clowns and, as the poets and playwrights of Ireland gave Ireland its best identity, the clowns and cutups of America are giving America its most effective gathering-together of something like a collective nature—and Benny is one of the best of the clowns.

A clown at work for money? Is that it? Well, money's there, of course, but where would we prefer to have it? With the bankers alone? Hell, they're a humorless lot and there's no way we can think that they ever did a lot for us.

He makes me laugh, as the saying is. I thank him. You do too, most likely.

The Secret Letters of Julius Marx

Marx's origin, like so much about him (hair, socks, hangnails), is shrouded in mystery. Take, for example, so simple a matter as his birth. A careful search through Marx's entire correspondence reveals only one letter (to *The Journal of Oat Propagation*) which casts any light on his early years, viz.:

Gentlemen: I was born during a volcanic eruption in one of the banana countries of Central America. I don't remember which one. I don't even remember the bananas; in fact, I hardly remember the stalk.

At the age of three, an utter stranger apprenticed me to a basket weaver in Guatemala. I soon learned to weave with such dexterousness that, by the time my second teeth arrived, I was known throughout the village as the basket child of Guatemala.

After I was run out of Guatemala, I met two other fellows, named, I believe, Harpo and Chico. They are brothers but they are both strangers to me. As for Sam Marx of MGM, who reluctantly confesses to being their cousin—the truth of the matter is that he is their joint child by a former marriage.

Yours truly, Groucho Marx

Dear Irving: I have been toying with the idea of making you my child's godfather. Before doing this, I would like to see a notarized statement of your assets.

I don't intend to repeat the unhappy experience that befell my own parents late in the 19th century. At that time, there was an Uncle Julius in our family. He was five feet one, had a brown spade beard, thick glasses and a head topped off with a bald spot the size of a buckwheat cake. Now my mother somehow got the notion that Uncle Julius was very wealthy, so she told my father (who never did understand my mother) that it would be a brilliant piece of strategic flattery to make Uncle Julius my godfather.

Well, as happens to all men, I was born. And before I could say "Gesundheit," I was named Julius. At that very moment, Uncle Julius was in the backroom of a cigar store on Third Avenue, dealing them off the bottom. When word reached him that he had been made my godfather, he dropped everything, including two aces he had up his sleeve for an emergency, and rushed over to our flat.

In a speech so moist with emotion that he was blinded by his own glasses, he hinted that my future was irrevocably linked with his. At the conclusion of his speech, unable to see, he kissed my father, handed my mother a cigar and ran back to the pinochle game. Two weeks later, he moved into the house, paper suitcase and all.

As time went by, my mother became suspicious. She not only discovered that Uncle Julius was without funds but that he owed my father $34. Since he was only five feet one, my father volunteered to throw him out. Mother said, "Let's wait a little longer." She had read of cases where rich men live miserly lives, then leave tremendous fortunes.

Well, Uncle Julius remained with us until I got married. By this time, he had the best room in the house—and owed my father $84.

My mother finally admitted that Uncle Julius had been a hideous mistake and ordered my father to give him the bum's rush. But Uncle Julius had grown an inch over the years, while my father had shrunk proportionately. Father convinced my mother that violence was not the solution to the problem.

Uncle Julius solved everything by kicking off. His estate, when probated, consisted of a nine-ball he had stolen from a poolroom, a box of liver pills and a celluloid dickey.

I suppose I should be more sentimental about the whole thing, but it was a severe shock to all of us. If I can help it, that sort of thing is not going to happen to my child.

Well, son, that's the story. If you are interested, let me hear from you. And remember, a financial statement will expedite things considerably.

Yours, Groucho

Dear Friend: I have had a pretty busy time of it. First I did a Command Performance for the Army—no money. Then I auditioned a radio show—for free. Then I did a guest column—for nothing. Today I am recording a speech for a heart specialist in Chicago. The only thing I can get out of this is that some day I may be lucky enough to get a heart attack in the Loop.

Ever yours, Groucho

When *Copacabana* was previewed, Marx took one look, honed his trusty cutlass and wrote the Messrs. Wilson, Green and Sobol:

Gentlemen: I have labored long and hard in the theatrical vineyards, and, frankly, my career cannot stand the handicap of being seen in the same picture with three refugees from a packing house.

When America gets a glimpse of Variety's *editor,* Billboard's *circulation will double. Green, who comes over with all the virility of a floorwalker in a beauty parlor, once told me he was a compelling personality. He is. His appearance will compel millions to stay away from movies forever.*

Sobol, fortunately, is so tiny that it is difficult to see him with the naked eye—and I doubt whether many people will don glasses just for the purpose.

As for Wilson, he comes over as a cross between Rocky Graziano and Gertrude Stein. Wilson, your shape is against you. You are too fat for Rathbone parts and too thin for Green-street roles. Squat figures are a dime a dozen out here. Besides, most of Hollywood's ingénues are taller than you are.

Wilson, my advice to you is to steer clear of the movies. Perhaps if there's a sequel to The Yearling, *you might play the bear—but even that's a grisly thing to contemplate.*

Groucho

Wilson tried to mollify Marx, but Marx could be as bitter as Byron. In a letter which is preserved under glass at Liederkranz High, he wrote:

Dear Wilson: You say you recently went to see Duck Soup *and* Animal Crackers. *Since I have no financial interest in either of these pictures, it made me shudder to think of all that money flowing to Paramount.*

I am, first of all, an artist—but for some strange reason, I seem to become increasingly crazy about money. The thought that you are spending your dough to see something that adds nothing to my bank roll fills me with anguish, remorse and woe (which, by the way, wouldn't be a bad name for a vaudeville act).

The French you quote at the bottom of your letter is, I assure you, not the French I am interested in.

Groucho Marx

Who, since Gibbon, has written English with so elegant a cadence?

Like all geniuses, Marx was racked by melancholia. His very soul, his inner *geist*, as R. H. Macy once described it, was a battleground on which hope clashed with despair. One morning in August, 1948, for instance, the Master received a routine communication from his bank:

Dear Mr. Marx: I think you might be interested to know that twenty years ago you opened your account with the Guaranty Trust Company of New York.

We have enjoyed this long banking relationship and do not want this occasion to pass without telling you of our appreciation. We sincerely hope that we may have the privilege of serving you for many years to come. If ever we can be of assistance, please let us know.

Cordially yours, Joseph D. Dent, Assistant Secretary

To this Marx replied with a directness unequaled in English *lettres:*

Dear Mr. Dent: Frankly, the best assistance you can give me is to steal some money from the account of one of your richer clients and credit it to mine.

Yours truly, Groucho Marx

Marx was a stickler for exactitude. Nothing aroused his ire like exaggeration. When *Variety* loosely reported on the *réclame* his brothers Harpo and Chico were garnering as individual performers, our bard wrote the editor:

Dear Sir: You state that the Marx Brothers can get $20,000 a week working as a unit again. Apparently you are under the impression that the only thing that matters in this world is money. This is quite true.

Sincerely yours, Col. J. G. Quackenbush

The Opdyck-Beamish school suggests that, as a stylist, Marx is a wee bit *too* pure, like a mountain stream which is pure because it is cold. To such, one can only retort, "Faugh!" If there is anything the true lover of Marx knows, it is that his words cover untapped wells of emotion.

Consider, for instance, the famed epistle to his brother Chico, now recited daily in so many schoolrooms throughout our land:

Dear Ravelli: To begin with, you are a liar. You didn't write to me at all. I wrote you. Now that that's straightened out, I want to say that I have nothing to say.

I was happy to read that "Hurrah for Captain Spaulding" was so well sung by your political friends. You say that they knew it better than you. Frankly, do you know anyone who doesn't know it better than you?

Ravelli, I have never told you this, but as a pianist, I am no great admirer of yours. You are a handy man with a deck of cards, and I understand there have been times when you were facile with the galloping cubes, but as a musician, you leave a great deal to be desired. After sitting on the stage for 25 years, listening to you grope your way through the ivories, I realize that there is a wide margin between your piano playing and that of, say, Vladimir Horowitz. You have many other qualities I admire, but as a pianist, as they say in Paris, "Pouf."

This is a hell of a lot more than I planned on writing, but I am basically a garrulous fellow, especially when someone else is taking the dictation.

Rufus T. Flywheel

We end on a softer, nobler note. Behind the mordant pen, beneath the biting wit, there is the gentle heart of a fawnlike man. For Julius Marx wore the mask of flippancy to hide a charming naïveté. The inner Marx was a man lost in a dream of the past. And it is this Marx—dauntless, gallant—who stands revealed in one of his last reminiscences, a letter so thoughtful, so nostalgic, so filled with a sense of history and the glory of man's past that it will stand beside the best of Macaulay:

Dear Sam Zolotow: For the past nine weeks, I've been leading a life that parallels Swain's Rat and Cat Act. This offering, in case you are too young to remember, consisted of six rats dressed as jockeys, perched on six cats dressed as horses, galloping furiously around a miniature race track. It was an extraordinary act. Alan Dale wrote in the New York Journal *of September 8, 1931:*

"Last night, Swain's Rats and Cats gave a performance that for beauty and sincerity hasn't been equaled since Beerbohm Tree played King Lear at the Old Garrick."

Of course, I get more salary than Swain paid his actors. As a matter of fact, they didn't get any *salary—Swain paid them in cheese. Each rat got two pounds a week. With the country facing a three-hundred-billion-dollar deficit, this may not seem like much, but remember, it was all* net.

The rats didn't have an agent—they knew their own kind and booked themselves independently. They didn't even have to shop for their cheese—they just sat in their dressing room and waited for Swain to throw their salary over the transom.

Frankly, I don't see where I am as well off as they were. Oh, of course, I get paid in money—but most of it goes for fuel, shelter and taxes. With the pittance that remains, I, too, buy cheese. But I have no manager to throw it over the transom. I have to take a bus to the grocery and shop for mine.

If my next picture turns out disastrously (and there is no reason why it shouldn't), I am going to look up Swain and ask him if he would be interested in reviving his act. I could play one of the jockeys.

Groucho Marx

The Funnymen

BY LEO ROSTEN

The following humorous biographies were written by Leo Rosten: "How to See Red…Skelton That Is"; "Bob Hope: Gags and Riches"; "Fat, Sad and Funny"; and "Slapstick with Sex Appeal: The Martin and Lewis Bonanza." —Ed.

How to See Red . . . Skelton That Is

The Skeltons were once staying at the Whitman Hotel in Camden, N.J. Red would come home late at night, exhausted from humoring the Walkathon cretins, all sweated up and shivering from the cold. He didn't own an overcoat. Edna had acquired a small bulldog, of which she was very fond, and it was one of Red's responsibilities to walk the creature. He had a harness made without Edna's knowing it and got a long, long rope. After that, he lowered the bulldog out of the third-story window. The dog would walk up and down the street, at one end of the rope, while Skelton, at the other, reclined blissfully on his bed.

It might have gone on like that to this very day—if not for the Eighteenth Amendment. That was the nasty one about Prohibition. And when it was repealed, all hell broke loose with Skelton and his little bulldog. Why? Well, it seems that certain gentlemen, frequenting a near-by saloon, began to complain bitterly to the owner about the quality of the whiskey he was serving. After a drink or two of his rot-gut, they averred, you began to see flying dogs. The saloonkeeper, a sober, home-loving type, thought it was an open-and-shut case of mass hysteria. He investigated. And he saw a flying dog. No doubt of it. A bulldog, floating out of a hotel window, right down to the ground, where it walked back and forth, attended a lamp post, then ascended.

The saloonkeeper counted up to a hundred and entered the Whitman Hotel. He threatened to drag Skelton into every court in the land unless the lowering and raising of dogs from hotel windows ceased at once.

[Later, in Canada,] Skelton was the m.c. at the Lido—and he was green and young. The veterans of vaudeville ignored him, patronized him, up-staged him or insulted him. Skelton even suffered from acute attacks of inferiority complex. To restore his self-confidence, he hit upon a device which performed miracles. Each Monday morning, before opening a new show, Red welcomed the new performer from the States with the utmost enthusiasm. "It's wonderful, your coming all the way up here to Montreal," he would say. "You'll knock 'em dead. These audiences go crazy over anyone who speaks French."

"French?" The new performer would blink uneasily. "What do you mean, French?"

Skelton would blink back innocently. "Why, you give your act in French, don't you? These people are all French Canadians, you know. They don't understand a word of English."

Then Skelton would go out front and, as his rival watched from the wings in agony, Red would open the show in flawless "French"—doubletalk garnished with Gallic intonations. The audience, knowing Skelton, howled with delight. His competitor, not knowing French, went ashen with horror. "By the time I'd get done with my monologue," Skelton reminisces fondly, "some of those fellows'd be so scared they'd be speechless."

He [Skelton] suffers from an ailment, hitherto unrecorded in medical literature, known as telephonophobia. For years and years, he refused to talk on the telephone. It confused him. "I just don't hear so good on it," he says. "People used to call up and keep asking me to do things and I'd agree. I got into the darnedest trouble, promising people things. Some people are just out to take advantage of you. It was terrible."

Shortly after Red and Edna got to Hollywood, the telephone rang in their hotel room. Edna took it, as usual. It was Louis B. Mayer's brother, Jerry, calling from the MGM lot. The conversation went something like this: "Let me talk to Red."

"Red doesn't talk on the phone, Mr. Mayer. But he's right here. I'll relay the message."

A strange sound issued from the phone at MGM.

"Do you mean to tell me that Skelton is standing there next to you and knows I'm on the phone and still he won't talk to me?"

"Yes, sir. But that's because—"

"Tell him to come right over to the studio! And you come along!"

When Red and Edna reached MGM, twenty minutes later, Mayer said, "Now you two listen to me. It's too soon for you to start going Hollywood on us. Who do you think you are, pulling a gag like that, about not talking on telephones?"

Edna explained that Red had a deep psychological antipathy to Alexander Graham Bell's device.

"Do you expect me to believe that?" Mayer asked.

Red just nodded miserably.

"Well—but—dammit, if you don't answer the phone, how do you get any business done?"

"That's what Edna's for," said Red.

Mayer fixed Red with a cold eye. "Young man, let me ask you one question. *Who answered the telephone before you met Edna?*"

"Before I met Edna, no one ever called me."

Skelton has it within him to become one of the most appealing clowns of our time. Not the least touching thing about this very funny, very sad, hopelessly helpless man-child is that he considers himself to be the luckiest mortal alive. Impressed by the saga of the bitter years of his poverty, I asked him what he considered his first real break. He grinned.

"When the doctor held me up by the feet and slapped my little behind."

Bob Hope:
Gags and Riches

Bob Hope was born with a chin that jutted, a nose that swooped and a profile that followed the clean, classic lines of a can opener. His father muttered darkly that evil forces had removed the baby and left the stork. His mother never even mentioned the infant's profile—on the theory, no doubt, that if no one talked about it, it would go away. It didn't. Instead, it flowered along its own mysterious lines until it drove Hope into a career which, for fame and mazuma, has rarely been equaled in the belly-laugh league.

The man's every move invites amusement. Where other faces flow, his lurches. Where profiles protrude, his caves in. He struts before an audience like the original Personality Kid, bares his many teeth and commits jokes.

He calls debutantes "barebacks with greenbacks," and sailors "wolves in ship's clothing." He defines a lorgnette as "a sneer on a stick." He describes the Irish Sweepstakes as "the only way Americans can get their money out of England." He says, "When Republicans play Pin-the-Tail-on-the-Donkey, they use ice picks." Some mathematical wizards estimate Mr. Hope has racked up over $500,000 a year, 10 years in a row, with side-stitchers like that.

His comic style is ageless. He is the permanent juvenile, at home in a beanie or a blazer, an 1890 straw or a 1940 zoot suit. He is the perfect symbol of the man Fate is determined to make a jerk.

He brags and blusters, but there isn't a child over five who can't outwit him, disarm him or steal his pants. He tries to act sharp, but you know he thinks a *bon mot* is a piece of chocolate. He is the type who gets his pocket picked while trying to rig the numbers at a church bingo.

Now all of this is the consequence of art, not accident. Robert is a superb clown and master of farce. But because farce is broad in its impact, the subtleties of its method are often lost on the yokels. No one in show business gives a funnier characterization of the second-class male. You can close your eyes and get an accurate image of Hope's creation just from that brash and breezy voice.

He is the unabashed Show-Off, the Card, the snappy guy who gets off hot ones at shoe salesmen's conventions while they're waiting for the girls to show up. He's a scream at fraternity smokers. He has well-scrubbed cheeks, can wiggle his ears and is a riot on the old kazoo.

A tie-fumbler and a neck-stretcher, he ogles the dames and hints at midnight seductions, but you know he'll end up with candied cashew nuts and a uke. He is Penrod playing Don Juan. The minute a babe sails into view, he breaks into a leer, but he breaks into a sweat if the girl so much as flutters her lashes. His leer, indeed, shows the triumph of innocence over intention. *His* type gets seasick in a boudoir. His face is meant to be seen not near a nightie but over a jazzbo tie, preferably the kind that lights up. Endlessly, he chases Lamour or Lamarr or Jane Russell, and his wolfery ends not in conquest but in giggles.

This take-off of the adult wolf with adolescent impulses is admirable for its insight and its accuracy. What Mr. Hope really does, in his parody of passion, is to make safe and faintly ludicrous the lechery that resides in every man.

In his movie roles, Hope has made a monumental contribution to American culture: Singlehanded, he took the curse off being a coward. In fact, he makes cowardice lovable. After decades of strong, silent men who sneer at fear, it's a pleasure to be in the presence of a guy who faints at the sight of blood. Hope is the coward's coward. He makes cowards feel like Men.

What makes the masses love Bob Hope is the smell of sincerity that comes out of the kitchen where all that gall is cooking. He is a sucker, sure, but a sucker is a man with a soft spot in the head—and the heart. Hope tries to end each show with an appeal for some charity or other, and with a straightforward statement about peace or Christmas, the U.N. or blood banks.

With Pearl Harbor, he enlisted in a personal crusade. He visited every theater of war, by plane and by jeep, on flat-tops and by helicopter, to entertain the troops. He made six overseas junkets and tallied close to a million miles. He visited front lines and replacement depots and every hospital he could get to. He put on as many as 20 shows a day and gave over 1000 performances in one year.

More than any entertainer of our time, he became the GIs' idol. His wisecracks were passed around like nuggets. In London, he said, "The blackout in Edinburgh is wonderful. You should see the Scotchmen running around developing film."

During a desert sandstorm in Algiers, he remarked, "The field is gaining altitude faster than the pilot." In a mess hall in Italy, he cracked, "This place is so crowded you put your food in your mouth and go outside and chew it." In Guadalcanal, he boasted, "Boy, were the soldiers at the last camp glad to see me! They actually got down on their knees. What a tribute! What a spectacle! What a crap game!"

He was under enemy fire in Bizerte and Palermo. In Sicily, he regaled an audience of 19,000 men just behind the front. In one hospital, a boy began to weep when Frances Langford sang *Embraceable You*. His arm had been amputated. Hope broke the awful tension with a crack that went around the world: "Men, the folks back home are having a terrible time with eggs. They just can't get powdered eggs. They have to use the old-fashioned kind you break open."

In North Africa, 600 men walked 10 miles to catch his show, missed it and started back to camp. Hope put his cast in a fleet of jeeps, overtook the hiking soldiers and put on an hour of monkeyshines in a deluge.

He wrote a book about his travels called *I Never Left Home*, and John Mason Brown, a critic who has not always admired Hope's style, said: "It is more than a funny book. It is a gallant one." At the end of the war, the War Department gave Hope the Medal of Merit. He deserved it. John Steinbeck wrote, "There is a man. There is really a man."

Fat, Sad and Funny

He has a repertoire of at least 300 comedy skits and character "take-offs." He opens with a monologue and ends in a sketch that reminds you of the Keystone Cops in a firehouse. He acts, sings, hollers and does body flips. About the only thing Gleason hasn't tried to do on his show is swallow swords, and five will get you ten he could if he set his mind to it. "Soon," the envious complained a year ago, "he'll be sewing the costumes and composing the music."

Gleason has not yet gotten around to sewing the costumes, but he does pass on the gowns his dancers wear, and on the long-stemmed beauties who wear them; and he did write the haunting theme song of the show, plus half a dozen other ballads. While putting some show girls and stooges through their paces not long ago, Jackie said, "That's what this show is after—straight men and curved girls." *The Gleason Hour* packs a wallop with both.

Hollywood's Jack Warner, a collector of off-beat talent, laughed so hard at Gleason's shenanigans one night that he signed him up at $250 a week and shipped him to the movie dungeons on the West Coast. Since he was an up-and-coming comic, Gleason was cast as a gangster. For two years, he shot his way through films with Humphrey Bogart and other Warnerites. "According to my contract, I had to buy my own bullets."

In one movie, Gleason was somehow cast in the role of an Arab. This involved his riding a particularly high-spirited Arabian steed. Gleason had about as much know-how on a horse as Marilyn Monroe would have playing *Rebecca of Sunnybrook Farm*—but he'd be caught dead before admitting there was any side of show business he hadn't mastered. He assured the director of the film that the blood of sheiks

321

flowed in his veins, arranged his burnoose with a flourish, spurred the apprehensive horse right toward the camera—and fell off. The director recovered his voice and screamed, "You said you could ride!" "What's the matter," said Gleason coolly, "don't you know a stunt man when you see one?"

"All my characters are psychologically constructed," says Gleason, and I quote him *verbatim*. "Each is consistent. I don't stray from the mirrors of actuality. I give each character a saving grace, a touch of sympathy. The audience see themselves in the characters, and this takes the heat and embarrassment off them."

Even The Loudmouth (a man I would cheerfully caress with a meat ax) has a *soupcon* of sympathy in Gleason's eyes. "He is basically insecure. That's what he's trying to cover up. He heckles guys who are less secure."

Or take Reggie Van Gleason III. An alcoholic roué with an outlandish cape, a stovepipe hat and a smudge-pot mustache, he pursues lechery with a monumental gall. Reggie is a living affront to the 4-H ideal. Yet he endears himself to our kiddies by squaring off to let Ma have a kick in the slats, or by slugging Pa on the back so filially that he ends up halfway through the scenery. Jackie says that Reggie, too, is sympathetic. (Don't go away.) "Reggie is basically lonesome. He's suspicious of everyone. He thinks everyone is waiting to do to him what he does to them. He fights back at life—loudly and unfairly. He treats others the way life has treated him."

We talked about the fact that so many comedians come from broken or unhappy homes. Their comedy seems to reflect a deep need to be loved. "Do you know any happy comics?" I asked.

"I don't know any happy *people*," he said. After a moment, he added, "How can anyone be happy in the kind of world we live in?"

Slapstick with Sex Appeal: The Martin and Lewis Bonanza

One hot, sweltering July, two young men named Martin and Lewis set foot upon the stage of New York's Paramount Theater. Life has never been the same. Dean Martin reeked of virility, resembled Cary Grant and sang like Bing Crosby. Jerry Lewis—well, Jerry Lewis can cross one eye at a time, touch his nose with his lower lip, bark like a seal or walk like a zombie with the seven-year itch. He imitates anything from a baboon to a burst appendix. While Martin crooned, hanging the bobby-soxers on the chandeliers, Lewis created a pretty good facsimile of a typical, un-

wholesome American boy who couldn't make the squad at the booby hatch.

Vaudeville has produced many rowdy and electric personalities in its star-studded years. But none of them—not Jimmy Durante, not Olsen and Johnson, not Abbott and Costello—uncorked the kind of comic pandemonium that Martin and Lewis let loose in the Paramount.

What accounts for this fantastic popularity? Our fair land has never felt a shortage of hit-and-run buffoons. We have certainly produced about every known variety of clown, comic or comedy team. But not until Martin and Lewis did the lively arts produce a combination so young, bright and brash that it had the daring to cross slapstick with sex appeal. *That* was something new in the theatrical heavens: bedroom eyes and belly laughs.

In private life, the boys have a loopy charm all their own. They have a genuine sense of nonsense. They also have a 24-karat sense of publicity. They are likely to butter your necktie or doodle on your shirt sleeve. They nail shoes to the floor or glue socks to the ceiling. They grab scissors to cut off the suspender buttons of any dear friend within reach. They pour water into people's pockets or salt their hair or put mustard on their combs. They stick cigarets in their noses and celery in their ears. They ride in New York taxicabs standing up, their heads through the sliding roof, playing gin rummy all the while. They use lines like: "I was walking around, counting my nostrils." They announce that their next picture will be *My Friend Irma Bites Lassie*, or *Son of Spellbound*. They make long-distance calls which go: "Hello, Charley?" Charley says: "Yes." "I'll be seeing you," says Martin or Lewis—and hangs up.

If you demur about having your cheek licked, your glasses soaped up or your suspenders severed, the boys make amends with the most rampant and unnerving humility. They fall prostrate on the ground, like Oriental slaves. They offer to mend your socks or Simonize your car. They kiss your shoes and beg you to beat them, stamp on their faces, break their fingers or lash their backs with a cat-o'-nine-tails.

The Western: The Legend and the Cardboard Hero

BY PETER HOMANS

He is the hero of every Western that ever thundered out of the movie or TV screen, this Galahad with a Colt .45

Adapted from "Puritanism Revisited: An Analysis of the Contemporary Screen-Image Western," published by the University of Chicago Press as part of a series "Studies in Public Communication" 1957-1962 Copyright

who stalks injustice on the dusty streets of Dodge. Or Carson City. Or Virginia City.

Once he accomplishes his mission, he vanishes into the mists, as do all true heroes of all true legends. But where Hercules goes to Olympus and King Arthur to Avalon, this galoot rides Old Paint into the sunset.

With few variations, the movies have been telling this story for more than half a century. There have, in fact, been Western movies as long as there have been movies; the first American narrative film was a Western, *The Great Train Robbery*, made in 1903. Without the Westerns, it would be hard to imagine television today. Far outstripping the rowdy little boys who were its first enraptured audience, the Western has gone round the globe to become the youngest of the world's mythologies. From the endless number of Westerns we have all seen, a basic concept emerges:

The Western takes place in a desolate, abandoned land. The desert, as a place without life, is indispensable. The story would not be credible were it set in a jungle, a fertile lowland or an arctic wasteland. This desert effect is contradicted by the presence of a town. Among the slapped-together buildings with false fronts, lined awkwardly along a road forever thick with dust, only three stand out—the saloon, the bank and the marshal's office (the hero's dwelling).

The saloon is the most important building in the Western. It is the only place in the story where people can be seen together time after time. It thereby functions as a meetinghouse, social center, church. More important, it is the setting for the climax of the story, the gunfight. No matter where the fight ends, it starts in the saloon.

The bank is a hastily constructed, fragile affair. Its only protection consists of a sniveling, timid clerk, with a mustache and a green eyeshade, who is only too glad to hand over the loot. Has there ever been a Western in which a robber wondered whether he could pull off his robbery?

The "good girl" is another supporting type in the cast of characters. Pale and without appetite, she is from the East and is classically represented as the new schoolmarm. The "bad girl" is alone in the world and usually works for her living in the saloon as a waitress or dancer. Both girls have their eye on the hero.

The bartender observes the action, but rarely becomes involved in it. "The boys," those bearded, grimy people who are always "just there" drinking and gambling in the saloon, function as an audience. No hero ever shot it out with his adversary without these people watching.

We meet the hero in the opening phase of the action. He is, above all, a transcendent figure, originating beyond the town. He rides into the town from nowhere; even if he is the marshal, his identity is disassociated from the people he must save. We know nothing of any past activities, relationships, future plans or ambitions. There are no friends, relatives, family, mistresses—not even a dog or cat—and even with his horse, he has a strangely formal relationship.

The hero indicates no desire for women. He appears somewhat bored with the whole business. He never blushes, or betrays any enthusiasm. His monosyllabic stammer and brevity of speech clearly indicate an intended indifference.

In the drinking scenes, we are likely to see the hero equipped with the traditional shot glass and bottle. We seldom see him pay for more than one drink. He gulps his drink, rarely enjoys it and is impatient to be off.

There are hundreds of variations of the villain, but each is unshaven, darkly clothed and from the West. Like the hero, he is from beyond the town. He is inclined to cheat at cards, get drunk, lust after women who do not return the compliment, rob banks and, finally, shoot people he does not care for, especially heroes.

The impact of this evil one on the town is electric, suddenly animating it with vitality and purpose. Indeed, it is evil, rather than good, that actually gives meaning to the lives of these people. Nevertheless, they all know (as we do) that they are of themselves ultimately powerless to meet this evil. What is required is the hero—a transcendent power originating from beyond the town.

Notice what has happened to this power. Gone are the hero's indolence and lack of intention. Now, he is infused with vitality, direction and seriousness, in order to confront this ultimate threat. Once the radical shift has been accomplished, the hero (like the audience) is ready for the final conflict.

While the fight can take many forms (fistfight, fight with knives or whips, even a scowling match in which the hero successfully glares down the evil one), the classic and most popular form is the encounter with six-guns. It is a built-up and drawn-out affair. The two men must adhere to an elaborate and well-defined casuistry as to who draws first. Although the hero's presence makes the fight possible—i.e., he insists on obstructing the evil one in some way; it is the latter who invariably attacks first. Were the hero ever to draw first, the story would no longer be a Western. With the destruction of the evil one, the action phase is completed.

The Western is, as most people by this time are willing to acknowledge, a popular myth that sets forth certain meanings about what is good and bad, right and wrong. Evil, according to the myth, is the failure to resist temptation. Temptation consists of five activities: drinking, gambling, moneymaking, sex and violence. Gambling is a situation over which one has rather limited control—one loses, but the hero does not lose. He wins. Wealth is not seized, although it is available to him through the unguarded bank. And both good girl and bad girl seek out the hero, to no avail—he remains a hero.

The derelict professional is derelict, and the nonviolent Easterner is weak, precisely because they have failed to resist temptation in the manner characteristic of the hero. Because these two types originate in the East, they have something in common with the good girl. Everything Eastern in the Western is weak, emotional, feminine. This covers family life, intellectual life, professional life. Only by becoming Westernized can the East be redeemed. The Western therefore is more a myth about the East than it is about the West; it is a secret and bitter parody of Eastern ways.

The Western bears a significant relationship to puritanism, in which it is the proper task of the will to rule and contain the spontaneous, vital aspects of life. Whenever vitality becomes too pressing, and the dominion of the will becomes threatened, the self must find some other mode of control. The puritan will seek a situation that allows him to express vitality while appearing to resist it. The Western provides just this opportunity, for the entire myth is shaped by the inner dynamic of apparent control and veiled expression. Indeed, in the gunfight, the hero's heightened gravity and dedicated exclusion of all other loyalties present a study in puritan virtue, while the evil one presents nothing more or less than the old New England Protestant devil—strangely costumed, to be sure—the traditional tempter whose horrid lures never allow the good puritan a moment's peace. In the gunfight, there are deliverance and redemption.

Here, then, is the real meaning of the Western: It is a puritan morality tale in which the savior-hero redeems the community from the temptations of the devil. Tall in the saddle, he rides straight from Plymouth Rock to a dusty frontier town, and though he be the fastest gun this side of Laramie, his Colt .45 is on the side of the angels.

The Short Courageous Life of Brian Piccolo

BY GALE SAYERS
WITH AL SILVERMAN

Brian Piccolo and I began rooming together in 1967, and we became close friends. It's easy to make a big deal out of the fact that he was white and I'm black and to wonder how we got along. But there was nothing to it, although I admit at first we did feel each other out.

I first met Pick at the All America game in Buffalo, after my senior year. The Bears brought Pick up in 1966, and we lockered next to each other. ("I had Dick Gordon on my left," he once said, "Sayers on my right. I felt like an Oreo cookie.")

He meant a lot to the Chicago Bears. His work wasn't always noticed, though, because he'd play a lot of *his* good games when *I* was having a good game. Then when Ronnie Bull banged up his knee in the Detroit game, Piccolo was switched to fullback and played alongside me and did a helluva job.

But just about this time, he began to cough. It wasn't much at first. Then we played in Pittsburgh and he still had the cough, and in Atlanta it really got bad. But he played the whole game well, and he scored a touchdown.

The Tuesday after the Atlanta game, Pick decided that he had better see a doctor. And that's when they discovered it was a tumor. And it was malignant.

That night, the night before the Baltimore game, Mr. Halas [owner of the Chicago Bears] called me again. He said, "Gale, I think maybe you ought to say something to the team before we go out tomorrow, try to dedicate the game to Brian."

I had never in my life talked to a team. I just said, "As you all know, Brian Piccolo is very, very sick. If you don't know it, you should know it. He's very, very sick and he might never play football again. So I think each of us should dedicate ourselves to giving our maximum effort to win this ball game and give the game ball to Pick. Then we can all sign the ball and take it up to him."

Dr. Beattie told Pick the tumor figured to be the size of a baseball. When they got it out—after a four-and-a-half-hour operation—it was closer to a grapefruit.

Considering everything he had gone through, he looked well, and he was in his usual good spirits. He had gotten thousands of cards and letters and he was all excited about an autographed picture and album he had received from Frank Sinatra.

Shortly after, he went out to play in the Astrojet golf tournament in Phoenix, in which they pair a professional baseball player with a professional football player. When he came back from the golf tournament, he called me to tell me about it. He also said that he had to go back to New York for more tests. He had discovered a lump on his chest.

He went into New York, and they put him on medicine for a while. They hoped that the medicine would reduce the tumor, but finally they decided he had to be operated on again and, a few weeks later, he underwent a third operation.

It happened that I have the same blood type as Pick—B positive—so I gave a pint. A couple of days later, just before he was to undergo his third operation, he was telling friends about how Gale Sayers had given him blood. "I don't know what it is," he said seriously, "but lately I've gotten an awful craving for chitlins."

As much as they cut into this man, as much as he was afflicted with terrible pain and discomfort, as much as he suffered because of this wicked disease, as much as he was faced with all those tortures, his spirit would not be destroyed. This was the beautiful nature of Brian Piccolo.

The Life Story of Branch Rickey

BY ARTHUR MANN

Given a free hand, Rickey built up a farm system that totaled 27 minor-league teams at the peak. The system was directed by Branch Jr., who had started four years previously during the MacPhail regime.

It was in 1945 that Rickey's idea of recruiting top ballplayers—of any race—came to full fruition. Two years of secret scouting had located a Negro player who satisfied all requirements on and off the field. Rickey was determined to go ahead with his plan, even though it would plunge him, the Dodgers, the press, the public and the South into as big an uproar as any sport had ever known.

The Negro player's name was Jackie Robinson. A former all-around college athlete, Robinson then was playing with the Kansas City Monarchs after an honorable discharge from the Army as a lieutenant.

Robinson arrived for his momentous interview with Rickey on August 28, 1945. Rickey sat behind a massive desk, rocking back and forth in a swivel chair, fingering a cigar. "Do you know why you're here?"

"I heard something about a colored ball club at Ebbets Field," said Robinson. "Is that it?"

"No," said Rickey. "I'm thinking of starting you out in Montreal. If you make good, you'll get a chance with the Dodgers. I want to win pennants! We need ballplayers!" Rickey whacked the desk. "Do you think you can make good in professional ball?"

Robinson hesitated. "If I got the chance."

"It'll take more than playing," said Rickey. "I wish it was only a matter of hits and runs and errors." He got up and waved his arms and bellowed. "They'll shout insults at you. They'll come in with their spikes up. The pitchers will throw at your head. *What will you do?*"

"They've been throwing at my head for a long time," said Robinson.

Rickey drew back as if to charge. "It's a crucial game. The score is tied. Everyone is screaming. I rush into second. We both go down." Rickey shot his face within an inch of Robinson's. "And as I come up I yell, 'You dirty black son-of-a------!' *What do you do?*"

Robinson frowned. "Mr. Rickey, do you want a ballplayer who's afraid to fight back?"

"I want a ballplayer *with guts enough not to fight back!*" Rickey cried. He wheeled around and faced Robinson and posed as a clerk in a Southern hotel who insultingly refuses to put Robinson up for the night. *"What would you do?"*

Rickey went on like that for a while, and then, during a pause, Robinson said, "I've got two cheeks. Is that it, Mr. Rickey?"

After three hours, Robinson agreed to accept a bonus of $3,500 to sign with the Montreal Royals at $600 a month. Rickey swore Robinson to secrecy. "Tell your mother or your girl—but no one else. No one at all!"

On October 23, Jackie Robinson flew to Montreal and signed with the Royals. And the lid blew right off baseball's roof. William Bramham, president of the minor leagues, issued a scathing statement: "Father Divine will have to look to his laurels—we can expect a Branch Rickey Temple to be built in Harlem. It is carpetbaggers of the white race who, under the guise of helping the Negro, use him for their own selfish ends. . . . " Dixie Walker, the popular outfielding star of the Dodgers, issued a prophetic statement from Birmingham: "As long as Robinson isn't with the Dodgers, I'm not worried."

Writers bombarded Rickey with questions, asking him whether he intended to sign more Negro players. Rickey replied: "I have looked at many, and I might find more." No one believed this—until Rickey threw another bombshell into baseball by signing Don Newcombe, Roy Campanella and two Negro pitchers for his minor-league clubs.

Rickey voluntarily made special arrangements to house Negro players around Florida's spring-training camps. He wished to observe local segregation laws and practices. He worried about Montreal's manager, Clay Hopper, who came from Mississippi and would be Robinson's boss.

One day, Rickey sat next to Hopper, watching a game at Daytona Beach. Rickey kept chuckling and jabbing his elbow into Hopper's side whenever Robinson made a brilliant play. When he exclaimed, "No other human being could have made *that* play!" Hopper turned and cried with deep emotion. "Mr. Rickey, do you really think niggers are human beings?"

Jackie Robinson

BY TIM COHANE

Before a series with the Brooklyn Dodgers, the Cincinnati Reds held a meeting.

Now I Know Why They Boo Me!

BY JACKIE ROBINSON

Last season, in a year when every game counted, I lost my head more than I ever had in my eight years as a major-leaguer. Fans—and some sportswriters—began calling me a "sorehead" and a "loudmouth," who wanted every break to go my way. I have puzzled for a long time now, and maybe I've got it figured out.

I admit that I challenge umpires and tell off opposing players. But I'm no more aggressive in this respect than Ty Cobb or John McGraw or Frankie Frisch. Leo Durocher and Eddie Stanky kick up fusses all the time. But if I do it, I'm stepping out of line. Many people think that a Negro, because he is a Negro, must always be humble—even in the heat of sports competition. But, in my case, maybe it goes deeper than that.

They have resented me especially ever since I came up to the Dodgers, not just because I am a Negro but because I was *the* Negro who broke the color line in baseball. It's a theory that is not entirely mine too. Tom Meany once wrote: "When he protests a decision, it becomes an issue. When Roy Campanella, Larry Doby or Monte Irvin protest, not too much is made of it. Robinson is simply paying the price which always accompanies a trail blazer."

I was on the spot when Branch Rickey signed me, the first Negro to get a chance in organized baseball. He told me that one wrong move on my part would not only finish the chance for all Negroes in baseball, but it would set the cause of the Negro in America back 20 years. So, in my first year in organized baseball with Montreal, the Brooklyn farm team, I had to hold my temper.

My wife Rachel and I spent our honeymoon at the Montreal spring-training camp in Daytona Beach. We moved to Sanford to complete training and the third day we were there, we had to pack and move in a hurry because a white mob was threatening to run us out of town. Several times that spring, exhibition games were canceled because Jackie Robinson, a Negro, was in the line-up—the local authorities wanted to avoid trouble. I was deeply embarrassed and upset by the trouble I was causing the Montreal club; I wanted to quit baseball before the season opened. But Rachel and Mr. Rickey talked me out of it.

Mr. Rickey told me that I could expect to be thrown at, and that a runner coming into second base might run a little harder because Robinson was playing the bag. He was right. In my first year with the Dodgers, a few players did ride me consistently and played it rough. The Cardinals were awfully tough base runners. Ben Chapman of the Phillies called me unprintable names from the dugout, egging his players on to do the same.

Throughout these two seasons, I had to keep my mouth shut and take it. I couldn't protest to an umpire and I couldn't get back at players who taunted and insulted me with racial remarks. Keeping myself in hand while I was playing ball was tough enough, but I also had to be extra careful about my life outside of the ball park. While traveling with the club, I was afraid to accept invitations to parties in strange towns or even to eat in a restaurant where I wasn't known. I worried about getting into a situation that would result in bad publicity. I was on guard night and day.

This Was Our Life

BY GENE SHALIT

For thousands of years, nobody had time to invent television, which set the stage for Thomas A. Edison. In 1923, Dr. Vladimir Zworykin, tired of being asked if he was the last word in the dictionary, patented the Iconoscope, which, I am willing to believe, is essential to television technology. By 1930, RCA had an experimental station, W2XBS, on the air. The Columbia Broadcasting System came along in 1931 with its gala premiere telecast, featuring Milton Watson and New York's Mayor Jimmy Walker. NBC put its antenna on top of the Empire State Building. CBS' was on top of the Chrysler Building. My grandfather was on top of the local Five & Ten, and my grandmother had to go out with a ladder to get him down. He was like that. When ABC launched its network telecasts in 1945, it featured a program called *Ladies Be Seated.* NBC responded with the Japanese surrender aboard the U.S.S. *Missouri.* By 1947, there were more than 16,000 TV sets in America—and two billion repairmen, all of whom had to take the set back to the shop. Then, on December 27, 1947, a day that will live in infancy, an event occurred that was to lead to a new paragraph:

Howdy Doody premiered on NBC! This kiddy show starred a freckled marionette who looked like a less intelligent Alfred E. Neuman, a clown called Clarabell, and cheering tots in the peanut gallery. Impresario Buffalo Bob Smith figured that if he could keep the show going long enough, by the time the tots got to college, he could tour the campuses and cash in on nostalgia. CBS countered with Ed Sullivan and, as far as I know, ABC was still doing OK with *Ladies Be Seated.* That kind of diversity cried out for prizes, so the Emmy Awards were created. They were presented at the Hollywood Athletic Club for the 1948 season. Top prize for America's "Most Outstanding Television Personality" went, of course, to Shirley Dinsdale and her puppet, Judy Splinters. This was also the year of the first "Special Award." Louis McManus got it for designing the Emmy statuette. It was either give him the prize or pay him.

The following year, Milton Berle was voted "Most Outstanding Kinescope Personality," which didn't bother him since he knew that by 1971 nobody would even remember what "kinescope" meant. His *Texaco Star Theater* had sprung from NBC the previous spring, and now, in 1949, Berle's gags were on everyone's lisps. In just two years, TV had completed its first decade.

It was TV's Golden Age. But not to Fred Allen. He said that television was called a medium because nothing on it was well done.

A "Golden Age"! Live drama! Comedy! Stars! Novelty! The giant life-size seven-inch screen! It was great to be young and an ophthalmologist. Did I ever tell you about the time it began to rain in New York one morning? Ernie Kovacs had a show on WCBS-TV, and he announced that anyone who wanted a free umbrella had only to call me at LOOK. That's the kind of thing that made Kovacs so popular and me so short of umbrellas. The hottest tickets in town in those days were the free passes to Sullivan's Sunday afternoon rehearsals. It was more fun than the show, and you got to overhear the stars' glamorous conversation ("How do I look?"). Sullivan was remarkable: never mind the jugglers, he presented just about every popular personage in the performing arts. Just being allowed to take a bow from his audience made you a big shot. ("And in

our audience, Pretty Niki Narky, who has just waded from Dayton, Ohio. Take a bow, Pretty Niki." Clap clap whistle wave.) Others bestrode the set. Jack Paar on *Tonight* "Disturbed the normal retiring habits of a nation," Abel Green wrote in *Variety.* His midnight iconoclasm made him a show-biz phenomenon. Paar had a touch for taking nobodies and making them rich and famous—Charley Weaver, Dody Goodman, Alexander King, Jack Paar. If television got people to stay up late, it also got them up early. While most stations were snoozing behind their test patterns, NBC leaped up at 7 a.m. with a daily network program called *Today.* Critics (who enjoyed sleeping late) said no one would watch TV at seven in the morning. Only millions.

When Paar walked off his show, he landed on Page One of the New York *Times.* Arthur Godfrey never left *his* shows, but when he fired members of his cast for excessive non-humility he made front-page banners everywhere. In those days, TV was news. *Headline:* Quiz Contestant Charles Van Doren knows all the answers. He also knows all the questions. *Headline:* Snooky Lanson, Dorothy Collins, Raymond Scott and *Your Hit Parade* go off the air, buried by an avalanche of rock. *Headline:* NBC teams Chet Huntley and David Brinkley on new news program. In 1956, NBC had revolutionized the coverage of political conventions with this newly formed team and with backpacked reporters scooting about the convention floor. Now Chet and David were to be on every weekday night. There was some early skepticism about their chances for success, but good night!, they leaped to the top of the ratings and became an American institution. CBS' journalistic superstar was Edward R. Murrow, who not only gave the news, he *was* the news. His documentary about Sen. Joseph McCarthy significantly influenced American history. His *See It Now* was an ornament of television, and he even had a long entertainment run: *Person to Person* showed how famous people live when their homes are overrun by TV cameramen.

During the '50's, each TV season offered 39 weeks of new shows, and 13 weeks of repeats (R). Slowly, the ratio has reversed. The ultimate goal may be a one-week season, 50 weeks of repeats, and one week off for good behavior.

The fifties were frequently funny. Sid Caesar and Imogene Coca scored on *Your Show of Shows*, with scripts by Mel Brooks, Neil Simon and Carl Reiner. The Jackie Gleason hour was written by a small army of driven young men, few as gifted as Marvin Marx. On many nights, I saw Marvin pacing Seventh Avenue near Gleason's Park Sheraton Hotel headquarters, sweating out a skit idea and wondering if on Saturday, the day of the night of the show, Gleason might throw out the whole script and tell everybody to start over. Kovacs was the most inspired comic artist on television, perhaps the only one who knew how to use the new technology. I will not forget his silent Special, in which he poured water crooked, and a copy of *Camille* coughed. Groucho flicked his cigar through *You Bet Your Life*, leering at contestants who had trouble with "Who's buried in Grant's Tomb?" Phil Silvers had no trouble with Sergeant Bilko, Lucille Ball became inseparable from Lucy, Red Skelton was underrated, and Bob Hope's troupes trooped the world like a comedy act of Congress. Everybody was a comedian: even Bishop Fulton J. Sheen was funnier than hell. But not everything was a joke. Live drama brought a vitality and an anxiety to television (like the time the dead man jumped up before the camera was off him). But *Studio One, Playhouse 90* and *Philco-Goodyear Playhouse* gave a vast forum to playwrights. A single night on TV drew a bigger audience than a ten-year run on Broadway. And they delivered the plays: *Patterns, Requiem for a Heavyweight, Marty, The Comedian, The Catered Affair*.

As the decade decreased, things were looking up. The prize for the Best Single Program went, in three consecutive years, to two live *Playhouse 90*'s and *An Evening With Fred Astaire*. Sometimes Emmy's categories grew tortuous, as in 1957 when "Best Continuing Performance (Male) in a Series by a Comedian, Singer, Host, Dancer, MC, Announcer, Narrator, Panelist, or Any Person Who Essentially Plays Himself" was won, mercy me, by Jack Benny. It was all nutty. Imogene Coca lost as best comedienne in 1951, but was voted best actress—beating out Helen Hayes! A year earlier, Miss Hayes had lost out to Gertrude Berg of *The Goldbergs*. Helen Hayes finally made it in 1952, when all she had to beat was other actresses. There was singing, there was dancing, and there was Arthur Murray. Perry Como proved that a man could sleep while awake. There were cops and docs and dicks and flacks, cowboys, plowboys, rubes and boobs. Contestants beat clocks, found secrets, told the truth and guessed my lines. As TV's popularity grew, "Going out" meant staying home.

Bert Parks' teeth, Senator Kefauver's hearings, Marie Wilson's, well, Marie Wilson, Kukla, Fran and Ollie—how did it all begin? For thousands of years, nobody had time to invent television, which set the. . . . (R).

A CARNIVAL
OF STYLE

For decades the female legions of the world have faced temporary panic each season: What will the new styles be? Women gasp or groan or fume; but in the end they conform. No new style is so bizarre as not to prevail (at least for a while), and no mode is as obsolete as yesterday's.

In recent years, however, some resistance to arbitrary style changes has developed, and the dictates of haute couture seem less imperious (remember the financial fiasco of the midi?). Yet some things in life remain constant. Fashions may be affected, absurd, fantastic; but whatever their design, they express a basic human impulse—the desire to beautify the ordinary.

To photographers, the couturiers of Paris and New York offer superlative subject matter—colorful, fanciful variations on the fertile theme of costume. Fashion, the glorification of vanity, is forever fascinating. —Ed.

RICHARD NOBLE

A mountain nymph, clad in Oscar de La Renta's sarong with matching scarf, lazes in the glow of an Acapulco sunset.

◄ A creation fit for Scheherazade—or an oil magnate's daughter. The gown is by Tina Lesor; the setting is the Grand Mosque of Herat in Afghanistan.

A superb conception—to reproduce
famous paintings with modern models
and props: Vermeer's immortal *The
Girl with a Red Hat* and its lovely
re-creation (above), Manet's *Boating*
and its novel simulation (opposite, top),
and an uncanny reprise of Degas's
extraordinary *Lady with Chrysan-
themums* (opposite, bottom).

For make-up artists inspired by Pop and
Op Art, the human form became a canvas
on which to experiment with arresting
colors and patterns.

This glorious shot of a cashmere gown and cloak was photographed beside an ancient stupa at the Erdeni Dzuu lamasery in Mongolia.
(far right). Chester Weinberg's dramatic, modern version of Cossack/Tartar garb was photographed against a background of the legendary warrior horsemen of Afghanistan.

In a shot that required energy as well as ingenuity, the light, structural grace of an early airplane
emphasizes the elegant, flowing gown by Rappi.

Only Homo sapiens cooks. Apes cannot bake, nor can fish make a sauce. It was a brave (or desperate) man who first ate a snail.

One of the great phenomena of the twentieth century is the extraordinary internationalization of cookery. A plethora of cookbooks has appeared on the market, allowing the adventurous to explore the endless variety of the world's cuisine in their own kitchens and dining rooms. Every day, would-be gourmets sign up for cooking courses or follow—and seek to duplicate—the culinary triumphs of television chefs as they demonstrate the intricacies of everything from French omelettes to Chinese hot and sour soup. French cuisine edifies Akron, and Italian pasta inspires Memphis and Morro Bay. Escoffier's influence cannot compare with that of Julia Child.

—Ed.

JOHN VACHON

Flask, peppermill, eggs—the commonplace as art.

◄ The convolutions of the artichoke in a prize-winning photograph.

A still life as beautifully composed as a Dutch painting.

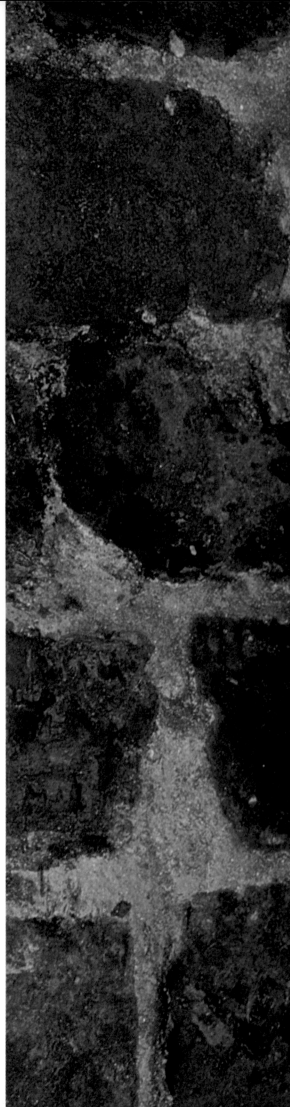

For piquancy, a palette of herbs and spices.

The fig is as delicious as Eve's leaf was decorous.
Here the fruit of Eden rests upon folds of thin prosciutto.

◄ Is there a Greek who does not love to eat—even in
an alleyway in Chios?

ARTHUR ROTHSTEIN

Peaches and the Chinese/Japanese character for "fruit" form a graceful Oriental composition.

◀ A tureen of New Orleans black-bean soup.

Sushi, the great raw-fish favorite of Japan, alluringly arranged.

◄ Insalata alla pescatori—a mariner's salad of squid,
shrimp, mussels, and clams.

Design has burst all bonds, affected every area of life: bridges, houses, high-rise apartments, motorcycles, lamps, chairs, napkins, forks, watches. Our eyes are beguiled by endless novelties. New materials introduce new textures, fresh forms, wholly modern concepts of comfort. Design concepts used in the latest, most exclusive luxury artifacts are soon applied to mass-produced articles. Even conservative consumers are in debt to such innovators as Frank Lloyd Wright, Ludwig Mies van der Rohe, Buckminster Fuller, Le Corbusier, Philip Johnson—and to their numberless disciples, who have so thoroughly transformed the way we live. —Ed.

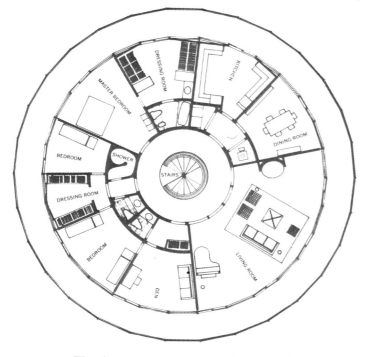

The floor plan of the 3,900-square-foot Carrousel House. The rooms can be opened to natural light or screened off for privacy, simultaneously or individually.

PHILLIP HARRINGTON

Structurally innovative, spatially efficient, visually exciting—in America's heartland, the State Capitol Bank of Oklahoma illustrates the versatility and vibrancy of modern architecture.

◀ The remarkable revolving Carrousel House in Wilton, Conn., designed and owned by Richard T. Foster. For the annual cost of running a refrigerator, a 1½-horsepower motor turns the 250-ton house 360 degrees every 48 minutes.

(overleaf).
Montreal's Expo 67 electrified architects, town planners, designers, and engineers, and the millions who thronged to see the pavilions of 68 nations aglow with original displays in the largest and most innovative of world's fairs.

DOUGLAS KIRKLAND

(top to bottom).
A Leonardo da Vinci design inspired the roof of Air Canada's pavilion.

Roofed with transparent plastic, the West German pavilion resembles a huge circus tent.

Buckminster Fuller's geodesic dome points the future to "Man and His World," the theme of Expo 67.

The Union Jack glows above the austere but dramatic British tower.

Israel-born architect Moshe Safdie designed Habitat 67 to bring space, privacy, and a sense of the outdoors to apartment living. His bold concept blueprints a brilliant new way of urban living.

355

OUR FAITHS,
OUR CULTS

G eorge Bernard Shaw, the most celebrated agnostic of the century, remarked: "There is only one religion, but a hundred versions of it."

All the evidence of history and anthropology indicates that Faith, whether in God or gods (or, in our time, political "isms"), remains an impregnable fortress to those who find meaning and solace within its walls. Any society must rest upon a consensus of morality, a code of right and wrong, and a structure of power—law—that dispenses justice and punishes transgressors. Voltaire understood this when he gibed, "If God did not exist, it would be necessary to invent him."

—Ed.

Undaunted by rain, the Reverend Billy Graham, the most famous modern-day representative of the Christian evangelical tradition, exhorts a crowd to join in his world-wide crusade.

A head-shaven priestess at the beginning of the three years of self-denial and contemplation that are a traditional part of the discipline of Zen Buddhism. Women and men are regarded as equals in her highly individualized religion.

◀ The consecrated wine, the embodiment of Christ's blood, at the climax of the Mass.

Shofar, tallit, mahzor, and a view of
Jerusalem. The ram's horn, the prayer
shawl, and the prayer book—three sancta
of the Judaic faith seen against the background of the Holy City.

361

An ordained minister of the Disciples of
Christ, Birdie ("Cousin Birdie") Farrar
Omer, officiates at a baptism in Danville,
Kentucky. "We love everyone," she says, "but
we believe in baptizing by *total* immersion."

The "Jesus Movement" has won many believers
among the young. Spurning established churches
and liturgy, they proclaim the ecstasy of Love and Peace
on Earth and the imminent return of the Saviour.

A penitent flays himself in Taxco's Holy
Week procession. During a surreal,
macabre ceremony, the sight of such raw
flesh is a commonplace.

Mountain folk in Tennessee assert the
power of faith in a ritual with poisonous
snakes. This cheerful celebrant survived
many bites—but others in the sect died.

364

In days as tormented as ours, mystical
cults, faith-healers, and even witchcraft
are being revived. Above, a witches'
coven in San Francisco.

Anton LeVay, high priest of the First
Church of Satan, preaches that selfishness
is sacred.

LOOK
TREASURY

The Vatican:
The Power and the Glory
Are Passing

BY JOSEPH RODDY

It seemed a good place for a miracle—Saint Peter's Basilica in Rome, and in the winter of 1965 after Vatican Council II closed there were many Roman Catholics who thought a miracle of sorts had happened in the vaulting central shrine of their faith. Twenty-four hundred bishops who had gathered there from all over the world, men whose skill at business administration was certain but whose ardor for theological change was faint, had somehow moved an ancient church with medieval ways into the modern world. Not all of them had helped, of course. There were resisters and obstructors, bishops who smelled heresy in the house and cardinals who felt God-summoned to save their Church from its popes. Still, as the bishops went back to their chanceries after the Council, a Catholic looking about could not help but be astonished at what God—or was it the bishops?—or was it a small band of willful men behind the scenes?—had wrought.

A creed that had claimed its ways timeless had found the time right to change its ways. It would be a true *aggiornamento*, a renewal, an opening out. From then on it would worship in vernaculars and forgo a dead Latin. It would retire cultic pietisms and accent the dignity of prayer. It would look to the rights of other faiths in officially Catholic states. In no state would it countenance oppression in this life with allusions to a good life after death.

It would search for ecumenical reunion with all sects calling themselves Christian. It would lift the charge of deicide from the Jews, and even foresee divine mercy for those who deny divine order. And it would do an amazing thing to its governing structure: its popes, instead of carrying on as absolute monarchs long after the age of kings had passed, would share their power with the universal college of bishops, the same twenty-four hundred very mortal men with their vanities and virtues about them in Saint Peter's. The bishops' new power was called "collegiality," and those who inquired about it were told to regard collegiality as the needed counterbalance to the primacy and infallibility of the pope, attributes of his office that few bishops had even thought to contest.

In prospect, collegiality was the Vatican Council's greatest accomplishment. In practice, it was to evaporate without a trace the first chance it had to work. That was only a few months after the Council. At an audience with Italian gynecologists, Pope Paul VI re-proclaimed his faith's old stand against contraception. The theological, medical and population experts whose advice he sought advised him not to do it, and the laity had plainly been disregarding it. Long before the bishops defined their collegial function with him, Paul had said he would hear all the advice but decide the birth-control issue himself. That he still decided it himself after collegiality became Church law was only a maladroit reminder of papal power. Had he accepted the counsel of his advisers to change birth-control teaching, and then invited the bishops to join with him in changing it, the Pope would have set collegiality off to a good start. But to reject the counsel and then bypass the bishops was an act of desperation. The Roman Catholic Church has been in disorder ever since.

The prospect now is that the Vatican Council the Catholics were so proud of may have accomplished little more than the trivialization of their beliefs. The liturgy of the Mass, shorn of its Latin, has degenerated in places into speech and song at its most primitive, crying out for the noble cadence of a *Dominus vobiscum*. In no country has the religious liberty of other creeds improved through the efforts of the Catholics. No non-Communist government has had its moves called immoral even when they were at the edge of, or into, genocide. The momentum has gone, and with it the heart, from the ecumenical movement toward Christian unity. Jews the world over felt Rome turn remote at the start of the Six Day War. And the unbelieving who looked for a few years with some interest at the faith because it gave the world such a good and true man as Pope John, have mostly turned from it now as just one more light that failed.

The Pope's long-awaited words on contraception included the stunning claim that his Church's teaching on birth control had at no time been in any question. But if it had never been in any question, then why had the Pope gathered around him banks of experts to draft the cases for and against changing it? That question drove Father Charles Davis, the leading young Catholic theologian in England, to answer that the Pope lied, and that under Paul, the Church was hopelessly irreformable. Davis then made his own exit from Roman Catholicism with regrets. There has been a steady flood of defections from the clergy since then, including two U.S. bishops, at least 11,000 priests by the Vatican's count, and an incalculable number of laymen and laywomen who may never be counted among those who have given up their faith—for, in fact, most haven't given it up at all. What they have given up is their allegiance to a besieged institution—that once-august, ecclesiastic principality whose temporal strength was reckoned at all the parliaments of great power "A noble, a venerable superstructure," Silone wrote. "But what happens to poor Christ in such a superstructure?"

There are now two irreconcilable Roman Catholic churches and an array of others between them, sharing one ancient foundation. There is the Pope's fortress church behind the Vatican walls, with outposts in most dioceses where bishops minister to comfortable flocks unaffected by the suffering about them. And there is the servant church of the Christ-ridden, some of them baptized Catholics, some not, but all ill at ease in their skins because they care deeply about the suffering they combat. Ignored by the servant church with no center, the Pope's fortress church is what remains of a once-solid structure now cracked in many places, its foundation not yet fragmented perhaps, but not very far from it either.

There are Roman Catholics uncertain that God exists, who believe the Word just became semantics. Once a Mass was the same, sound for sound, sign for sign, whether in the center of Brazil or the hamlets of the Great Plains. Now there may well be drumbeaters at one, folk-rock singing at the other, and at neither can a worshiper be sure that the priest isn't planning to marry—if he doesn't already have a wife.

Of the more than 40 priests suspended in the Washington, D.C., area three years back because they said they found papal teaching on birth control insupportable, most have left the active ministry, some of them to get married, and, once married, in all likelihood to violate Church teaching on birth control. The Vatican's Sacred Congregation for the Clergy made a compromise settlement for 14 who have remained priests, and by its terms they seem still free not to support the Pope's stand. Better priests who disagree, it seems now even in Rome, than no priests.

The priests who remain speak out—sometimes from the day they become priests. Two young Jesuit seminarians whom Cardinal Terence Cooke was ordaining in New York this spring told him, and all those in a Fordham University chapel, that they could not exchange any kiss of peace with him until he resigned as the armed forces' military vicar. In Chicago, 144 priests announced their censure of Cardinal John Cody and five of his auxiliary bishops because they did not speak up in defense when priests were criticized at the last bishops' conference. When five missionaries working in the slums in St. Louis learned that Cardinal John Carberry had refused to ordain them, they arranged to be ordained instead by a bishop from Ghana on a visit to the U.S. A priest in Fresno was consecrating tacos until the bishop stopped him.

Because the White Fathers taught more than the catechism, and gave refuge to Mozambique liberationists, their missionary work was found subversive by the state, and the state's bishops were not heard to disagree. For Father Theo van Asten then, the choice was to leave at once, or to shift his priests from the servant church in deep trouble with the police to the fortress one in a holy communion with a colonial power. He and his priests chose to leave. "A muzzled Church," he explained, "can remain a worthwhile sign in a regime where the Church is officially persecuted. But she becomes a counter-witness in a country that openly proclaims itself Catholic and Protector of the Church, but in the long run uses the Church for aims which have nothing to do with the gospel.

"The Church should be the conscience of the world, and not be a diplomatic church. In Mozambique, it was because the Church did not speak up, and the hierarchy did not speak up, that I spoke up. In Portugal and Rome too, they say that the Roman Catholic Church should not mix in politics. But what they call politics, I don't. So if priests speak out against social injustices, they say, 'You are against the government.' If we did not speak out, the people in Mozambique would say, 'You are accomplices of this government.'"

The fortress church worships in a much different world. Within it, the massive problem is the decline of celibacy in its priests. But in the servant church, that problem has passed, or lacks importance, or never existed. The servant church knows the massive problem before Christians is justice in the world, and knows that the fortress church cannot get any farther with it at the Synod than the hierarchy of Portugal. The fortress church is set on working things out with civil governments that find the need growing to put servant-church priests in jail. By civil law, most of those jailed deserved to be there. They are enemies of states that are enemies of Christian ethics, or human freedom, or just enemies of life.

The non-Catholic Christian sects have no near-equivalent to the fortress church's Vatican. Their neat and edifying and traditionless counterpart is the World Council of Churches in Geneva. As an ecumenical gesture, Paul VI visited there two years back and was welcomed, but some thought apprehensively, as Mao Tse-tung might be received at the U.N. He said that the question of his Church's membership in the World Council was not yet mature, and that it needed to be studied, and around Geneva the Vaticanologists divided on whether his emphasis had been on the first or the second objection. All know the Church of Rome will not join the World Council unconditionally. While the World Council is not a church but an organization, the Vatican is effectively both. And as an organization, it is quite plainly not collegial but authoritarian, while the World Council is deliberative, or at most, parliamentary. And if the World Council is a trace antiseptic for lacking the odor of nationality, the complaint falls the other way at the Vatican, which is still and ever will be Italian. Looming almost inconceivably large as the obstacle to Christian unity is Rome's pope—his primacy, which is protocol, and his infallibility, which is the touchiest but no longer an untouchable dogma in Christendom.

There are visionaries around the World Council's offices who will die happy only if they achieve full Christian unity. But if they are pessimistic right now, and they are, it is because of the emanations from their friends in Rome. There, they think the entire Church structure is so shaky at present that the Vatican cannot risk another *aggiornamento* move of any sort, least of all a move toward Geneva, and into equality with the Protestant sects. Rome had anathematized them as apostates four centuries back when Martin Luther set off the Reformation. The position of the Holy Office only 20 years ago was that "true reunion can only come from the return of dissidents to the one, true Church of Christ." Since the Vatican Council, the non-Catholic Christians have been gently called "separated brethren," though with the accent leaning heavily on the adjective. This is not the pope to shift it, because in Geneva, the feeling is wide-spread that the never-popular Paul VI—though he may have done more than John XXIII did to move his Church into the world as it really is—is not the pontiff to cross the bridge to unity.

Misunderstanding is plentiful on just what that doctrine of infallibility means. It has never meant that everything the pope says must be believed and observed by Roman Catholics wishing to remain in good standing with their Church. Nor does it mean that until it was defined as Church dogma a hundred and one years ago, popes were unaware of their own infallibility. Though it does not turn up in ecclesiological settings until the fourteenth century at the earliest, the word "infallible" from its Latin root meant simply "not liable to err." When Vatican Council I in 1870 made it the exalting attribute of the papacy, most theologians thought it made the pope incapable of error whenever he undertook to define doctrines of the Church. Legally, it had a touch of the conundrum about it even then, for only if it worked retroactively could the doctrine of infallibility itself be infallible doctrine.

One young man who has made it his holy mission in life to get the fortress church to abandon papal infallibility, to let that most cumbersome dogma fall of its own swaying weight, is the Swiss-born Catholic theologian, Father Hans Küng. Küng's recent book, *Infallible? An Inquiry*, though less an inquiry than a polemic, is so tightly reasoned that the Pope has asked that it be examined closely by the Congregation for the Doctrine of the Faith. There, they describe the assignment as "a necessary part of the constant dialectic that is aimed at clarifying issues." The book clarifies the issue perfectly, and what is lacking is a rebuttal from the Vatican worthy of the book. "There is a solid front against Hans Küng now in Rome," a magistral figure at the World Council said, "but I think it will collapse. The infallibility issue wants out. The problem is Küng himself, as a theologian. Those Catholics who say he has become a Protestant are not entirely wrong. So what Küng needs to show yet is how his view of the infallibility problem is really a Catholic view."

Küng is in such good graces outside of Rome through the servant church that he lectures under Catholic auspices all over the world between classes at the University of Tübingen in Germany, where he is professor of Catholic dogma. What chance, old Romans ask, has Catholicism to flourish where the young come to study it with a Protestant set on diminishing it? Küng says he is not diminishing it at all, only paring from it those pious or foolish encrustations that have no New Testament texts for support.

"There is plenty of confidence that the truth of the Church will go on. But the whole problem is whether we can accept infallibly guaranteed statements, or guaranteed infallible statements. And I think that anyone who will accept them has the onus to get out the arguments in their defense. I think the traditional arguments are really destroyed by my book—maybe 'destroyed' is not a good word—those arguments are demonstrated as invalid. They are not real arguments, though we are still in a very heavy debate on this. But I would be very content if the Pope and the bishops—and theologians, too, of course—would be a little more cautious, have a little more consciousness, about realizing that they can always err. With the Pope and bishops, what is often much more influential is to give the aura of infallibility. They do not often use the power to make a statement infallible. They just give the impression of being infallible.

Küng went on to lament the ways in which Catholic teaching is a prisoner of its past. "We have this wrong decision on birth control only because the Pope is the prisoner of teachings of previous popes." If the decision on birth control were left to the bishops, Küng thinks it would have been a more favorable one than the Pope's. The religious-liberty position arrived at by the last Council contradicted a Church position taken a century earlier that religious pluralism in civil societies was inadmissible. "So at the last Council, the infallibility of the earlier doctrine on religious liberty was . . . well, it was neglected," Küng said. "It was put aside. 'Oh, let us not talk too much about what was in the nineteenth century,' the bishops said. In the matter of birth control, we probably would have had the same development. We would certainly have had a more liberal statement from the Council, even if it had not been an ideal one." Küng paused then to look pleased. "But it was the Pope's statement on birth control that brought so many of us back to the infallibility problem.

"The drama of Paul VI is that he has been educated in this very narrow Roman theology. He tries practically all the time to come out of it, he has serious feelings that it is not enough. And he has read a great deal in others. But I think it is not possible for him to have a new foundation for his own theology. So he comes back all the time to traditional solutions. Where he is not bound, like in the questions of peace, or justice, or the Third World—where he has no difficulties with past doctrinal statements, or with the traditional Roman theology—he is always much freer. He can even be rather progressive because the subjects have not been treated in his textbooks."

Küng remembered then a remark of Pope John's while he talked about the powers of the papacy to a group of Greek seminarians in Rome. "'I'm not infallible,' he said. 'I'm infallible only when I speak *ex cathedra*. But I'll never speak *ex cathedra*.' And he never did," Küng added. "You see, I think Pope John showed very clearly that it was possible to be the unifier not only of the Catholic Church but of all Christianity without any prerogative of infallibility. And the opposite is clear, too, because Paul VI founded himself on the aura of infallibility and of infallible doctrines in the past. And he practically accentuates the polarization and the divisions between Christians. That is why they cannot accept Paul as a unifier, for in both the Eastern churches and in the Protestant churches, the main obstacle is still the doctrine of infallibility."

The obstacle is rarely set in the way, for the doctrine of infallibility has been used only once since its promulgation. That was in 1950, when Pius XII proclaimed the Assumption, the doctrine that the body of Mary, the mother of Jesus, had been transported in physically complete form to Heaven. "The most notoriously problematical of dogmas," Jesuit theologian Avery Dulles has called it. Notoriously problematical it might be, but it has not been theologically provocative, and the silence around it seemed pained. If the infallibility doctrine was to be challenged, the Assumption case lacked dimension. Dimension is what the birth-control case had, but unfortunately no pope had ever got around to declaring that teaching infallible.

Papal history has its particularly woeful areas, and the follies to be found in them range from the Index of Forbidden Books (496)—which are no longer forbidden, but are often not worth reading either—to the condemnation of Galileo (1633)—whose rehabilitation in Rome was undertaken in 1968.

Infallibility, it seems at times, might have toppled by now under the foolishness written about it. But Küng's tactic is to make a case against infallibility that rarely alludes to what others have said about it. Because articles of faith are propositions, he begins, and all propositions are formed with words that (1) fall short of reality, (2) are open to misunderstanding, (3) can be translated only up to a point, (4) are in motion, and (5) are "ideology-prone," it follows that propositions are not as clear in their meaning as they seem to be. They are often ambiguous and understood differently. Küng does not think this linguistic problem should stop the Church from making pronouncements, only from claiming that the infallible pronouncements it makes are forever infallibly true, and can never become plainly false.

Can the collapse of any visible symbol cause all the falling away that has happened? The Roman Catholic Church has three classes of members—the hierarchy, the clergy and the laity, in whom the devastation is enormous. The heirarchy held all the attention until after Vatican Council II came to an end. The shining time for the clergy began then, and their lives and times as priests will start the discussion going at the Synod. Interest in priests' problems should be at its peak soon, and then start to fade. Now the laity is beginning to feel its voice rising and maybe its anger. The devout, and once devout, in the parishes are tired of hearing that the priest in the next parish has just taken a wife, and that the bishop is planning to attend another unity meeting with the Lutherans. And they are tired of dissemblings about trifles when the substance of life is coming apart all around them.

There may never be any Christian unity, but just in case there is, the laity have been getting ready for it by abandoning many of the religious practices that once marked them Catholic. They have given up confession almost altogether. Once in a while they go to communion. Contraception is practiced by Catholics as guiltlessly as by non-Catholics. Divorce is almost common now with Church members, and the strictures about remarrying are going. The seminaries are very short of candidates for ordination, and the ordained—well, they are raising quite a few families.

In Rome there were fierce theological colloquies on doctrinal content in times past, but now there are arch little matters of good form being nattered over, such as whether a priest who goes over the wall should feel bound to marry the girl he was dating. When the Church was triumphant and medieval, not so many years ago, and the questions in dispute had a fire-and-brimstone fear to them, those colloquies ended with a hard Vatican answer—"Rome has spoken, the case is closed." Those words could have a sadder meaning now.

What Is an Agnostic?

BY BERTRAND RUSSELL

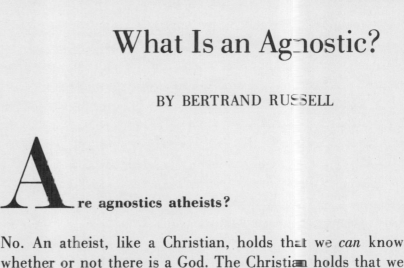

Are agnostics atheists?

No. An atheist, like a Christian, holds that we *can* know whether or not there is a God. The Christian holds that we can know there is a God; the atheist, that we can know there is not. The agnostic suspends judgment, saying that there are not sufficient grounds either for affirmation or for denial. At the same time, an agnostic may hold that the existence of God, though not impossible, is very improbable; he may even hold it so improbable that he is not far removed from atheism.

Since you deny "God's law," what authority do you accept as a guide to conduct?

What passes as "God's law" varies from time to time. The Bible says both that a woman must not marry her deceased husband's brother, and that, in certain circumstances, she must do so. If you have the misfortune to be a childless widow with an unmarried brother-in-law, it is logically impossible for you to avoid disobeying "God's law."

How do you know what is good and what is evil?

The agnostic is not quite so certain as some Christians are as to what is good and what is evil. He does not hold, as most Christians in the past held, that people who disagree with the government on abstruse points of theology ought to suffer a painful death. He is against persecution, and rather chary of moral condemnation.

Does an agnostic do whatever he pleases?

No one but a fool indulges every impulse, but what holds a desire in check is always some other desire. A man's anti-social wishes may be restrained by a wish to please God, but they may also be restrained by a wish to please his friends, or to win the respect of his community, or to be able to contemplate himself without disgust. But if he has no such wishes, the mere abstract precepts of morality will not keep him straight.

How does an agnostic regard the Bible?

An agnostic regards the Bible exactly as enlightened clerics regard it. He does not think that it is divinely inspired; he thinks its early history legendary, and no more exactly true than that in Homer; he thinks its moral teaching sometimes good, but sometimes very bad. For example: Samuel ordered Saul, in a war, to kill not only every man, woman and child of the enemy, but also all the sheep and cattle. Saul, however, let the sheep and cattle live, and for this we are told to condemn him.

How does an agnostic regard Jesus, the Virgin Birth and the Holy Trinity?

Since an agnostic does not believe in God, he cannot think

that Jesus was God. Most agnostics admire the life and moral teachings of Jesus as told in the Gospels, but not necessarily more than those of certain other men. Some would place him on a level with Buddha, some with Socrates and some with Abraham Lincoln. Nor do they think that what He said is not open to question, since they do not accept any authority as absolute.

Can an agnostic be a Christian?

If you mean by a "Christian" a man who loves his neighbor, who has wide sympathy with suffering and who ardently desires a world freed from the cruelties and abominations which at present disfigure it, then, certainly, you will be justified in calling me a Christian. And, in this sense, I think you will find more "Christians" among agnostics than among the orthodox. But, for my part, I cannot accept such a definition. Apart from other objections to it, it seems rude to Jews, Buddhists, Mohammedans and other non-Christians, who, so far as history shows, have been at least as apt as Christians to practice the virtues which some modern Christians arrogantly claim as distinctive of their own religion. If the word "Christianity" comes to be generally used to mean merely a kind of morality, then it will certainly be possible for an agnostic to be a Christian.

Does an agnostic believe in a hereafter?

The question whether people survive death is one as to which evidence is possible. Psychical research and spiritualism are thought by many to supply such evidence. An agnostic, as such, does not take a view about survival unless he thinks that there is evidence one way or the other. For my part, I do not think there is any good reason to believe that we survive death, but I am open to conviction if adequate evidence should appear.

Are you never afraid of God's judgment in denying Him?

Most certainly not. I also deny Zeus and Jupiter and Odin and Brahma, but this causes me no qualms. I observe that a very large portion of the human race does not believe in God and suffers no visible punishment in consequence. And if there were a God, I think it very unlikely that He would have such an uneasy vanity as to be offended by those who doubt His existence.

How do agnostics explain the beauty and harmony of nature?

I do not understand where this "beauty" and "harmony" are supposed to be found. Throughout the animal kingdom, animals ruthlessly prey upon each other. Most of them are either cruelly killed by other animals or slowly die of hunger. For my part, I am unable to see any very great beauty or harmony in the tapeworm. Let it not be said that this creature is sent as a punishment for our sins, for it is more prevalent among animals than among humans.

If you abandon religious principles, could mankind exist?

The existence of base and cruel passions is undeniable, but I find no evidence in history that religion has opposed these passions. On the contrary, it has sanctified them, and enabled people to indulge them without remorse. Cruel persecutions have been commoner in Christendom than anywhere else. What appears to justify persecution is dogmatic belief. Kindliness and tolerance only prevail in proportion as dogmatic belief decays. In our day, a new dogmatic religion, namely, communism, has arisen. To this, as to other systems of dogma, the agnostic is opposed. The persecuting character of present-day communism is exactly like the persecuting character of Christianity in earlier centuries. I think that anybody who surveys past history in an impartial manner will be driven to the conclusion that religion has caused more suffering than it has prevented.

Is not faith in reason alone a dangerous creed?

No sensible man, however agnostic, has "faith in reason alone." Reason is concerned with matters of fact, some observed, some inferred. But matters of fact alone are not sufficient to determine action, since they do not tell us what ends we ought to pursue. In the realm of ends, we need something other than reason. The agnostic will find his ends in his own heart and not in an external command.

Do agnostics think that science and religion are impossible to reconcile?

The answer turns upon what is meant by "religion." If it means merely a system of ethics, it can be reconciled with science. If it means a system of dogma, regarded as unquestionably true, it is incompatible with the scientific spirit, which refuses to accept matters of fact without evidence, and also holds that complete certainty is hardly ever attainable.

What kind of evidence could convince you that God exists?

I think that if I heard a voice from the sky predicting all that was going to happen to me during the next twenty-four hours, including events that would have seemed highly improbable, and if all these events then proceeded to happen, I might perhaps be convinced at least of the existence of some superhuman intelligence. I can imagine other evidence of the same sort which might convince me, but so far as I know, no such evidence exists.

Can a Scientist Believe in God?

BY WARREN WEAVER

WHAT IS SCIENCE?

It is the activity whereby man gains understanding and control of nature. It is practiced professionally and intensely by a few, but practiced to some degree by every person. It proceeds by observing and experimenting, by constructing theories and testing them; by discarding the theories that do not check with the facts, and by improving good theories into better ones. It is never perfect, never absolute, never final; but it is useful and it improves.

Not every scientist would accept this definition. Almost every scientist would want to change it a little, and a few would change it a lot. But, by and large, a scientist is ready to define science. He doesn't feel the need (as he would in trying to define religion) to qualify his statement by saying, "This is *my* kind of science—this is what science means to me."

WHAT IS RELIGION?

Religion is a highly personal affair. I can only tell you what I mean by the word.

Religion, to me, has two main aspects. It is, first and foremost, a guide to conduct. Second, it is the theory of the moral meaning of our existence.

Do not be surprised that this definition of religion involves a practical aspect, which touches every act of every day, and a more "intellectual" aspect, which comes into play relatively seldom. This double answer is to be expected from a scientist, as we shall see. And scientists are precisely the kind of people who should not be surprised if these two aspects are not "consistent" with each other.

Science tries to answer the question "How?" How do cells act in the body? How do you design an airplane that will fly faster than sound? How is a molecule of insulin constructed?

Religion, by contrast, tries to answer the question "Why?" Why was man created? Why ought I tell the truth? Why must there be sorrow or pain or death?

Science attempts to analyze how things and people and animals behave; it has no concern as to whether this behavior is good or bad, is purposeful or not. But religion is precisely the quest for such answers: whether an act is right or wrong, good or bad, and why.

I realize that when theologians define religion they emphasize more abstract considerations. They would probably say that "religion is the service and adoration of God" or "a system of faith and worship"; or that religion is primarily "an apprehension, awareness, or conviction of the existence of a supreme being . . . controlling man's destiny and nature's."

HOW DO YOU DEFINE GOD?

Some regard God in very human terms, as a father who is kind but nevertheless subject to spells of wrath. Others assign to God a lot of other human qualities (love, anger, sympathy, knowledge, etc.) but expand these qualities beyond human possibilities (limitless love, infinite wisdom, total knowledge, etc.). Still others take a mystical attitude toward the concept of God: God is a spirit, and it is not useful or possible to describe God in any other way.

I am sure that each of these ideas has well served different persons at different times. But my own concept of God is rather different.

The difficulty I find with the three conceptions of God just summarized is not that they are vague; not that they depend on faith rather than reason; not that they may even involve contradiction. I think that vagueness is sometimes not only inevitable but even desirable; that faith, in certain realms of experience, is more powerful than logic. And scientists accept such contradictions more readily than most people think.

My difficulty with the views of God sketched above is simply that though they bring comfort on the emotional plane, they do not seem to bring satisfaction on the intellectual plane. When I take any such idea of God and try to work with it mentally, try to clarify it or think it through, I find myself getting confused or embarrassed, using words with which I am not fundamentally content, words which cover up difficulties rather than explain them. It therefore gratifies me to use additional ways of thinking about God—ways which seem to me intellectually satisfying, and consistent with the thinking I try to do along other lines—scientific or not. Indeed, it is these additional ways which very directly relate to scientific thinking and scientific theories. Let me illustrate this.

When I am troubled or afraid, when I am deeply concerned for those I love, when I listen to the hymns which go back to the loveliest memories of my childhood, then God is to me an emotional and comforting God—a protecting Father.

When I am trying to work out a problem of right and wrong, then God is a clear and unambiguous Voice, an unfailing source of moral standard. I do not in the least understand how these things happen; but I know perfectly well, if I listen to this Voice, what is the right thing to do. I have many times been uncertain which course of action would best serve a certain practical purpose; but I cannot think of a single instance in my life when, asking what was the really *right* thing to do, the answer was not forthcoming.

These two statements cover my everyday relation with God. I do not find it helpful—or necessary—to try to analyze these statements in logical terms. They state facts of *experience.* You can no more convince me that there is no such God than you can convince me that a table or a rock is not solid—in each case the evidence is simple, direct and uniform.

As a scientist who is familiar with the detailed explanations of the atomic structure of, say, the table and the rock, it does not surprise me, nor disturb me, that these everyday concepts of God do not offer me detailed logical explanation. God on an intellectual plane (corresponding to the theoretical plane of the physicist) is something else.

That "something else," just as a scientist would expect, is very abstract: on the intellectual level, God is, to me, the name behind a consistent set of phenomena, all of which are recognizable in terms of moral purpose and which deal with the control of man's destiny. I shall explain this in greater detail in a moment.

CAN A SCIENTIST BELIEVE IN GOD?

Some persons think that scientists simply can't believe in God. But I think scientists have unique advantages here—for scientists are precisely the persons who believe in the unseeable, the essentially undefinable.

No scientist has ever seen an electron. No scientist soberly thinks that anyone ever could. In fact, "electron" is simply the name for a set of things that happen under certain circumstances. Yet nothing is more "real" to a scientist than an electron. Chairs and tables and rocks—these are in fact not very "real" to a scientist, if he is thinking deeply. A table, viewed with the precise tools of the atomic physicist, is a shadowy, swirling set of electric charges, these electric charges themselves being very vague and elusive. So viewed, the table completely loses its large-scale illusion of solidity.

In fact, the modern scientist has two sets of ideas about the world, which he carries in his head simultaneously. He uses the simpler set of ideas when it works, and he falls back on the more fundamental set when necessary. The simpler set of ideas deals with large-scale objects—you, me, tables, chairs, rocks, mountains. For these large-scale objects, the scientist has a workaday set of ideas about solidity, location, reality, etc. In these everyday terms, a rock is solid and real because it hurts your toe when you kick it. You know how to measure where a star is and how it is moving. These ideas are extremely useful. If a scientist got up some morning without these workaday ideas, he couldn't even succeed in getting his shoes on. Indeed, he would never figure out how to get out of bed.

But the scientist also knows that all these large-scale ideas simply *do not stand up under close examination*. When he forces his thinking down to basic levels, a wholly new and strangely abstract set of ideas comes into play. Solids are not really solid. "Real objects" are not even composed, as physicists thought a half-century ago, of submicroscopic atoms like billiard balls.

Consider the electron, for example. For a while physicists thought it was a particle. (You mustn't really ask what "particle" means, any more than you should ask just what it means when you say God has certain human characteristics.) Then physicists realized that electrons are wave motions. (Wave motions of *what?* Well, it isn't useful to ask this question, either.) Today, physicists think of electrons as being both (or either) particles or waves.

Further, you can't pin down this electron-object, whatever it is. If you ask the electron more and more insistently "Where *are* you?" you end up with less and less information about where it is going. Or, if you demand to know more and more accurately "Where are you *going?*" you end up with less and less information about where it *is*. I am not being facetious. Modern physics simply cannot tell both where a particle is and where it is going; it can answer one or the other, but not both.

Or suppose you carry out careful measurements and consult the best theories of physics to determine what an electron is going to do next. Well, it turns out that you can only say what it is *likely* to do next. Science can predict with great definiteness on large-scale, everyday sort of phenomena; but this definiteness fades away and vanishes as you proceed down the scale of size, to individual events. If a scientist is studying just two electrons, it turns out to be completely hopeless for him even to try to keep track of which is which.

All this may seem funny or ridiculous to you. But you had better not jump to unwise conclusions. Science may move on to more advanced views of the ultimate nature of things; but there is not the slightest promise that the "improved" view can be any less abstract. Most scientists, I think, have had to come to an entirely new concept of what "explaining," "understanding," or "defining" really mean. And this holds for science no less than religion.

To "explain" something used to mean that you described a strange situation in terms of more familiar situations; you "understand" the thing which was "explained" with more familiar ideas. But if you have any mental curiosity, you are bound to say "How about the more familiar ideas? Explain *them*! And then you run into a real dead end. For any "explanation," however useful and however comforting, finally comes to rest on the *unfamiliar*—because when you get to the bottom step of an explaining process there simply are no terms which you can use to become "familiar" with the bottom step.

Let's take stock of where we are. I am trying to explain whether or not a scientist can believe in God. To do this, I am trying to explain the way scientists think. And we find that a scientist is, by his training, specially prepared to think about things in two ways: the everyday way, and a second way which is a deep, logical, restless, and detailed way. In this second way of thinking, the scientist is forced to live with very abstract ideas. He has come to feel their value and their inevitability. He has developed skepticism concerning easy answers or the "obvious" nature of events. He is the last to expect that an "ultimate explanation" is going to involve familiar ideas. He is convinced, moreover, that reality is not simply denseness or visibility, hardness or solidity. To the scientist, the real is simply *what is universally experienced*.

Does this sound abstract and difficult? Of course it does: The scientist knows that when he is pushed back to a point at which his thinking should begin, he is forced to deal with difficult abstractions. A scientist is just the one who should not say that an abstract concept of God results in an "unreal" God. For the scientist knows that the everyday reality of the table and the rock is an illusion, and that reality is in fact a very subtle, evasive, and somewhat abstract business.

A scientist does not accept ideas just because they are abstract or unreal. He raises a very basic question: "Does this definition *work* successfully?" "Electron" is only the name behind a set of phenomena, but essentially all physicists agree as to what these electron-phenomena are; and there is a high degree of agreement on the rules which govern electron-phenomena. If there is this kind of consistency, then a definition "works"—and the scientist finds it acceptable and satisfying.

Man has not attained the same universal agreement, or consistent explanations, for what can be called God-phenomena. Yet I accept the idea of God for three reasons: First, in the total history of man there has been a most impressive amount of general agreement about the existence (if not the details) of "God." This agreement is not so logically precise as the agreements about electrons but far, far more people believe and have believed in God than believe or have ever believed in electrons.

Second, I know I cannot think through the realm of religious experience as satisfactorily as I can think through certain smaller and less important problems. The nuclear physicist today only has incomplete and contradictory theories. But the theories work pretty well, and represent the best knowledge we have on a very important subject.

Third, I accept two sets of ideas of God—the everyday concept of an emotional and intuitive God, and the intellectual concept of an abstract God—for the very solid reason that I find both of them personally satisfying. It does not at all worry me that these are two rather different sets of ideas: if an electron can be two wholly inconsistent things, it is a little narrow to expect so much less of God.

CAN A SCIENTIST BELIEVE IN THE BIBLE?

I think that God has revealed Himself to many at many times and in many places. I think, indeed, that he keeps continuously revealing Himself to man today. Every new discovery of science is a further "revelation" of the order which God has built into His universe.

I believe that the Bible is the purest revelation we have of the nature and goodness of God. It seems to me natural, indeed inevitable, that the human record of divine truth should exhibit a little human frailty along with much divine truth. It seems to me quite unnecessary to be disturbed over minor eccentricities in the record.

There are, of course, sincere and earnest persons who find it necessary to place a literal interpretation on every word in the Bible, and who accept every statement as divinely revealed truth. This attitude seems to me to lead to both spiritual and intellectual poverty.

The reports of miraculous happenings in Biblical times seem to me more reasonably understandable as poetic exaggeration, as ancient interpretations of events which we would not consider miraculous today, or as concessions (on the part of Christian writers) to the problem of competing with the magical claims of other religions.

CAN A SCIENTIST BELIEVE IN MIRACLES?

Put a kettle of water on the stove. What happens? Does the water get hot and boil, or does it freeze? The nineteenth-century scientist would have considered it ridiculous to ask this question. But scientists today, aware of the peculiarities of modern physical theories, would say, "In the overwhelming proportion of the cases, the water will get hot and boil. But in one of a vast number of trials, it is to be expected that the water will *freeze* rather than boil."

Modern science recognizes the exceedingly rare possibility of happenings—like water freezing on a hot stove, or like a brick spontaneously moving upward several feet—which so contradict the usual order of events that

they can be called "miracles." No one can logically hold that science rules out "miracles" as impossible.

If my religious faith required miracles, my scientific knowledge would not necessarily deny them. But my religious faith does not at all rest on the validity of ancient miracles. To me, God gains in dignity and power through manifestations of His reason and order, not through exhibitions of caprice.

CAN A SCIENTIST BELIEVE IN "LIFE AFTER DEATH"?

Scientists are very heavily (but not exclusively, as some claim) influenced by evidence: If there is good evidence for a statement, they accept or believe the statement; if there is good evidence *against*, they reject. If it seems impossible to produce any evidence—either for or against a statement —the scientists tend to consider such statements as unprofitable matters of inquiry.

So far as I am concerned, "life after death" is a matter in which I can neither believe nor disbelieve. To date, at least, I have been too much interested in this life to feel any urge to indulge in pure speculation about another.

With Oppenheimer

BY THOMAS B. MORGAN

It was 21 years since the laboratory at Los Alamos, N.M., organized, directed and inspired by Oppenheimer, exploded the first atomic bomb.

It was 12 years since the Federal Government withdrew his security clearance while judging him a "loyal citizen" in what was probably the most wasteful exercise of the McCarthy era. His real sin was his failure to enthuse over the H-bomb strategy of massive retaliation, which he felt might weaken his country. Today, most Americans recognize the inadequacy of that strategy—and we have adopted a philosophy of flexible response not unlike the one prematurely advocated by Oppenheimer in the early fifties.

And it was only three years since President Lyndon B. Johnson presented Oppenheimer with the AEC's Enrico Fermi prize, accompanied by $50,000, for "especially meritorious contribution to the development, use or control of atomic energy." The prize neither restored Oppenheimer's clearance nor compensated the nation for the loss of his counsel in government. But it was something of a vindication. Commenting on the prize, Oppenheimer had said: "Most of us look to the good opinion of our colleagues and to the goodwill and confidence of our Government. I am no exception." To see him now was to be reimmersed in all this, the tragedy of science in politics that has been one of the central dramas of our century.

He possessed a particular ability to frame good questions and maintain a steady theme—the dilemma of values, or the problem of making better use of scientific knowledge or, in a word, change. He had a vision of "common discourse," of continuous interplay between the world of scientists and the world of "people at large"—artists, farmers, lawyers and political leaders. In 1947, he wrote, ". . . because most scientists, like all men of learning, tend in part also to be teachers, they have a responsibility for the communication of the truths they have found." In his view, expressed in 1960, men in "high intellectual enterprise" must contribute to "the common culture, where we talk to each other, not just about the facts of nature . . . but about the nature of the human predicament, about the nature of man, about law, about the good and the bad, about morality, about political virtue, about politics in the Aristotelian sense. . . ."

He said he had been thinking a great deal about the explosion and fragmentation of knowledge and reminded me that of all the scientists who had ever lived, 95 percent of them were alive at this moment. "My whole feeling," he said in a gritty voice, "is to try to create a unity, to encourage and nourish understanding. The point is to simplify and to order knowledge. The profession I'm part of has as its whole function the rendering of the physical world understandable and beautiful. Otherwise, you have only tables and statistics. The measure of our success is our ability to live with this knowledge effectively, actively and, eventually, with delight. If we succeed, we will be able to cope with our knowledge and not create despair. There are antiscientists who say that science has nothing to do with values and is therefore not of interest. There are also scientists who say that physics alone is basic. I oppose both. Science is not everything. But science is very beautiful."

Last winter, he had commented that the Treaty of Moscow, the limited-test-ban treaty, was "a tentative, but to me, very precious, declaration that reason might still prevail." Now, he said: "The central question is this—how to encompass this part of the human story in judgments of good and evil—how to subject the development of weapons to a notion of what is right. This absence of the ethical is what I'm talking about," he said. "What are we to think of a civilization that has not been able to talk about the prospect of killing almost everybody, except in prudential and game-theoretical terms? Very great evil is inherent in weaponry—and where there is great evil is the opportunity for great good. We have forgotten now but right after the war, this is what people were saying: that the discovery of atomic power was good, that, among other things, it created an opportunity for great human grandeur because one was dealing with such great dimensions of evil. Atomic power is *not* the same old problem of evil with which man has always been confronted, but you lose an essential dimension when you view it without considering good and evil."

Oppenheimer paused. I waited. Lacking international control of atomic energy, the world's A-bomb club had grown to include the U.S., U.S.S.R., China, France and Great Britain. West Germany has nuclear weapons without triggers. Both India and Israel and others might decide to join the club at any time. "The only hope for discouraging proliferation," Oppenheimer said, "is our own commitment to the transitory character of our reliance on these weapons. As long as we say, 'It is all right for us, but don't you do it,' efforts to prevent proliferation aren't going to be very effective.

"I have been much concerned that in this world we have so largely lost the ability to talk to one another. In the great succession of deep discoveries, we have become removed from one another in tradition and. in a certain measure, even in language. We have neither the time nor the skill nor the dedication to tell one another what we have learned, nor to listen, nor to learn, nor to welcome its enrichment of the common culture and the common understanding. Thus, the public sector of our lives, what we have and hold in common, has suffered, as have the illumination of the arts, the deepening of justice, and virtue, the ennobling of power and our common discourse. We are less men for this. Our specialized traditions flourish; our private beauties thrive; but in those high undertakings where man derives strength and insight from public excellence, we have been impoverished. We hunger for nobility: the rare words and acts that harmonize simplicity and truth. I see some connections with the great unresolved public problems: survival, liberty, fraternity."

He allowed that his writing had lately developed a new emphasis. For one thing, the word "responsibility" appeared more and more frequently—his devotion to it seemed almost religious to me. Oppenheimer said I did not have that quite right.

"The use of the word 'responsibility,'" he said, "is almost a secular device for using a religious notion without attaching it to a transcendent being. I like to use the word 'ethical' here. I am more explicit about ethical questions now than before—although these were very strong in me when I was working on the bomb. I was more concerned then with doing what I should than chattering about it. Now, I don't know how to describe my life without using some word like 'responsibility' to characterize it, a word that has to do with

379

choice and action and the tension in which choices can be resolved. I am not talking about knowledge, but about being limited by what you can do. . . . There is no meaningful responsibility without power. It may be only power over what you do yourself—but increased knowledge, increased wealth, leisure are all increasing the domain in which responsibility is conceivable. . . ."

Oppenheimer said that he was by no means hopeless about the prospects for peace, only "temporarily gloomy."

"It is a bad time," he said. "I think peace should be far more prominent in our thoughts, talk and deeds as it tended to be toward the end of the last war. One of the responsibilities of a national government is to see to it that this attention is maintained and not betrayed. Not many governments in this much-governed world satisfy this condition. . . . Still, a great deal can be learned from the irreversible changes in the relations between the United States and the Soviet Union in the past 12 years. Things have gotten better in a way that would be hard to change back. The attitudes of the bitterest cold-war days have not returned, despite trouble. Altogether, this teaches that peace must be approached through cooperation and non-national ways of doing things that gradually take the power and the burden from the nation-state."

On the way out, I walked down a corridor past several tiny study cubicles where young scientists sat alone, thoughtfully staring out at what was left of that beautiful day.

A Reflection

BY ARCHIBALD MacLEISH

Men's conception of themselves and of each other has always depended on their notion of the earth. When the earth was the World—all the world there was—and the stars were lights in Dante's heaven, and the ground beneath men's feet roofed Hell, they saw themselves as creatures at the center of the universe, the sole, particular concern of God—and from that high place they ruled and killed and conquered as they pleased.

And when, centuries later, the earth was no longer the World but a small, wet, spinning planet in the solar system of a minor star off at the edge of an inconsiderable galaxy in the immeasurable distances of space—when Dante's heaven had disappeared and there was no Hell (at least no Hell beneath the feet)—men began to see themselves, not as God-

directed actors at the center of a noble drama, but as helpless victims of a senseless farce where all the rest were helpless victims also, and millions could be killed in world-wide wars or in blasted cities or in concentration camps without a thought or reason but the reason—if we call it one—of force.

Now, in the last few days, the notion may have changed again. For the first time in all of time men have seen the earth: seen it not as continents or oceans from the little distance of a hundred miles or two or three, but seen it from the depths of space; seen it whole and round and beautiful and small as even Dante—that "first imagination of Christendom"—had never dreamed of seeing it; as the twentieth century philosophers of absurdity and despair were incapable of guessing that it might be seen. And seeing it so, one question came to the minds of those who looked at it. "Is it inhabited?" they said to each other and laughed—and then they did not laugh. What came to their minds a hundred thousand miles and more into space—"half way to the moon" they put it—what came to their minds was the life on that little, lonely, floating planet: that tiny raft in the enormous, empty night. "Is it inhabited?"

The medieval notion of the earth put man at the center of everything. The nuclear notion of the earth put him nowhere—beyond the range of reason even—lost in absurdity and war. This latest notion may have other consequences. Formed as it was in the minds of heroic voyagers who were also men, it may remake our image of mankind. No longer that preposterous figure at the center, no longer that degraded and degrading victim off at the margins of reality and blind with blood, man may at last become himself.

To see the earth as it truly is, small and blue and beautiful in that eternal silence where it floats, is to see ourselves as riders on the earth together, brothers on that bright loveliness in the eternal cold—brothers who know now they are truly brothers.

The Moon Landing

BY C.P. SNOW

We have seen a wonder. There has never been one quite like it. What first steps in human history would one have chosen to witness, if one could travel in time? The Vikings coming ashore wherever they did come ashore—Newfoundland?—in North America? Or the first little boat from Columbus' ship scraping the land under her keel?

We have seen something unique. It is right that it should have looked like something we have never seen before. In science-films, perhaps—but *this was real*. The figure, moving so laboriously, as though it was learning, minute by minute, to walk, was a man of our own kind. Inside that gear there was a foot, a human foot. Watch. It has come, probing its way down—near to something solid. One expects to hear (there is no air, one could hear nothing) a sound. At last, it has come down. Onto a surface. Onto the surface of the moon.

Well, we have seen a wonder. We ought to count our blessings.

This is the time when we might try to clear our minds about the whole project. There will never be a better time. If the landing had failed, we shouldn't have been in a mood to be even moderately detached. But now we are happy, admiring and basking in a kind of reflected moonlight. If we can't ask sensible questions now, we never shall.

It is important to ask the right questions, though. One is, have we gained anything, and, if so, what? And what effect is the landing going to have on us? Will it change our lives? How, and to what extent?

As for the first, yes, we have gained something. The most important part of it is a moral gain. We are compelled to spend so much time in this jagged century looking at the worst in other people and ourselves. We should be stupid and guilty if we didn't. But it is just as well that we should have the occasional spectacle forced upon us of men being clever, competent and brave.

There is also a clear scientific gain. We now know beyond doubt a good deal about the constitution of the moon; soon, we shall know more. This means that before long, we shall solve some tough scientific problems about how the solar system was formed. Further, we shall before long be able to erect laboratories on the moon or a space platform. That doesn't sound dramatic, but the result may be very dramatic. At the moment, cosmogonists are arguing and guessing about the nature of the universe. Observation outside the earth's atmosphere should tell us some of the answers. So far, so good. But will the landing change our lives?

I am afraid that in the long run, perhaps a generation, perhaps longer, it will have a bad effect. It will give us the feeling, and the perfectly justified feeling, that our world has finally closed in. This is forever the end of the mortal frontier.

I dislike saying what I have just said, and am going on to say. No one is fond of stating a negative opinion. Too many such opinions, even by men we consider tremendously wise, have turned out to be wrong.

Yet I feel it would be cowardly not to speak my mind. There are some things on which we deceive ourselves very easily. Science presents us with many horizons to which we can't see the end. Fine. That doesn't mean that all horizons are infinite. I am sure this one isn't. (Yes, I know all about tachyons, those hypothetical particles moving faster than the speed of light.) The horizon is limited because of the size of the universe and the shortness of a human lifetime.

This is the only point on which I flatly disagree with the space enthusiasts. They speak as though reaching the moon (and the other possible spots in the solar system) is going to liberate the human imagination as the discovery of America did. I believe the exact opposite, that the human imagination is going to be restricted—as to an extent it was when the last spots on the globe had been visited, the South Pole and the summit of Everest. Nowhere on earth for adventurous man to go. Very soon, there will be nowhere in the universe for adventurous man to go.

The analogy with the discovery of America is a very bad one. The Spaniards and Portuguese found riches, marvels, above all, people, in the American land. When Armstrong trod on the moon, he found lumps of inorganic matter, as he might have done at the South Pole. The South Pole is a pretty accurate analogy.

The trouble is, the solar system is a desperately disappointing place. Scientists have known this for a long time; it is now being confirmed in concrete, only too concrete, fact. Our planet is a peculiar fluke in a dead system. Before the end of the century, Americans and Russians will have landed on Mars. It is conceivable that they will discover traces of primitive organic life. Scientifically, that will be exciting. But that is the very most that we can anticipate. A little lichen on a barren world.

Where else can we go? One can tick off the possibilities on the fingers. One or two of the major planets, perhaps. Just imaginably, but only just, one or two of the moons of Jupiter. Those, we can predict, will be more barren lumps of inorganic matter. Then we come to the end. That is the frontier. There is nowhere else in the entire universe where man can ever land, for so long as the human species lasts.

This has been scientifically obvious for long enough. The solar system is dead, apart from our world: and the distances to any other system are so gigantic that it would take the entire history of mankind from paleolithic man to the present day to traverse—at the speed of Apollo 11—the distance to the nearest star. So that the frontier is closed. We can explore a few lumps in our system, and that is the end. This has been, as I say, scientifically obvious for a good many years. But it takes the evidence of eyes and hands and feet—the eyes, hands and feet of Armstrong and his successors—to translate the scientific certainties into common knowledge. In the domain of space travel, I reckon that this will take from 30 to 100 years. Then disappointment, the sense of confinement, a kind of cosmic claustrophobia will set in.

We had better be prepared for it. Science-fiction writers

(at least those who have scientific knowledge and insight, of whom there are plenty) have been fighting a rearguard action against the inevitable. One of the casualties of the moon landing will be science fiction, at least as applied to space travel. You can write scientifically about what you know to be improbable, but you can't write scientifically for long about what you know to be impossible. Science-fiction writers will be driven inward, not outward, and will turn their attention to human biology and psychology. There is plenty to occupy them there for more than a hundred years.

Nevertheless, they will be driven inward. So will the imaginations of the rest of us. It is a paradox. The greatest exploration — that pioneers have been looking forward to so long. The greatest exploration. The pioneers weren't to know the realization that would afterward gradually dawn upon us. The realization that, as well as being the greatest exploration, it was very near the final one.

That is a pity. We badly need something to take us out —not constantly but for part of our time—out of this, our mundane life. The naïve idea of heaven did that for generation after generation, when people could believe that heaven was somewhere above us, up there beyond the sky. To secular minds, the prospect of space, the other worlds to find, other lives to meet, has been a substitute. To many, a substitute of almost equal power. Now that will fail us too. As a result of supreme technological skill and heroism, we are faced not with the infinite but with the immovable limits. The limits of our practical condition. We now know that the only lives we shall ever meet turn out to be our own.

Astrology:
Fun, Fraud or Key-hole
to the Future?

BY ISABELLA TAVES

I've just emerged, slightly rumpled, from the hip pocket of the occult. In New York, my first contact with it was Maurice Woodruff, the clairvoyant-astrologer imported from England to star in Metromedia's new hour-long TV prediction show. He told me I was going to go to California and would have a swollen left ankle. A couple of weeks later, just as I was about to take off to hunt psychics in California,

a friend looked at me and said, "What's wrong with your left ankle? It's swollen."

Astrology is insidious. It supposes a rhythm in the movement of the planets that affects each human being differently, so that if you know your own pattern, which can be worked out through an individual horoscope, you can avoid many missteps. But lots of astrologers believe that the daily forecast columns that appear in newspapers and the monthly magazine horoscopes are just vague generalities.

If you want a really personalized horoscope, everything gets more complicated. You must give the astrologer not only the date of your birth, but the place, hour and preferably the minute, based on the instant you took your first breath. And if you aren't going to tell the truth, you might just as well have stood in bed.

The price of a horoscope done by a serious white-collar astrologer is usually $25 or $35. The fee includes drawing up the chart, which takes some time, and interpreting it, apparently the real trick, to the client. This is why flesh-and-blood astrologers regard the much-advertised $20 horoscope done by computer with disdain. Actually there seems to be considerable clairvoyance connected with intrepretation of a chart, even though the astrologer sometimes prefers to call it ESP or intuition.

But few astrologers get rich on clients alone. The handful who make good money get it from TV and radio appearances, the lecture circuit, regular astrology columns or, less likely, books and astrology magazines.

Why, then, does anyone become an astrologer? Many I met had transferred from other, more lucrative, fields. Keith Clayton was in public relations. Doris Kaye was a reporter in San Francisco. The answer seems to be that these people are hooked too. Astrology works for them, and they believe it is the answer for everyone.

There is also the sense of helping people, which can be translated into power. Movie stars, politicans, government figures, foreign heads of state, doctors and stockbrokers are among their clients. Astrologers suggests days favorable for operations, buying stock, getting married and even begetting children. I heard of a couple in Los Angeles who have been waiting for two years for his astrologer to find a propitious date for their marriage.

There is too little money in astrology to attract big-time phonies. Most astrologers think that once a year is enough for a client to come in and have his horoscope gone over, unless special problems come up. They don't want people to become dependent; I heard Maurice Woodruff tell a client over long distance, "Now, your good sense will tell you the man will never marry you. You didn't need to bother me." They also deplore the super-hooked fringe, like the Chicago music critic who won't leave his house on days the aspects are bad, or the New York woman executive who calls her astrologer before she makes a hair appointment. Pauline

Messina, who has supported herself and raised two children by astrology, told me, "I have only one word for them—NUTS."

Tougher than many psychiatrists because they've had to be, infinitely cheaper, astrologers prefer to call astrology a road map, which allows free will to operate after you get what is indicated.

Does astrology really provide a keyhole to the future? I talked to doctors who are by no means scoffers; they feel that since links have been established between weather and the movements of the planets, we can't deny out of hand that living organisms can be affected. Dr. Joseph Henderson, a psychiatrist in San Francisco, a Virgo happily married to a Virgo—something the astrologers usually take a dim view of—says he finds the zodiac signs do have some meaning when he is treating certain patients. A belief in reincarnation, which is often considered part and parcel of astrology, also helped a patient whom he was treating for depression. Much as she considered suicide, she would not kill herself because of the penalty that would be imposed in her next reincarnation if she did.

I embarked on this project a cool cat, a hard-nosed Virgo. But I did have one experience that continues to give me pause. I found an old friend, now living in California, who is almost my astrological twin; that is, we were born the same month and year, within two days of each other (her birthplace was Mexico City and mine was Nebraska). We are exactly the same height. We have the same Dufy reproduction in our living rooms, the same India print on our beds and our living rooms are in the same colors (what Carroll Righter calls Virtuous Virgo earth colors): brown, dark green, the flaming orange-red of leaves in autumn. We both even like to start to the airport a couple of hours early, just in case.

Coincidence? Of course, it could be. And the astrology boom could be due to a breakdown in our society. It could be a sign of our decadence; it was in the last chaotic period of the Roman Republic that people took to horoscopes "like drugs." The increased interest also could have something to do with the frail role religion is playing in the lives of so many people today, the lack of communication between men of the cloth and the layman.

My personal conviction is that astrology is providing a guideline to many people, a rope they can hang on to in an insecure world, as they work their way up—or down—to that inevitable end. Whether the rope is real doesn't matter; the important thing is believing in it. And if knowing the zodiac sign of your husband or your children or your parents makes you a little more understanding of their problems and their difficult periods, then it's all to the good even if the whole thing is superstition.

MAGIC OF
THE LENS

CAL BERNSTEIN

Arizona's Canyon de Chelly.

◄ Manhattan skyscrapers.

JOHN VACHON

(overleaf). Harvested fields in the Midwest.

New York City composition.

Stonehenge, on Salisbury Plain, England.

ART KANE

The Piazza di San Marco, Venice, in a photographer's doubled image.

A mossy forest in Ireland.

A terraced hillside in China.

The text of this volume was set in Bodoni Book, a modern recutting of a face designed by Giambattista Bodoni in the eighteenth century. The text was photocomposed by JM Typographic Services Inc., New York. The type for the chapter openings and captions was photocomposed by Cardinal Type Service, Inc., New York. The display type is Modern No. 20, a characteristic English face. It was set by Jo-Electro Film Typography Inc., New York.

The book was printed in five-color offset by Universal Printing Company, St. Louis, Missouri. The four-color separations were supplied by DC & S Incorporated, New York. The illustrations were printed on 80-pound Flokote, manufactured by the S. D. Warren Company, Westbrook, Maine, and supplied by Lindenmeyr Paper Corporation, New York. The text sections were printed on 80-pound Carnival Offset, laid finish, supplied by Nationwide Papers, Moonachie, New Jersey. The book was bound by Rand McNally and Company, Hammond, Indiana.

JOHN F. KENNEDY • NORMAN M
ENE • MARGARET MEAD • NORMAN M
ICHEN • DOUGLAS KIRKLAND • MARVIN NEWMAN • J
RY • WILLIAM ATTWOOD • LORD SNOWDON • ARTHUR
PMANN • PHILLIP HARRINGTON • ART KANE • YOUSUF
UCK • MILTON GREENE • JOHN VACHON • STANLEY TRET
ANCHESTER • S. J. PERELMAN • GALE SAYERS • ARCHIBA
QUELINE KENNEDY • GLORIA STEINEM • ROBERT FRÉSO
E SHALIT • ARTHUR ROTHSTEIN • JOSEPH RODDY • JAM
MARX • EDWARD M. KENNEDY • CORNELL CAPA • ARCH
NEWMAN • EUGENE O'NEILL • ART KANE • YOUSUF KARS
FFER • WILLIAM SAROYAN • EDWARD STEICHEN • DOUG
N • WILLIAM F. BUCKLEY, JR. • MARC RIBOUD • TIM COI
N GUNTHER • STANLEY KUBRICK • JOHN F. KENNEDY • M
LLSBERG • ADLAI STEVENSON • GLORIA STEINEM • ROB
N • MICHAEL VACCARO • JULIAN HUXLEY • MRS. WILLIA
MAILER • RICHARD AVEDON • EDWARD STEICHEN • DOU
L • ERNST HAAS • HARRY S TRUMAN • GROUCHO MARX
S TRUMAN • STANLEY TRETICK • MARVIN NEWMAN • JA
SCO • MARSHALL McLUHAN • S. J. PERELMAN • LEO ROS
S • ARCHIBALD MacLEISH • ALLEN DRURY • WILLIAM AT
ORNELL CAPA • ARCHIE LIEBERMAN • BERTRAND RUSS
N NEWMAN • JACKIE ROBINSON • ERNEST HEMINGWAY
YOUSUF KARSH • WEEGEE • IRVING PENN • WALTER LIF
RD SNOWDON • ARTHUR MANN • DANIEL ELLSBERG • A
BOUD • TIM COHANE • MILTON GREENE • LEO ROSTEN
M. F. ASHLEY MONTAGU • FRED MAROON • JOHN GUNT
H RODDY • JAMES KARALES • ARNOLD NEWMAN • EUGE
ERT FRÉSON • PEARL S. BUCK • GENE SHA
DOUGLAS DUNCAN • C